"THE FUTURE IS A WATERSLIDE
THAT LASTS FOREVER."

-INSPIROBOT

IMAGE COMICS, INC. • Robert Kirkman: Chief Operating Officer • Erik Larsen: Chief Financial Officer • Todd McFarlane: President • Marc Silvestri: Chief Executive Officer • Jim Valentino: Vice President • Eric Stephenson: Publisher / Chief Creative Officer • Jeff Boison: Director of Publishing Planning & Book Trade Sales • Chris Ross: Director of Digital Services • Jeff Stang: Director of Direct Market Sales • Kat Salazar: Director of PR & Marketing • Drew Gill: Cover Editor • Heather Doornink: Production Director • Nicole Lapalme: Controller • IMAGECOMICS.COM

• Deanna Phelps: Production Artist for CROWDED •

VOLUME TWO
GLITTER DYSTOPIA

CHRISTOPHER SEBELA
::.SCRIPT + DESIGN.::

RO STEIN + TED BRANDT
::.LINE ART.::

TRIONA FARRELL
::.COLORS.::

CARDINAL RAE
::.LETTERS.::

JULIETTE CAPRA
::.EDITS.::

YLAN TODD
::.LOGO.::

YESFLATS
HOLLEY MCKEND
RICHEL TAGYAMON
::.COLOR FLATTING.::

::.CREATED BY SEBELA, STEIN, BRANDT, FARRELL, RAE & CAPRA.::

CHAPTER SEVEN

TIME TO PRETEND

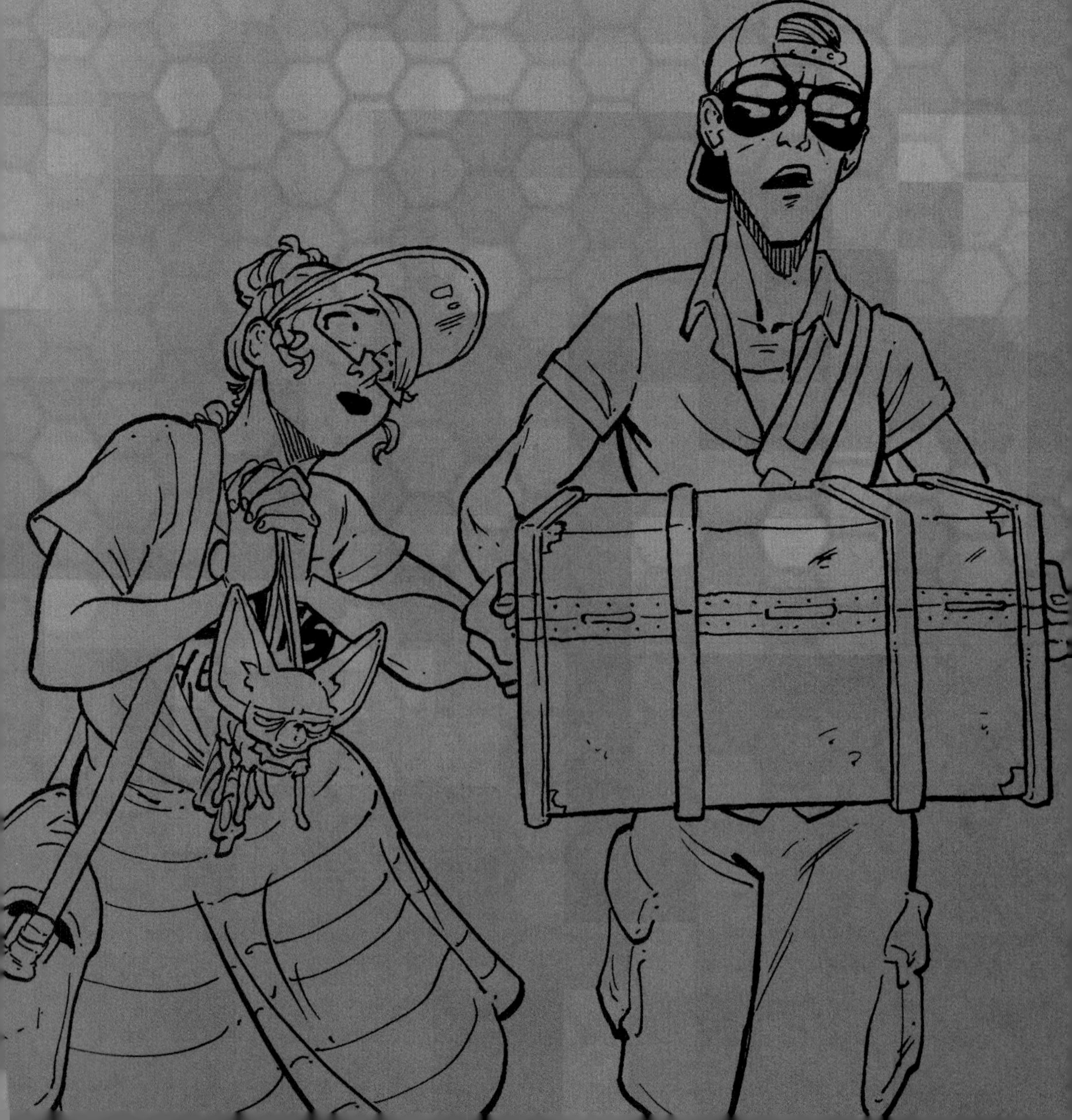

ÜberTube

reapr million dollar girl trotter

$2 million dollar girl escapes, trotter gets cancelled on his own stream LOL

1,812,008 views

40.3k   16.6k

Reapr Shade
Published 20 hours ago

SUBSCRIBE 5.2 M

Charlie Ellison, the Two Million Dollar Girl, has been on the run for days since her Reapr campaign was started against her and all along, everyone was waiting for Killstreamer, Trotter, to finish her off in style. But Ellison hired this Dfender who turns out to be Vita Slatter (yes *that* Vita Slatter) and she just beat the hell out of Trotter on his own killstream. Here's all the best highlights, including footage of their escape. No one knows where Ellison and Slatter are headed now so be sure to smash the like and subscribe button and hit the notification bell for all the latest sightings from your best sourced source for Reapr drama on übertube. Donate to the Hatreon and check out all the new merch in our store, featuring

Up next

Elderly woman in custody claims her dog was stolen by Reapr target Charlie...

Million dollar girl invades my BFF's bachelorette party and all hell breaks loose (PICS)

10 Reasons Why Librarians Definitely Shouldn't Be Screwed With

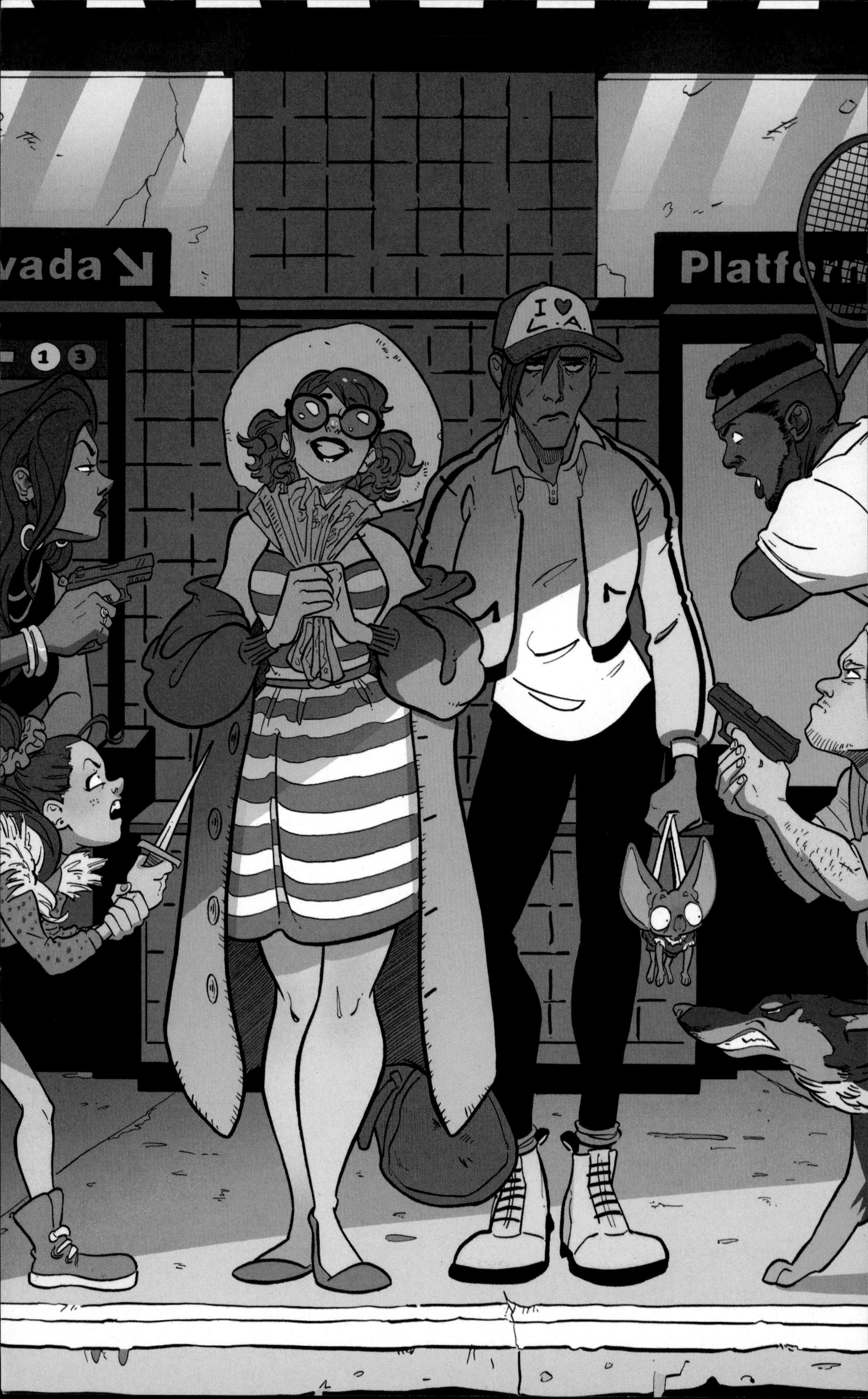

vada
1 3
Platfor
I ♥ L.A.

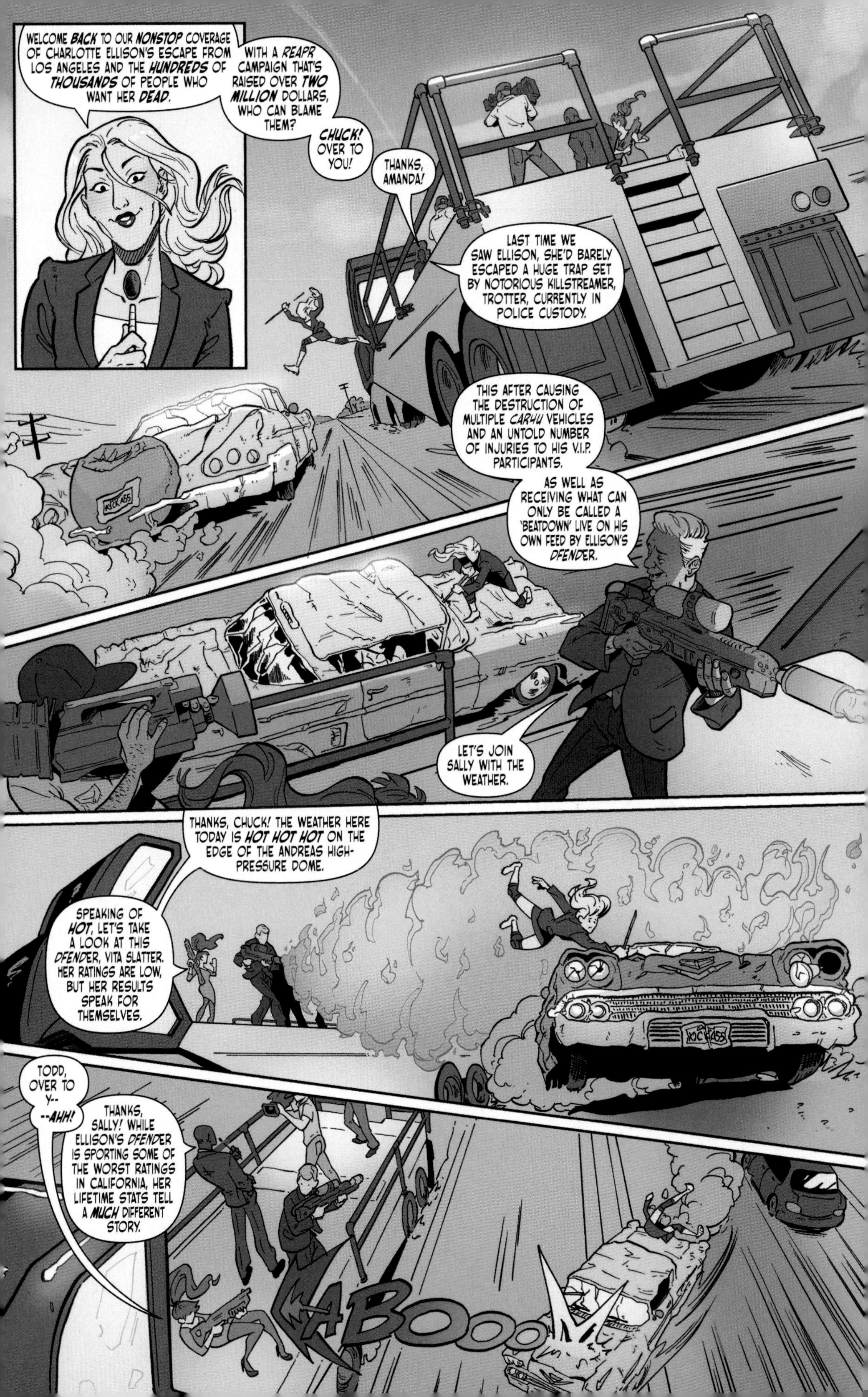
WELCOME BACK TO OUR NONSTOP COVERAGE OF CHARLOTTE ELLISON'S ESCAPE FROM LOS ANGELES AND THE HUNDREDS OF THOUSANDS OF PEOPLE WHO WANT HER DEAD.
WITH A REAPR CAMPAIGN THAT'S RAISED OVER TWO MILLION DOLLARS, WHO CAN BLAME THEM?
CHUCK! OVER TO YOU!
THANKS, AMANDA!
LAST TIME WE SAW ELLISON, SHE'D BARELY ESCAPED A HUGE TRAP SET BY NOTORIOUS KILLSTREAMER, TROTTER, CURRENTLY IN POLICE CUSTODY.
THIS AFTER CAUSING THE DESTRUCTION OF MULTIPLE CAR4U VEHICLES AND AN UNTOLD NUMBER OF INJURIES TO HIS V.I.P. PARTICIPANTS.
AS WELL AS RECEIVING WHAT CAN ONLY BE CALLED A 'BEATDOWN' LIVE ON HIS OWN FEED BY ELLISON'S DFENDER.
LET'S JOIN SALLY WITH THE WEATHER.
THANKS, CHUCK! THE WEATHER HERE TODAY IS HOT HOT HOT ON THE EDGE OF THE ANDREAS HIGH-PRESSURE DOME.
SPEAKING OF HOT, LET'S TAKE A LOOK AT THIS DFENDER, VITA SLATTER. HER RATINGS ARE LOW, BUT HER RESULTS SPEAK FOR THEMSELVES.
TODD, OVER TO Y--
--AHH!
THANKS, SALLY! WHILE ELLISON'S DFENDER IS SPORTING SOME OF THE WORST RATINGS IN CALIFORNIA, HER LIFETIME STATS TELL A MUCH DIFFERENT STORY.
KABOOOOO

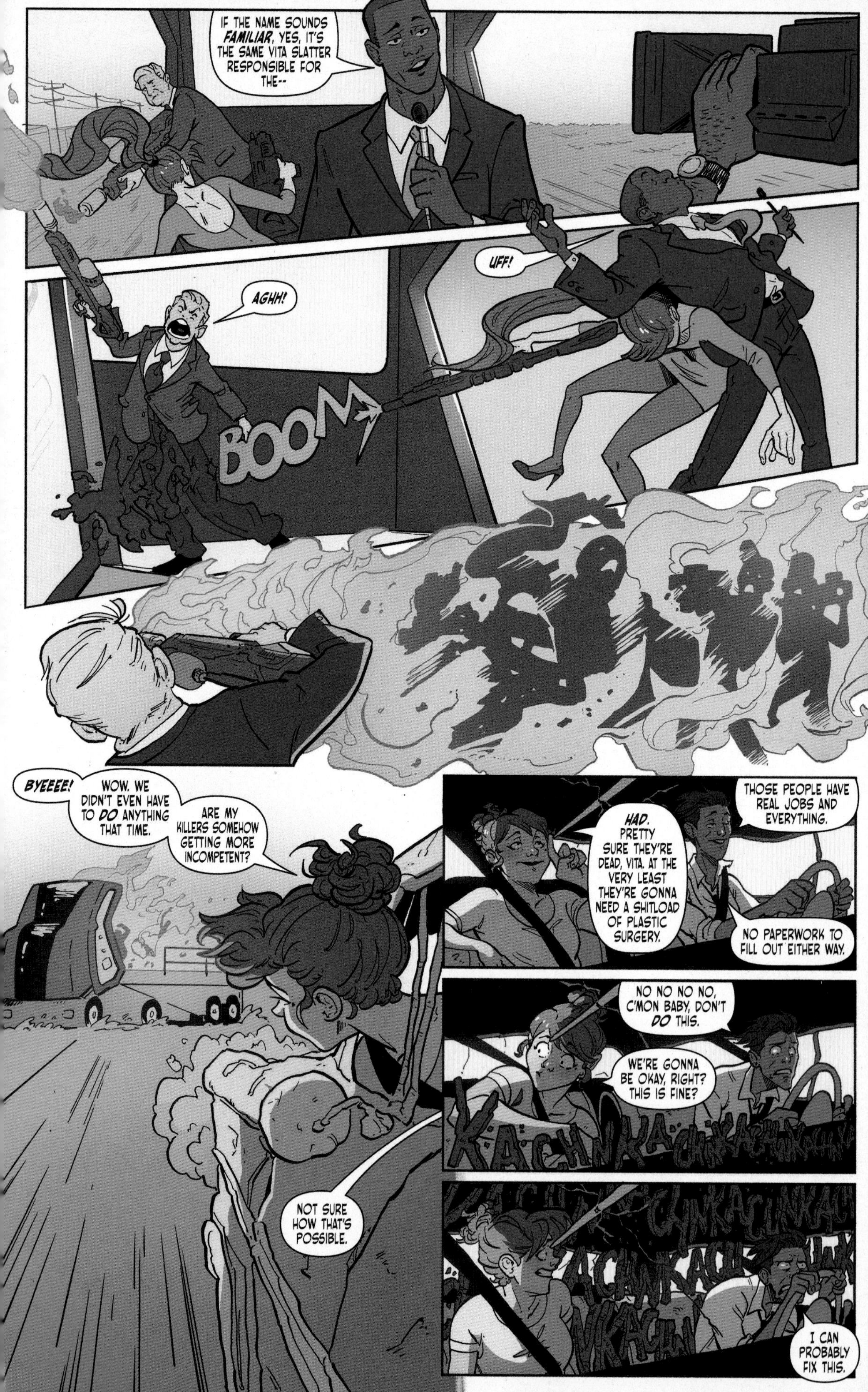
IF THE NAME SOUNDS FAMILIAR, YES, IT'S THE SAME VITA SLATTER RESPONSIBLE FOR THE--
UFF!
AGHH!
BOOM
BYEEEE!
WOW. WE DIDN'T EVEN HAVE TO DO ANYTHING THAT TIME.
ARE MY KILLERS SOMEHOW GETTING MORE INCOMPETENT?
NOT SURE HOW THAT'S POSSIBLE.
THOSE PEOPLE HAVE REAL JOBS AND EVERYTHING.
HAD. PRETTY SURE THEY'RE DEAD, VITA. AT THE VERY LEAST THEY'RE GONNA NEED A SHITLOAD OF PLASTIC SURGERY.
NO PAPERWORK TO FILL OUT EITHER WAY.
NO NO NO NO, C'MON BABY, DON'T DO THIS.
WE'RE GONNA BE OKAY, RIGHT? THIS IS FINE?
KACHNKA
I CAN PROBABLY FIX THIS.

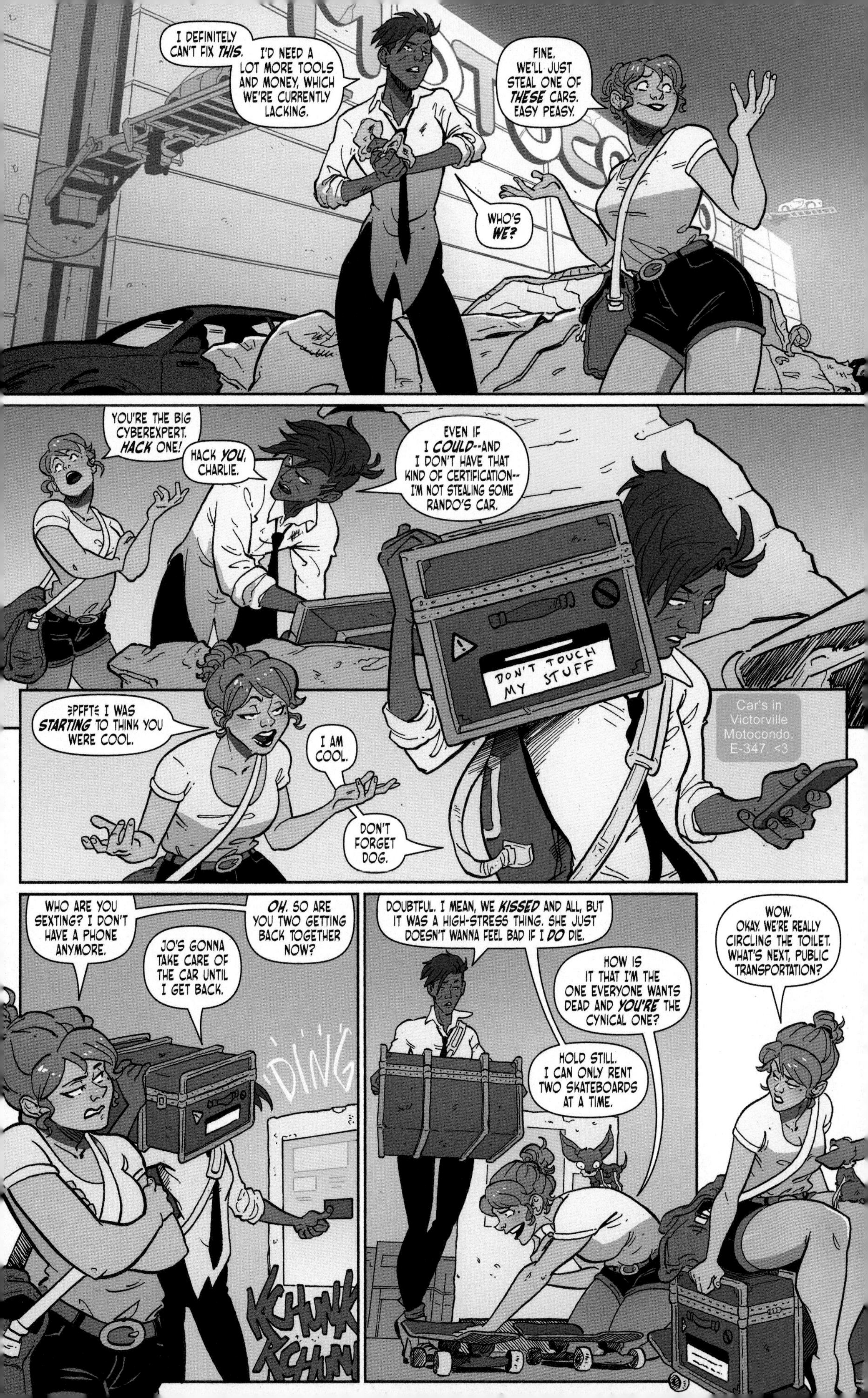
I DEFINITELY CAN'T FIX *THIS*.
I'D NEED A LOT MORE TOOLS AND MONEY, WHICH WE'RE CURRENTLY LACKING.
FINE. WE'LL JUST STEAL ONE OF *THESE* CARS. EASY PEASY.
WHO'S *WE?*
YOU'RE THE BIG CYBEREXPERT. *HACK* ONE!
HACK *YOU*, CHARLIE.
EVEN IF I *COULD*--AND I DON'T HAVE THAT KIND OF CERTIFICATION--I'M NOT STEALING SOME RANDO'S CAR.
DON'T TOUCH MY STUFF
ƎPFFTƐ I WAS *STARTING* TO THINK YOU WERE COOL.
I AM COOL.
DON'T FORGET DOG.
Car's in Victorville Motocondo. E-347. <3
WHO ARE YOU SEXTING? I DON'T HAVE A PHONE ANYMORE.
JO'S GONNA TAKE CARE OF THE CAR UNTIL I GET BACK.
OH. SO ARE YOU TWO GETTING BACK TOGETHER NOW?
DING
KCHUNK KCHUNK
DOUBTFUL. I MEAN, WE *KISSED* AND ALL, BUT IT WAS A HIGH-STRESS THING. SHE JUST DOESN'T WANNA FEEL BAD IF I *DO* DIE.
HOW IS IT THAT I'M THE ONE EVERYONE WANTS DEAD AND *YOU'RE* THE CYNICAL ONE?
HOLD STILL. I CAN ONLY RENT TWO SKATEBOARDS AT A TIME.
WOW. OKAY. WE'RE REALLY CIRCLING THE TOILET. WHAT'S NEXT, PUBLIC TRANSPORTATION?

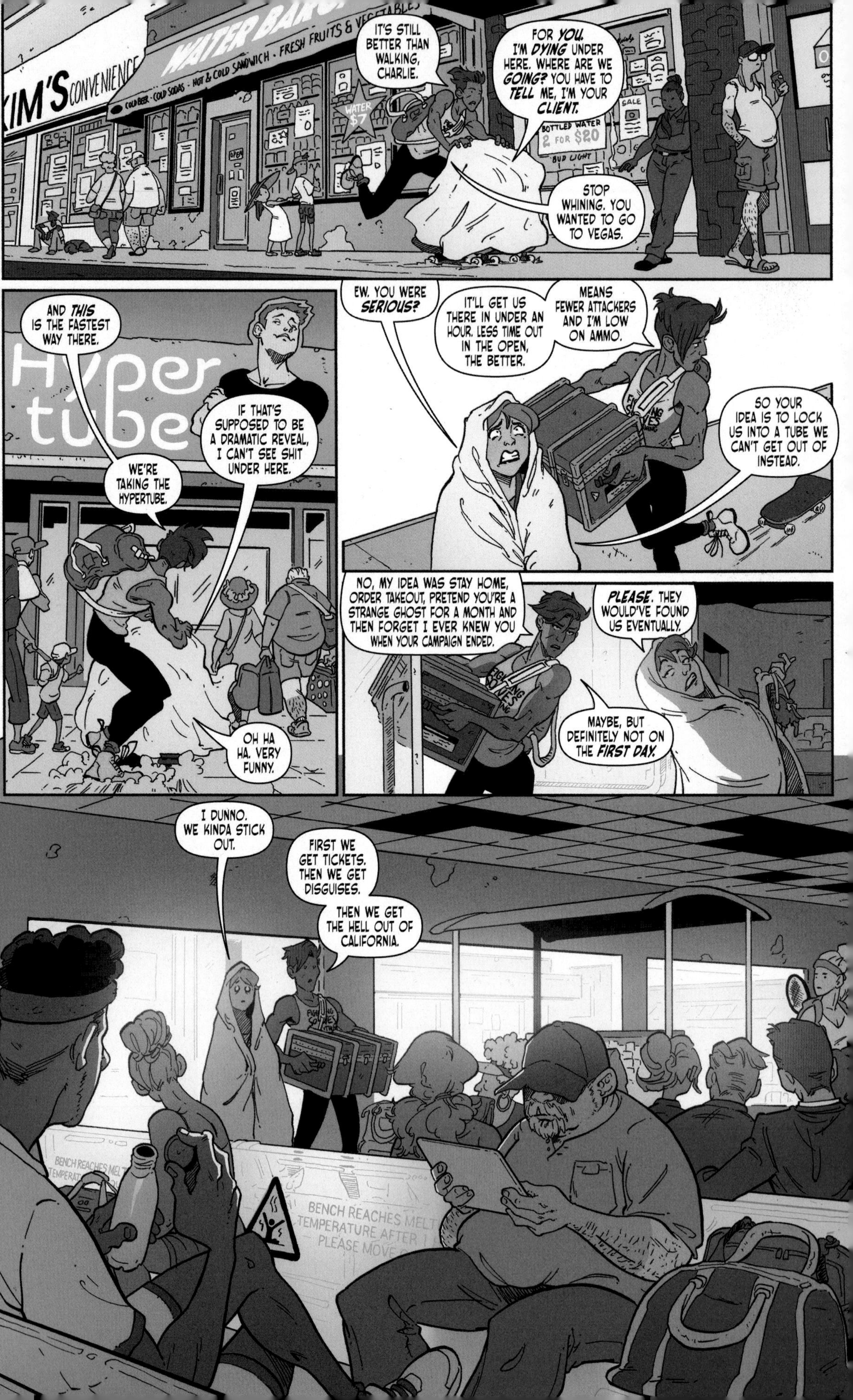
KIM'S CONVENIENCE
COLD BEER · COLD SODAS · HOT & COLD SANDWICH · FRESH FRUITS & VEGETABLES
WATER $7
IT'S STILL BETTER THAN WALKING, CHARLIE.
FOR YOU. I'M DYING UNDER HERE. WHERE ARE WE GOING? YOU HAVE TO TELL ME, I'M YOUR CLIENT.
BOTTLED WATER 2 FOR $20
BUD LIGHT
SALE
STOP WHINING. YOU WANTED TO GO TO VEGAS.
Hyper tube
AND THIS IS THE FASTEST WAY THERE.
IF THAT'S SUPPOSED TO BE A DRAMATIC REVEAL, I CAN'T SEE SHIT UNDER HERE.
WE'RE TAKING THE HYPERTUBE.
OH HA HA. VERY FUNNY.
EW. YOU WERE SERIOUS?
IT'LL GET US THERE IN UNDER AN HOUR. LESS TIME OUT IN THE OPEN, THE BETTER.
MEANS FEWER ATTACKERS AND I'M LOW ON AMMO.
SO YOUR IDEA IS TO LOCK US INTO A TUBE WE CAN'T GET OUT OF INSTEAD.
NO, MY IDEA WAS STAY HOME, ORDER TAKEOUT, PRETEND YOU'RE A STRANGE GHOST FOR A MONTH AND THEN FORGET I EVER KNEW YOU WHEN YOUR CAMPAIGN ENDED.
PLEASE. THEY WOULD'VE FOUND US EVENTUALLY.
MAYBE, BUT DEFINITELY NOT ON THE FIRST DAY.
I DUNNO. WE KINDA STICK OUT.
FIRST WE GET TICKETS. THEN WE GET DISGUISES.
THEN WE GET THE HELL OUT OF CALIFORNIA.

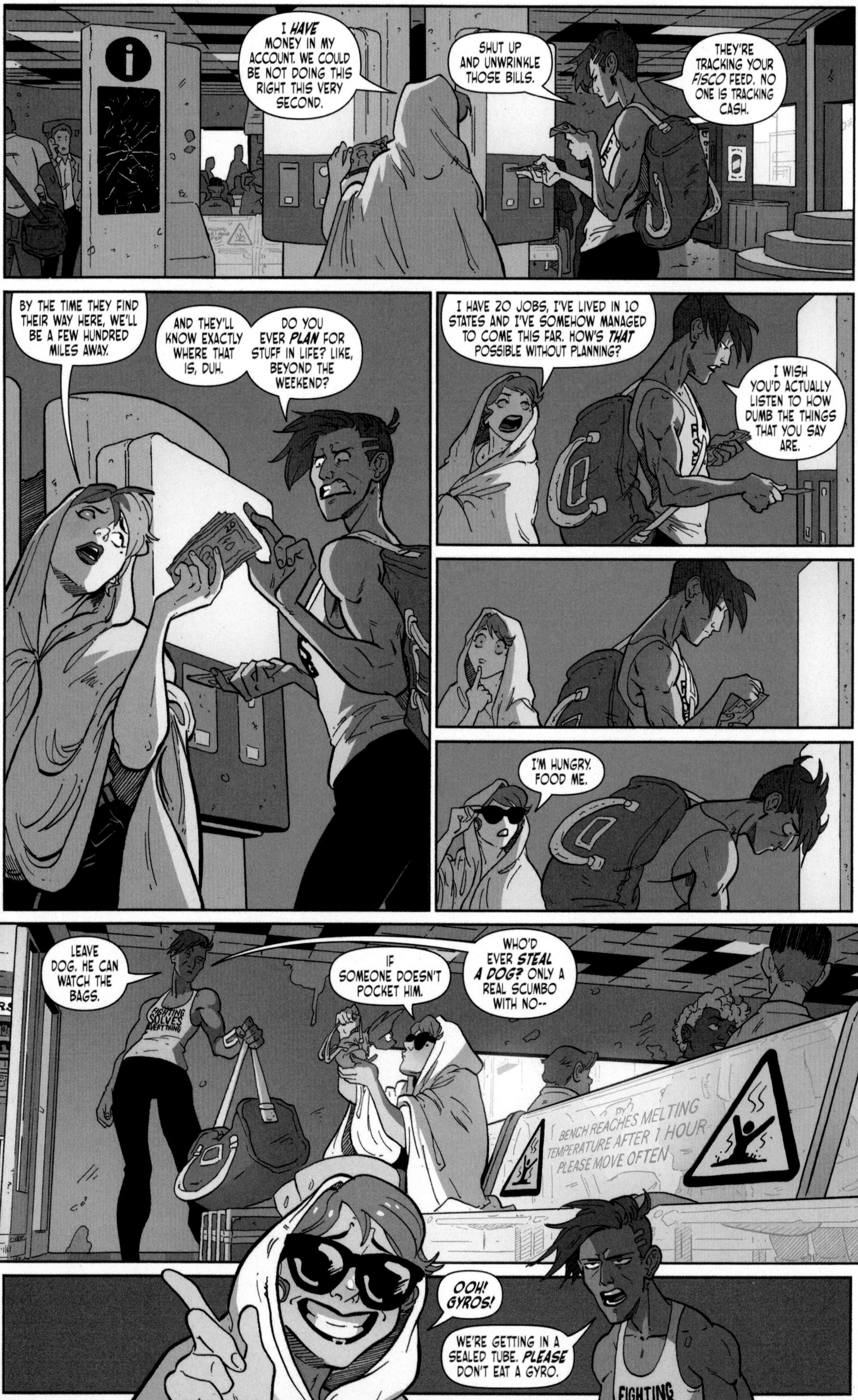

I HAVE MONEY IN MY ACCOUNT. WE COULD BE NOT DOING THIS RIGHT THIS VERY SECOND.
SHUT UP AND UNWRINKLE THOSE BILLS.
THEY'RE TRACKING YOUR FISCO FEED. NO ONE IS TRACKING CASH.
BY THE TIME THEY FIND THEIR WAY HERE, WE'LL BE A FEW HUNDRED MILES AWAY.
AND THEY'LL KNOW EXACTLY WHERE THAT IS, DUH.
DO YOU EVER PLAN FOR STUFF IN LIFE? LIKE, BEYOND THE WEEKEND?
I HAVE 20 JOBS, I'VE LIVED IN 10 STATES AND I'VE SOMEHOW MANAGED TO COME THIS FAR. HOW'S THAT POSSIBLE WITHOUT PLANNING?
I WISH YOU'D ACTUALLY LISTEN TO HOW DUMB THE THINGS THAT YOU SAY ARE.
I'M HUNGRY. FOOD ME.
LEAVE DOG. HE CAN WATCH THE BAGS.
IF SOMEONE DOESN'T POCKET HIM.
WHO'D EVER STEAL A DOG? ONLY A REAL SCUMBO WITH NO--
FIGHTING SOLVES EVERYTHING
BENCH REACHES MELTING TEMPERATURE AFTER 1 HOUR PLEASE MOVE OFTEN
OOH! GYROS!
WE'RE GETTING IN A SEALED TUBE. PLEASE DON'T EAT A GYRO.
FIGHTING

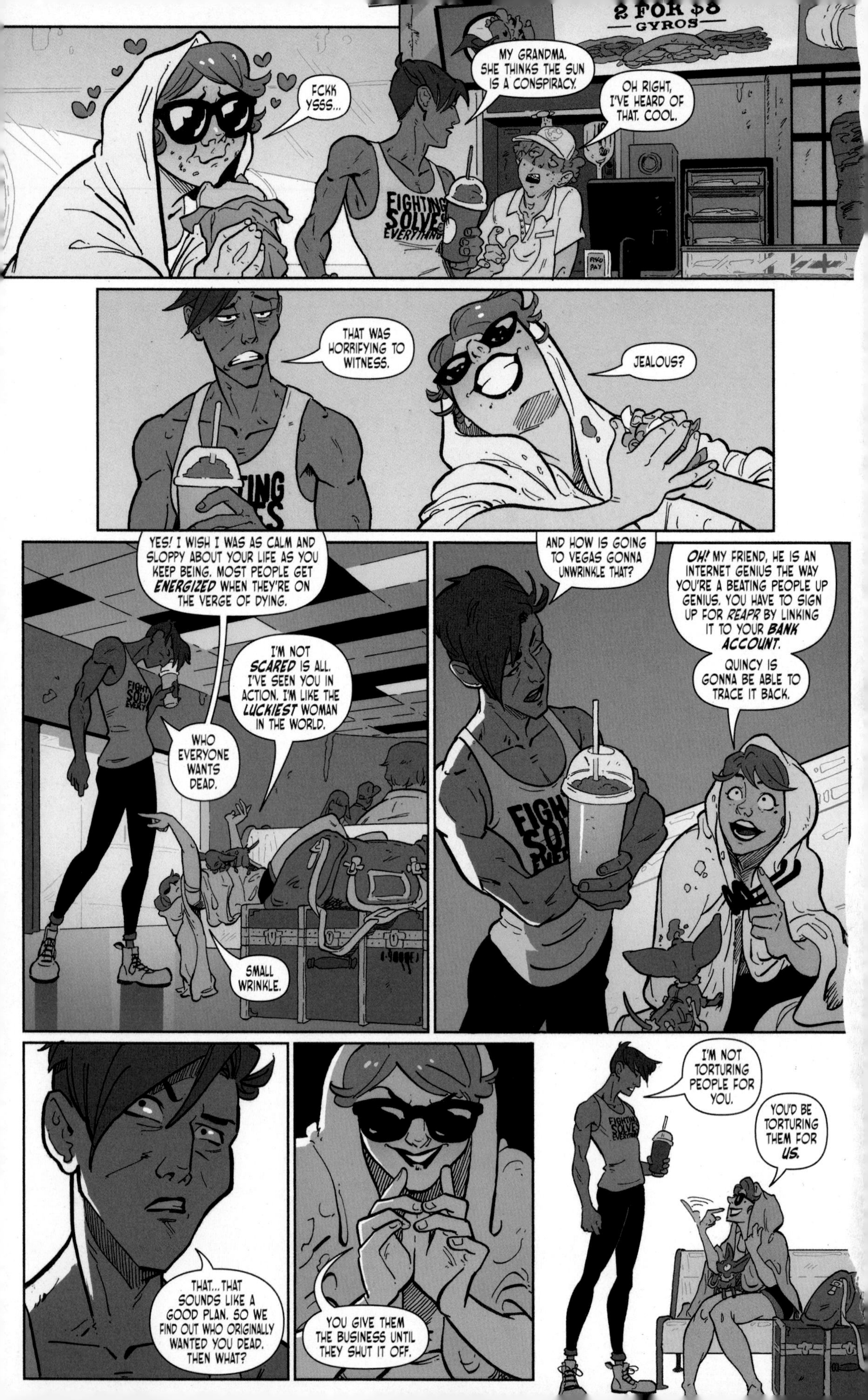
2 FOR $8
GYROS
FCKK YSSS...
MY GRANDMA. SHE THINKS THE SUN IS A CONSPIRACY.
OH RIGHT, I'VE HEARD OF THAT. COOL.
FIGHTING SOLVES EVERYTHING
THAT WAS HORRIFYING TO WITNESS.
JEALOUS?
YES! I WISH I WAS AS CALM AND SLOPPY ABOUT YOUR LIFE AS YOU KEEP BEING. MOST PEOPLE GET ENERGIZED WHEN THEY'RE ON THE VERGE OF DYING.
I'M NOT SCARED IS ALL. I'VE SEEN YOU IN ACTION. I'M LIKE THE LUCKIEST WOMAN IN THE WORLD.
WHO EVERYONE WANTS DEAD.
SMALL WRINKLE.
AND HOW IS GOING TO VEGAS GONNA UNWRINKLE THAT?
OH! MY FRIEND, HE IS AN INTERNET GENIUS THE WAY YOU'RE A BEATING PEOPLE UP GENIUS. YOU HAVE TO SIGN UP FOR REAPR BY LINKING IT TO YOUR BANK ACCOUNT.
QUINCY IS GONNA BE ABLE TO TRACE IT BACK.
THAT...THAT SOUNDS LIKE A GOOD PLAN. SO WE FIND OUT WHO ORIGINALLY WANTED YOU DEAD. THEN WHAT?
YOU GIVE THEM THE BUSINESS UNTIL THEY SHUT IT OFF.
I'M NOT TORTURING PEOPLE FOR YOU.
YOU'D BE TORTURING THEM FOR US.

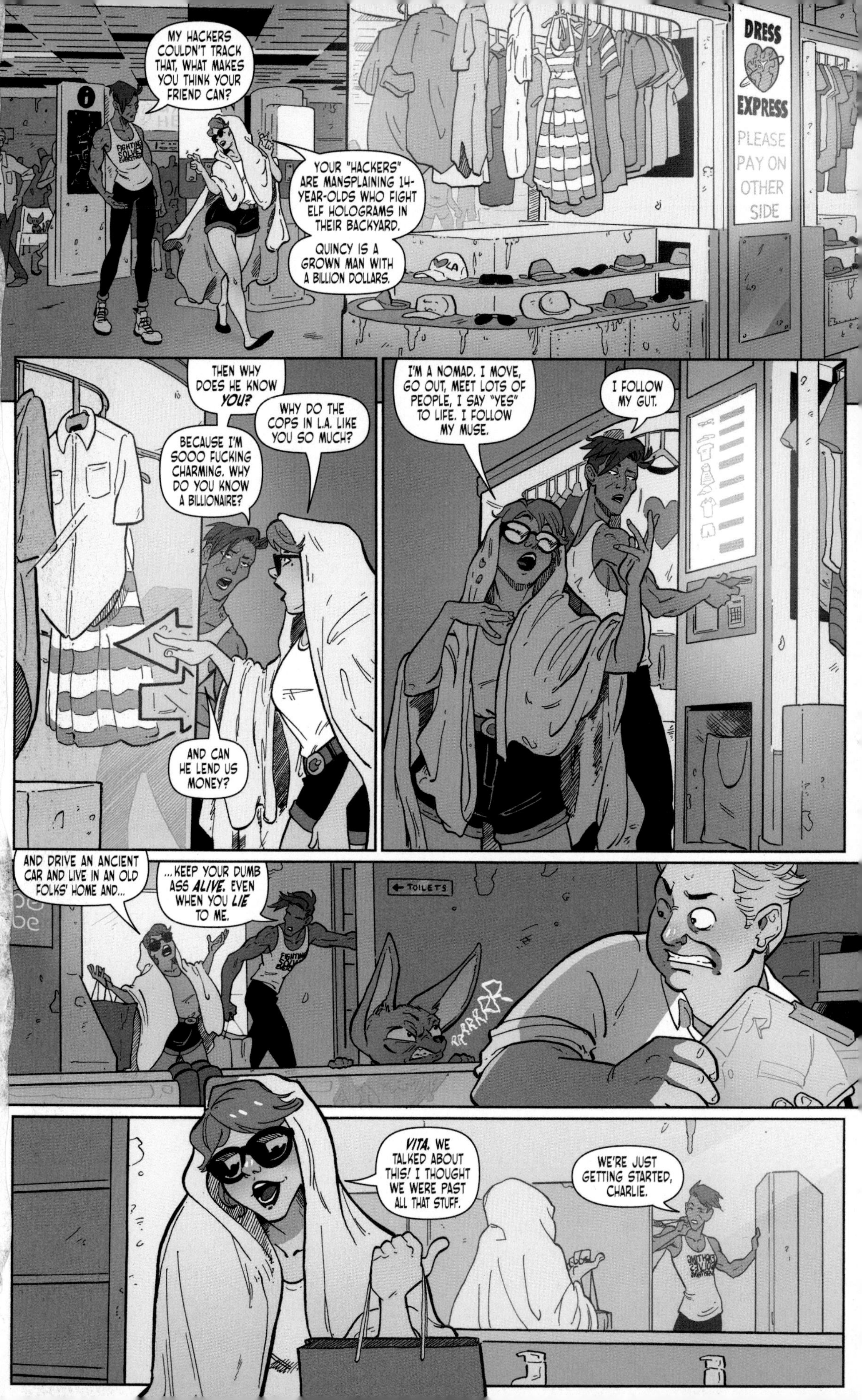
MY HACKERS COULDN'T TRACK THAT, WHAT MAKES YOU THINK YOUR FRIEND CAN?
YOUR "HACKERS" ARE MANSPLAINING 14-YEAR-OLDS WHO FIGHT ELF HOLOGRAMS IN THEIR BACKYARD.
QUINCY IS A GROWN MAN WITH A BILLION DOLLARS.
DRESS EXPRESS
PLEASE PAY ON OTHER SIDE
THEN WHY DOES HE KNOW *YOU?*
WHY DO THE COPS IN L.A. LIKE YOU SO MUCH?
BECAUSE I'M SOOO FUCKING CHARMING. WHY DO YOU KNOW A BILLIONAIRE?
AND CAN HE LEND US MONEY?
I'M A NOMAD. I MOVE, GO OUT, MEET LOTS OF PEOPLE, I SAY "YES" TO LIFE. I FOLLOW MY MUSE.
I FOLLOW MY GUT.
AND DRIVE AN ANCIENT CAR AND LIVE IN AN OLD FOLKS' HOME AND...
...KEEP YOUR DUMB ASS *ALIVE.* EVEN WHEN YOU *LIE* TO ME.
← TOILETS
RRRRRR
VITA. WE TALKED ABOUT THIS! I THOUGHT WE WERE PAST ALL THAT STUFF.
WE'RE JUST GETTING STARTED, CHARLIE.

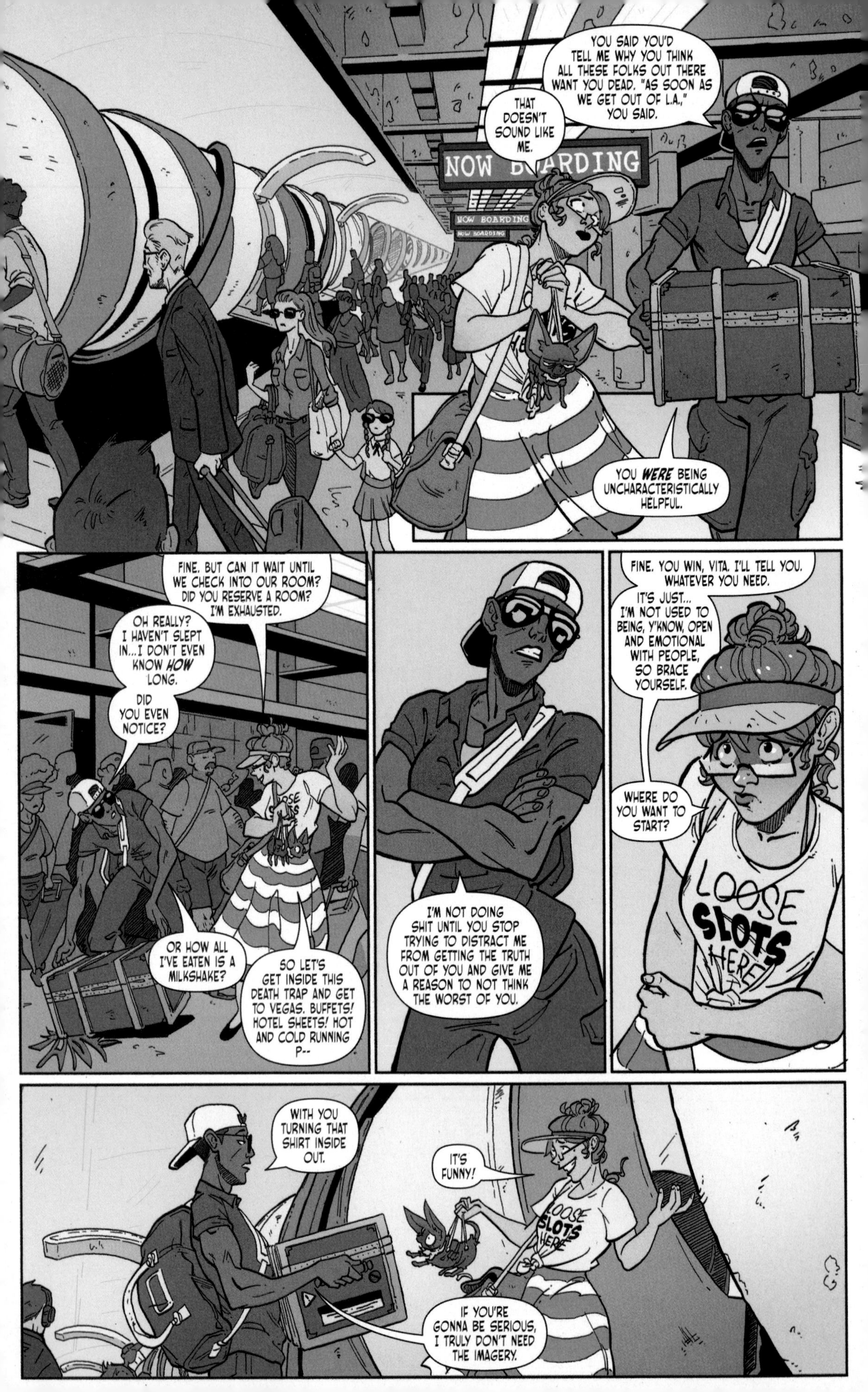
NOW BOARDING
YOU SAID YOU'D TELL ME WHY YOU THINK ALL THESE FOLKS OUT THERE WANT YOU DEAD. "AS SOON AS WE GET OUT OF L.A.," YOU SAID.
THAT DOESN'T SOUND LIKE ME.
YOU WERE BEING UNCHARACTERISTICALLY HELPFUL.
FINE. BUT CAN IT WAIT UNTIL WE CHECK INTO OUR ROOM? DID YOU RESERVE A ROOM? I'M EXHAUSTED.
OH REALLY? I HAVEN'T SLEPT IN...I DON'T EVEN KNOW HOW LONG.
DID YOU EVEN NOTICE?
OR HOW ALL I'VE EATEN IS A MILKSHAKE?
SO LET'S GET INSIDE THIS DEATH TRAP AND GET TO VEGAS. BUFFETS! HOTEL SHEETS! HOT AND COLD RUNNING P--
I'M NOT DOING SHIT UNTIL YOU STOP TRYING TO DISTRACT ME FROM GETTING THE TRUTH OUT OF YOU AND GIVE ME A REASON TO NOT THINK THE WORST OF YOU.
FINE. YOU WIN, VITA. I'LL TELL YOU. WHATEVER YOU NEED.
IT'S JUST... I'M NOT USED TO BEING, Y'KNOW, OPEN AND EMOTIONAL WITH PEOPLE, SO BRACE YOURSELF.
WHERE DO YOU WANT TO START?
LOOSE SLOTS HERE
WITH YOU TURNING THAT SHIRT INSIDE OUT.
IT'S FUNNY!
IF YOU'RE GONNA BE SERIOUS, I TRULY DON'T NEED THE IMAGERY.

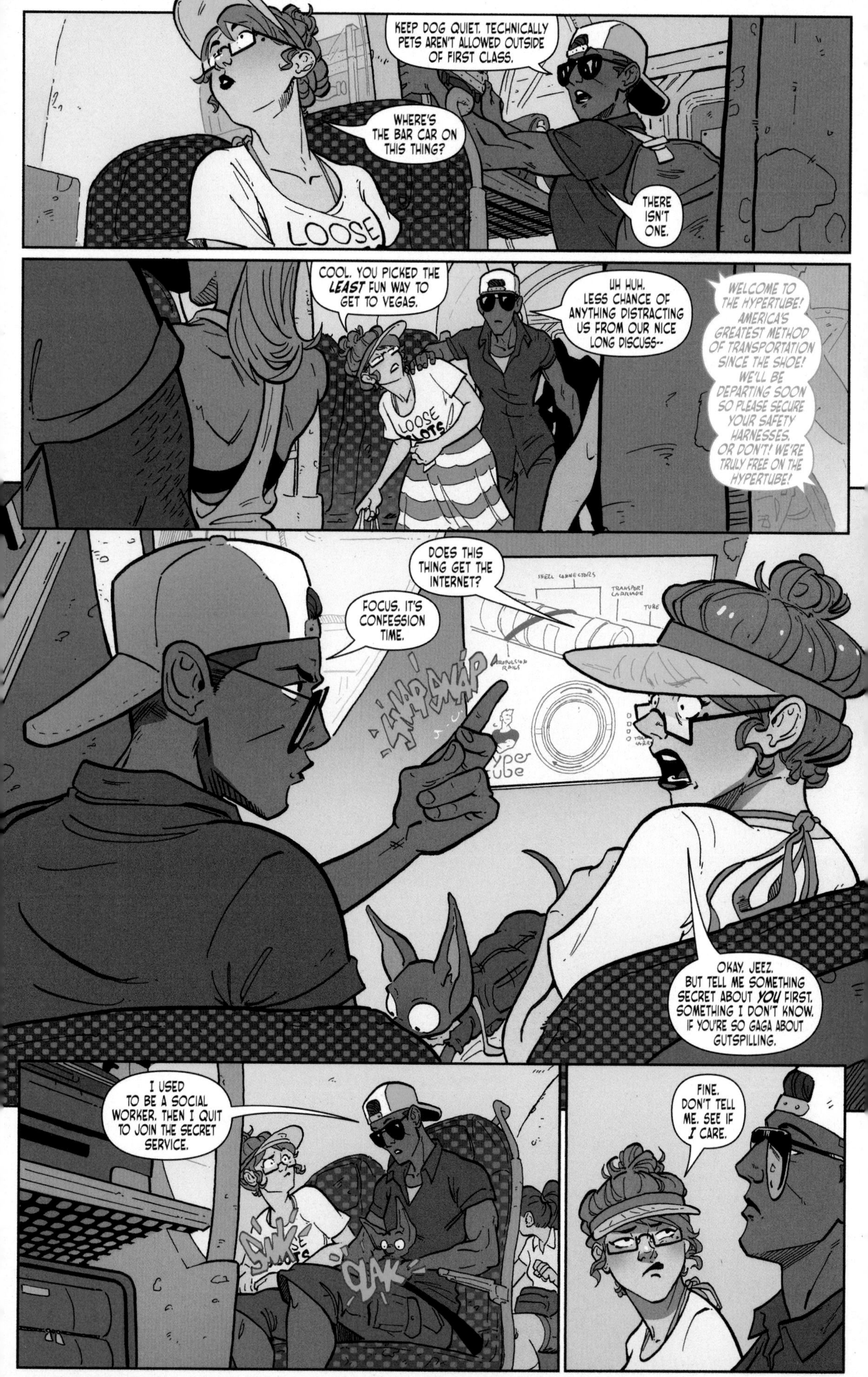
KEEP DOG QUIET. TECHNICALLY PETS AREN'T ALLOWED OUTSIDE OF FIRST CLASS.
WHERE'S THE BAR CAR ON THIS THING?
THERE ISN'T ONE.
LOOSE
COOL. YOU PICKED THE LEAST FUN WAY TO GET TO VEGAS.
UH HUH. LESS CHANCE OF ANYTHING DISTRACTING US FROM OUR NICE LONG DISCUSS--
WELCOME TO THE HYPERTUBE! AMERICA'S GREATEST METHOD OF TRANSPORTATION SINCE THE SHOE! WE'LL BE DEPARTING SOON SO PLEASE SECURE YOUR SAFETY HARNESSES. OR DON'T! WE'RE TRULY FREE ON THE HYPERTUBE!
LOOSE LOTS
DOES THIS THING GET THE INTERNET?
FOCUS. IT'S CONFESSION TIME.
SNAP SNAP
OKAY, JEEZ. BUT TELL ME SOMETHING SECRET ABOUT YOU FIRST. SOMETHING I DON'T KNOW. IF YOU'RE SO GAGA ABOUT GUTSPILLING.
I USED TO BE A SOCIAL WORKER. THEN I QUIT TO JOIN THE SECRET SERVICE.
CLAK
FINE. DON'T TELL ME. SEE IF I CARE.

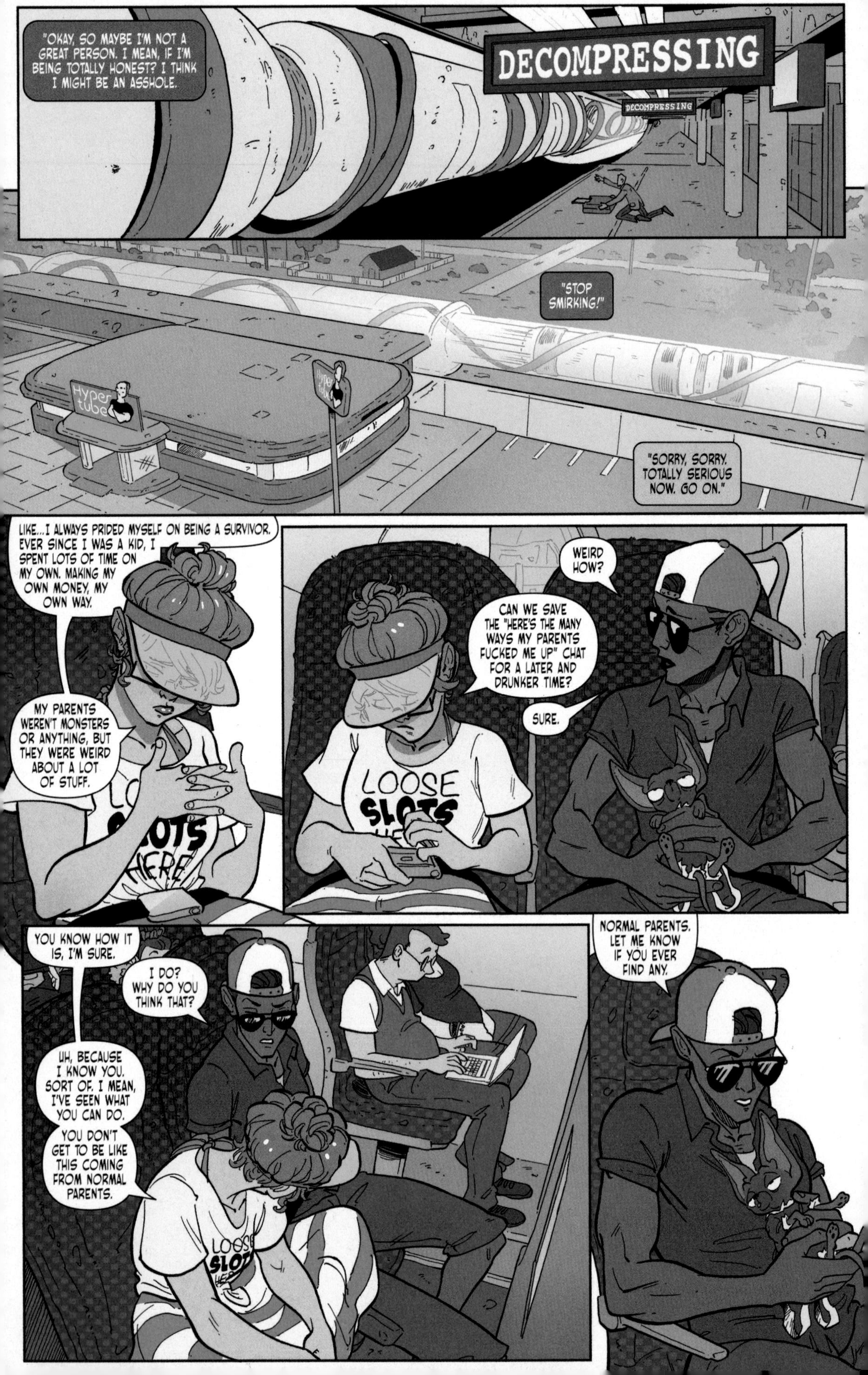
"OKAY, SO MAYBE I'M NOT A GREAT PERSON. I MEAN, IF I'M BEING TOTALLY HONEST? I THINK I MIGHT BE AN ASSHOLE.
DECOMPRESSING
DECOMPRESSING
"STOP SMIRKING!"
Hyper tube
"SORRY, SORRY. TOTALLY SERIOUS NOW. GO ON."
LIKE...I ALWAYS PRIDED MYSELF ON BEING A SURVIVOR. EVER SINCE I WAS A KID, I SPENT LOTS OF TIME ON MY OWN. MAKING MY OWN MONEY, MY OWN WAY.
MY PARENTS WEREN'T MONSTERS OR ANYTHING, BUT THEY WERE WEIRD ABOUT A LOT OF STUFF.
WEIRD HOW?
CAN WE SAVE THE "HERE'S THE MANY WAYS MY PARENTS FUCKED ME UP" CHAT FOR A LATER AND DRUNKER TIME?
SURE.
LOOSE SLOTS
YOU KNOW HOW IT IS, I'M SURE.
I DO? WHY DO YOU THINK THAT?
UH, BECAUSE I KNOW YOU. SORT OF. I MEAN, I'VE SEEN WHAT YOU CAN DO.
YOU DON'T GET TO BE LIKE THIS COMING FROM NORMAL PARENTS.
NORMAL PARENTS. LET ME KNOW IF YOU EVER FIND ANY.

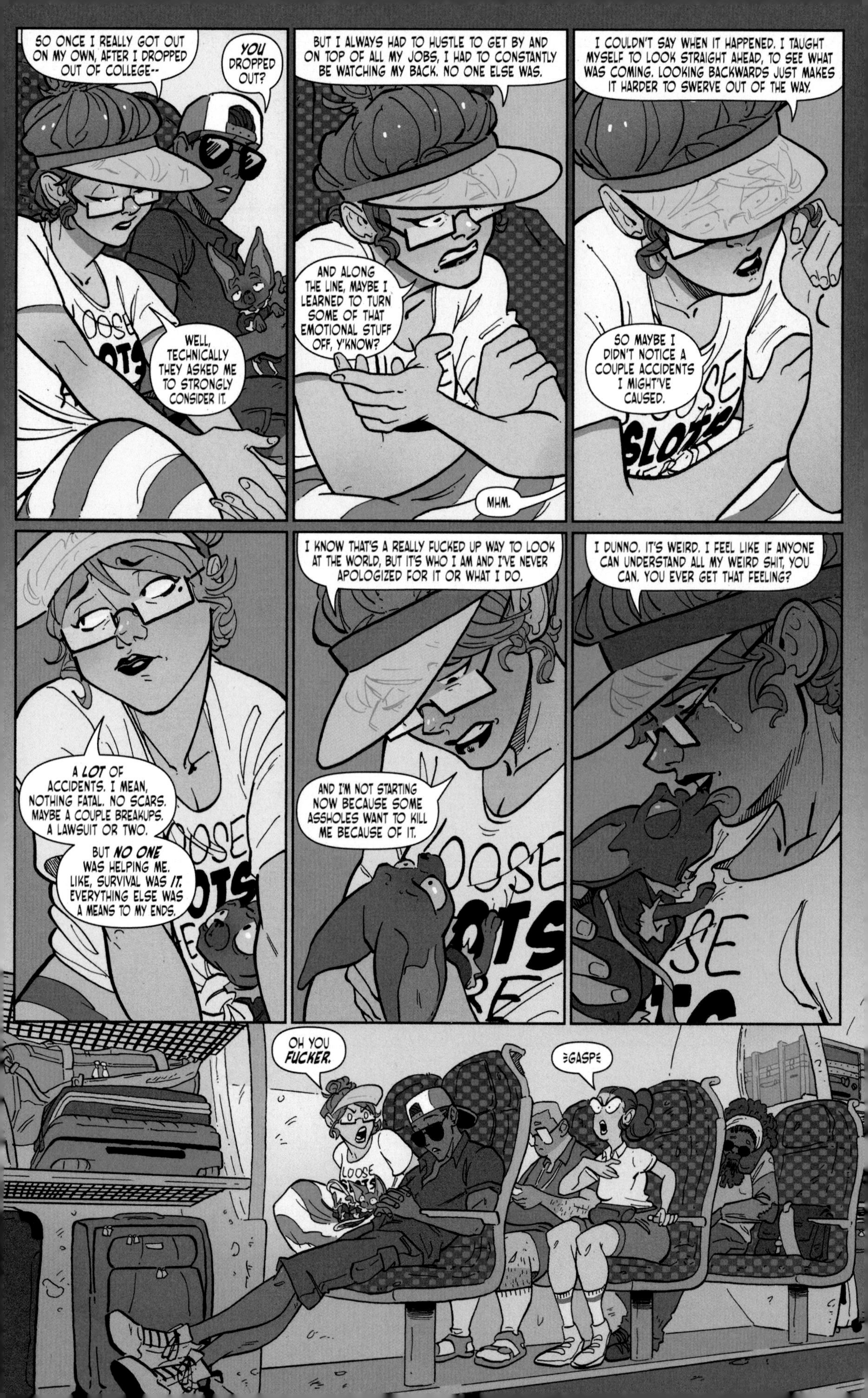
SO ONCE I REALLY GOT OUT ON MY OWN, AFTER I DROPPED OUT OF COLLEGE--
YOU DROPPED OUT?
WELL, TECHNICALLY THEY ASKED ME TO STRONGLY CONSIDER IT.
BUT I ALWAYS HAD TO HUSTLE TO GET BY AND ON TOP OF ALL MY JOBS, I HAD TO CONSTANTLY BE WATCHING MY BACK. NO ONE ELSE WAS.
AND ALONG THE LINE, MAYBE I LEARNED TO TURN SOME OF THAT EMOTIONAL STUFF OFF, Y'KNOW?
I COULDN'T SAY WHEN IT HAPPENED. I TAUGHT MYSELF TO LOOK STRAIGHT AHEAD, TO SEE WHAT WAS COMING. LOOKING BACKWARDS JUST MAKES IT HARDER TO SWERVE OUT OF THE WAY.
SO MAYBE I DIDN'T NOTICE A COUPLE ACCIDENTS I MIGHT'VE CAUSED.
MHM.
A LOT OF ACCIDENTS. I MEAN, NOTHING FATAL. NO SCARS. MAYBE A COUPLE BREAKUPS. A LAWSUIT OR TWO.
BUT NO ONE WAS HELPING ME. LIKE, SURVIVAL WAS IT. EVERYTHING ELSE WAS A MEANS TO MY ENDS.
I KNOW THAT'S A REALLY FUCKED UP WAY TO LOOK AT THE WORLD, BUT IT'S WHO I AM AND I'VE NEVER APOLOGIZED FOR IT OR WHAT I DO.
AND I'M NOT STARTING NOW BECAUSE SOME ASSHOLES WANT TO KILL ME BECAUSE OF IT.
I DUNNO. IT'S WEIRD. I FEEL LIKE IF ANYONE CAN UNDERSTAND ALL MY WEIRD SHIT, YOU CAN. YOU EVER GET THAT FEELING?
OH YOU FUCKER.
GASP

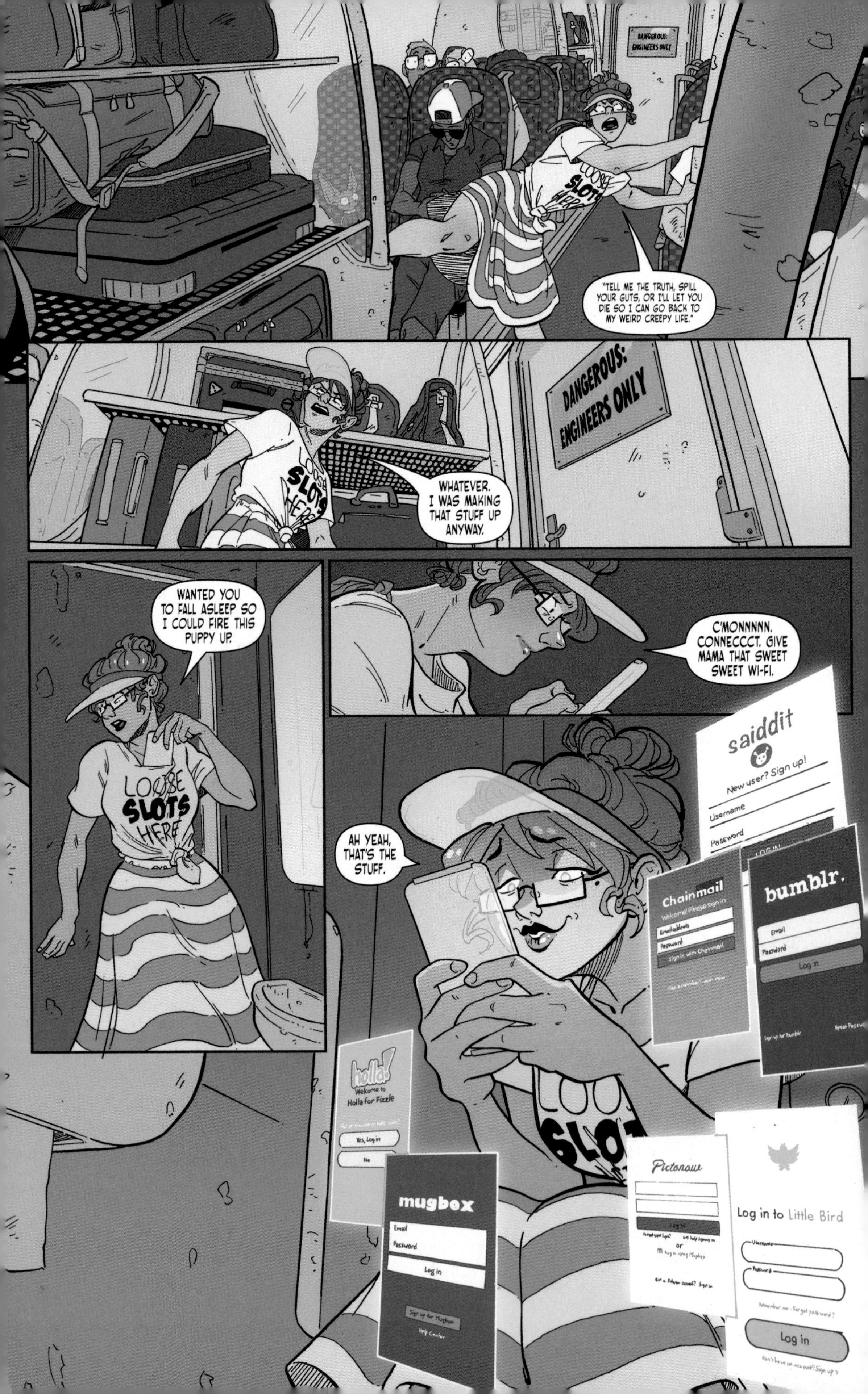

DANGEROUS: ENGINEERS ONLY
LOOSE SLOTS HERE
"TELL ME THE TRUTH, SPILL YOUR GUTS, OR I'LL LET YOU DIE SO I CAN GO BACK TO MY WEIRD CREEPY LIFE."
DANGEROUS: ENGINEERS ONLY
WHATEVER. I WAS MAKING THAT STUFF UP ANYWAY.
WANTED YOU TO FALL ASLEEP SO I COULD FIRE THIS PUPPY UP.
C'MONNNNN. CONNECCCT. GIVE MAMA THAT SWEET SWEET WI-FI.
AH YEAH, THAT'S THE STUFF.
saiddit
New user? Sign up!
Username
Password
Chainmail
Welcome! Please sign in
Email address
Password
Sign in with Chainmail
bumblr.
Email
Password
Log in
holla!
Welcome to Holla for Fizzle
Yes, Log in
No
mugbox
Email
Password
Log in
Sign up for Mugbox
Help Center
Pictonow
Log in
or
Log in to Little Bird
Username
Password
Remember me · Forgot password?
Log in
Don't have an account? Sign up?

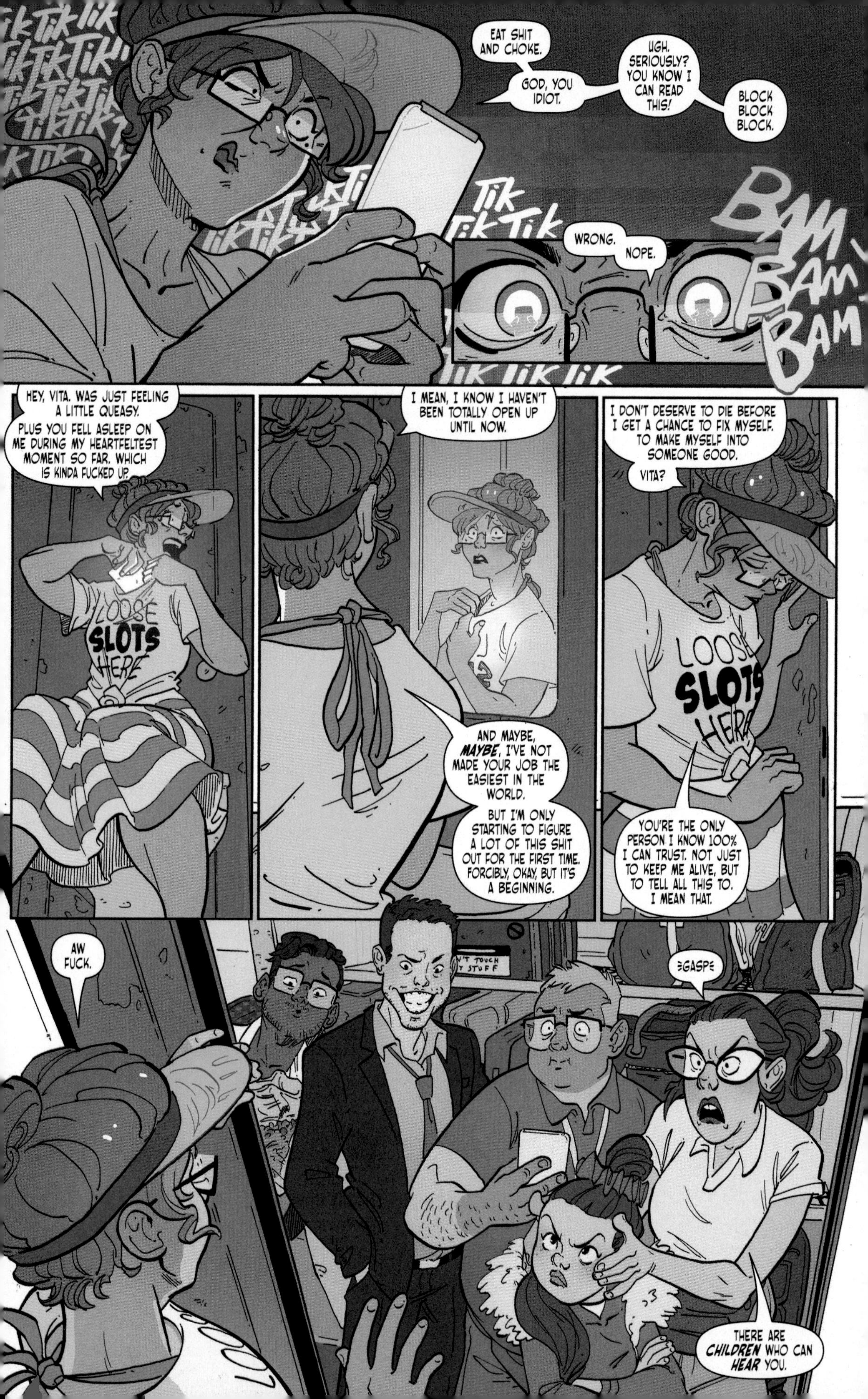
TIK TIK TIK TIK TIK
EAT SHIT AND CHOKE.
GOD, YOU IDIOT.
UGH. SERIOUSLY? YOU KNOW I CAN READ THIS!
BLOCK BLOCK BLOCK.
TIK TIK TIK
WRONG.
NOPE.
BAM BAM BAM
TIK TIK TIK
HEY, VITA. WAS JUST FEELING A LITTLE QUEASY.
PLUS YOU FELL ASLEEP ON ME DURING MY HEARTFELTEST MOMENT SO FAR. WHICH IS KINDA FUCKED UP.
LOOSE SLOTS HERE
I MEAN, I KNOW I HAVEN'T BEEN TOTALLY OPEN UP UNTIL NOW.
AND MAYBE, ***MAYBE***, I'VE NOT MADE YOUR JOB THE EASIEST IN THE WORLD.
BUT I'M ONLY STARTING TO FIGURE A LOT OF THIS SHIT OUT FOR THE FIRST TIME. FORCIBLY, OKAY, BUT IT'S A BEGINNING.
I DON'T DESERVE TO DIE BEFORE I GET A CHANCE TO FIX MYSELF. TO MAKE MYSELF INTO SOMEONE GOOD.
VITA?
LOOSE SLOTS HERE
YOU'RE THE ONLY PERSON I KNOW 100% I CAN TRUST. NOT JUST TO KEEP ME ALIVE, BUT TO TELL ALL THIS TO. I MEAN THAT.
AW FUCK.
=GASP=
THERE ARE ***CHILDREN*** WHO CAN ***HEAR*** YOU.

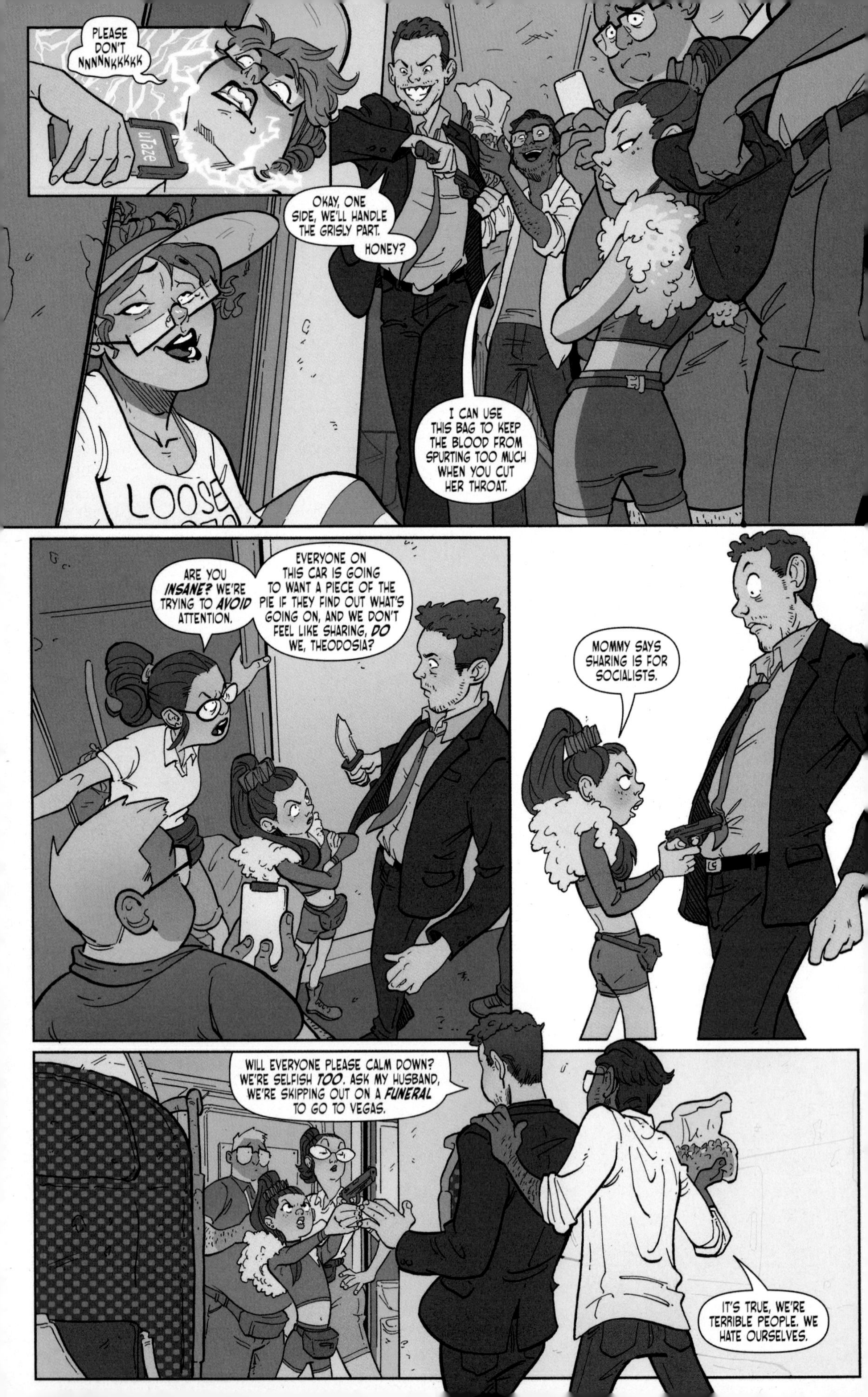
PLEASE DON'T NNNNNKKKKK
uTaze
OKAY, ONE SIDE, WE'LL HANDLE THE GRISLY PART.
HONEY?
I CAN USE THIS BAG TO KEEP THE BLOOD FROM SPURTING TOO MUCH WHEN YOU CUT HER THROAT.
LOOSE
ARE YOU INSANE? WE'RE TRYING TO AVOID ATTENTION.
EVERYONE ON THIS CAR IS GOING TO WANT A PIECE OF THE PIE IF THEY FIND OUT WHAT'S GOING ON, AND WE DON'T FEEL LIKE SHARING, DO WE, THEODOSIA?
MOMMY SAYS SHARING IS FOR SOCIALISTS.
WILL EVERYONE PLEASE CALM DOWN? WE'RE SELFISH TOO. ASK MY HUSBAND, WE'RE SKIPPING OUT ON A FUNERAL TO GO TO VEGAS.
IT'S TRUE, WE'RE TERRIBLE PEOPLE. WE HATE OURSELVES.

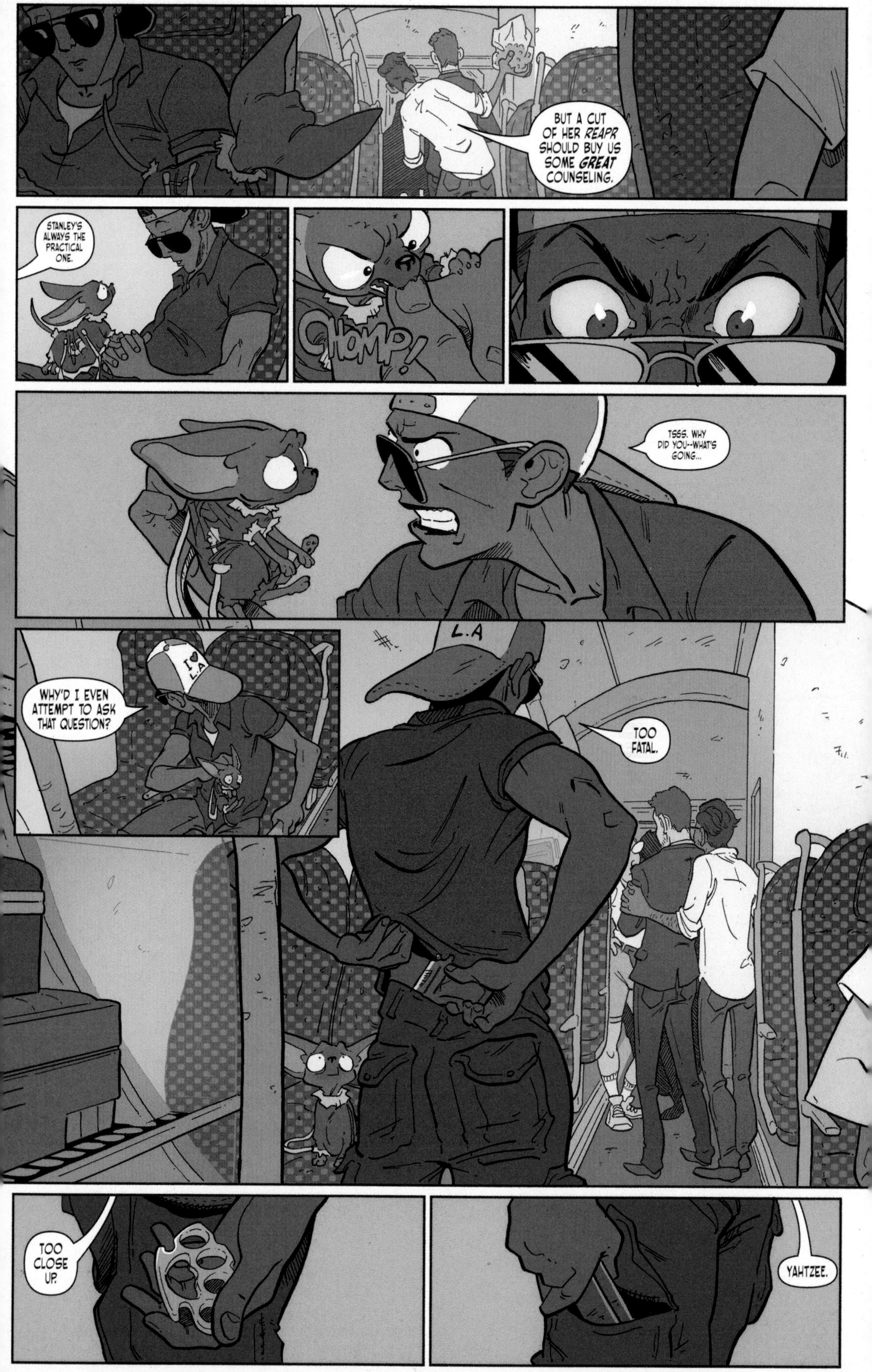
BUT A CUT OF HER *REAPR* SHOULD BUY US SOME ***GREAT*** COUNSELING.
STANLEY'S ALWAYS THE PRACTICAL ONE.
CHOMP!
TSSS. WHY DID YOU--WHAT'S GOING...
L.A
WHY'D I EVEN ATTEMPT TO ASK THAT QUESTION?
TOO FATAL.
TOO CLOSE UP.
YAHTZEE.

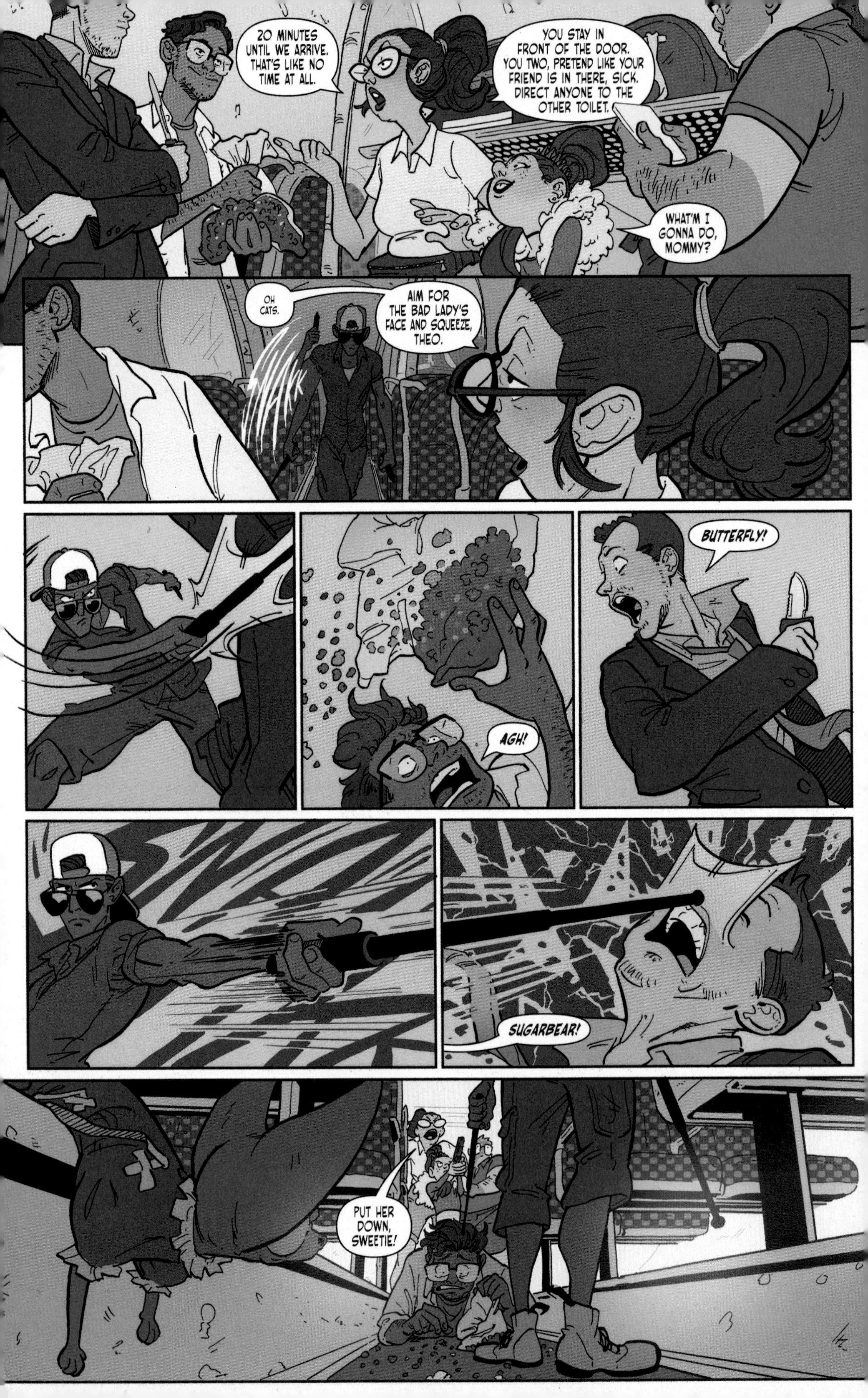
20 MINUTES UNTIL WE ARRIVE. THAT'S LIKE NO TIME AT ALL.
YOU STAY IN FRONT OF THE DOOR. YOU TWO, PRETEND LIKE YOUR FRIEND IS IN THERE, SICK. DIRECT ANYONE TO THE OTHER TOILET.
WHAT'M I GONNA DO, MOMMY?
OH CATS.
AIM FOR THE BAD LADY'S FACE AND SQUEEZE, THEO.
AGH!
BUTTERFLY!
SUGARBEAR!
PUT HER DOWN, SWEETIE!

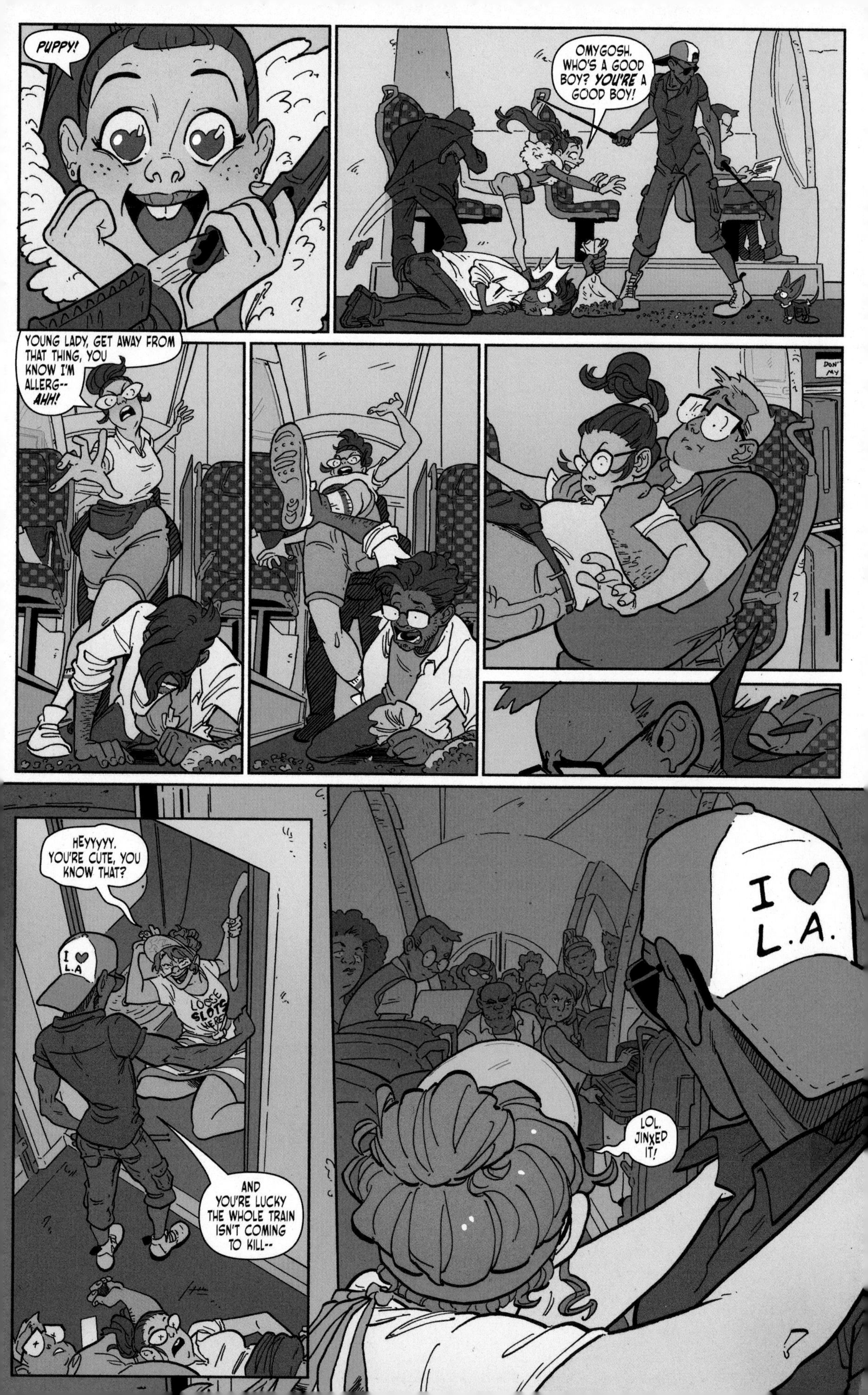
PUPPY!
OMYGOSH. WHO'S A GOOD BOY? YOU'RE A GOOD BOY!
YOUNG LADY, GET AWAY FROM THAT THING, YOU KNOW I'M ALLERG-- AHH!
DON'T MY
HEYYYYY. YOU'RE CUTE, YOU KNOW THAT?
I ♥ L.A
LOOSE SLOTS HERE
AND YOU'RE LUCKY THE WHOLE TRAIN ISN'T COMING TO KILL--
I ♥ L.A.
LOL. JINXED IT!

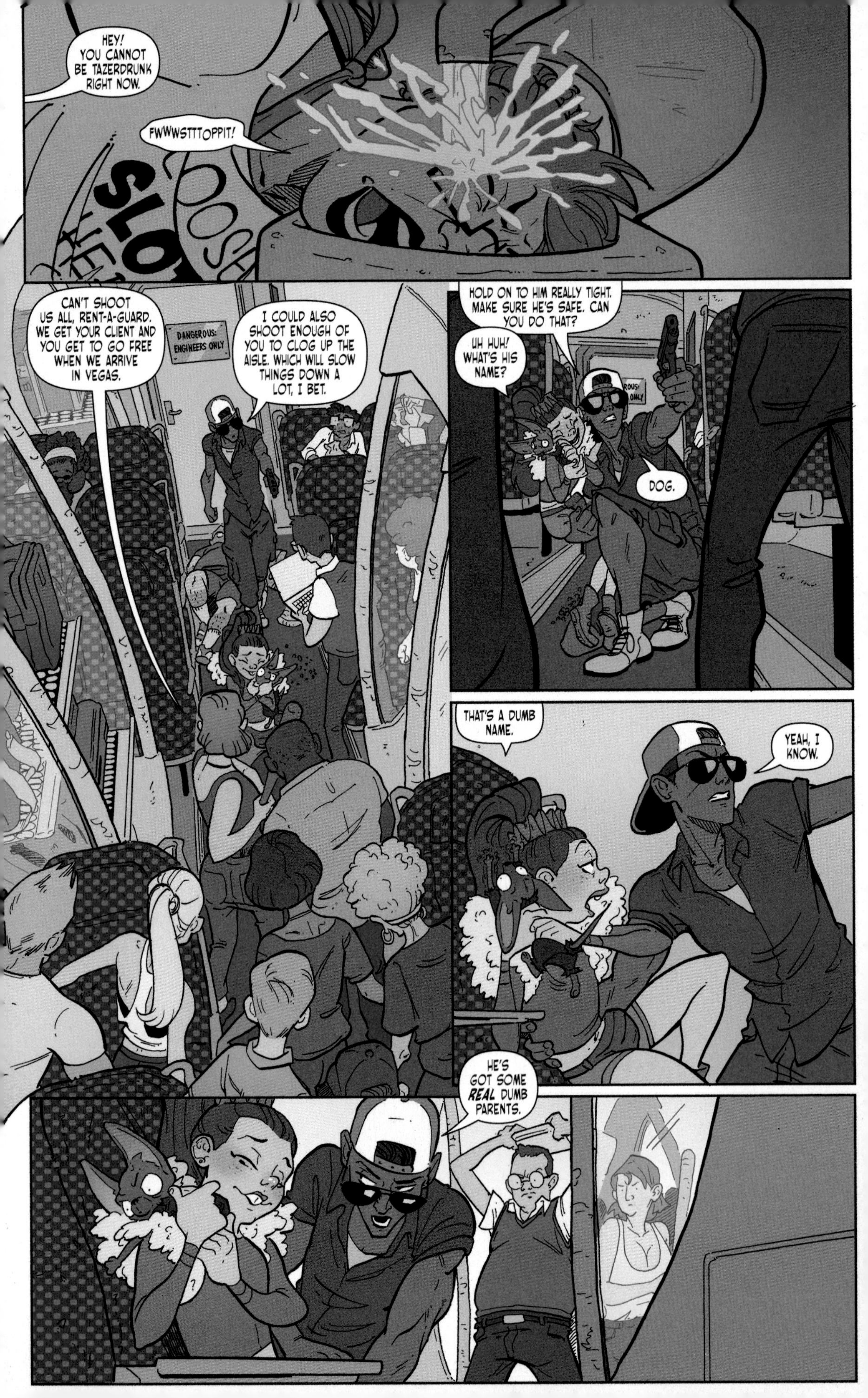
HEY! YOU CANNOT BE TAZERDRUNK RIGHT NOW.
FWWWSTTTOPPIT!
CAN'T SHOOT US ALL, RENT-A-GUARD. WE GET YOUR CLIENT AND YOU GET TO GO FREE WHEN WE ARRIVE IN VEGAS.
DANGEROUS: ENGINEERS ONLY
I COULD ALSO SHOOT ENOUGH OF YOU TO CLOG UP THE AISLE. WHICH WILL SLOW THINGS DOWN A LOT, I BET.
HOLD ON TO HIM REALLY TIGHT. MAKE SURE HE'S SAFE. CAN YOU DO THAT?
UH HUH! WHAT'S HIS NAME?
DOG.
THAT'S A DUMB NAME.
YEAH, I KNOW.
HE'S GOT SOME REAL DUMB PARENTS.

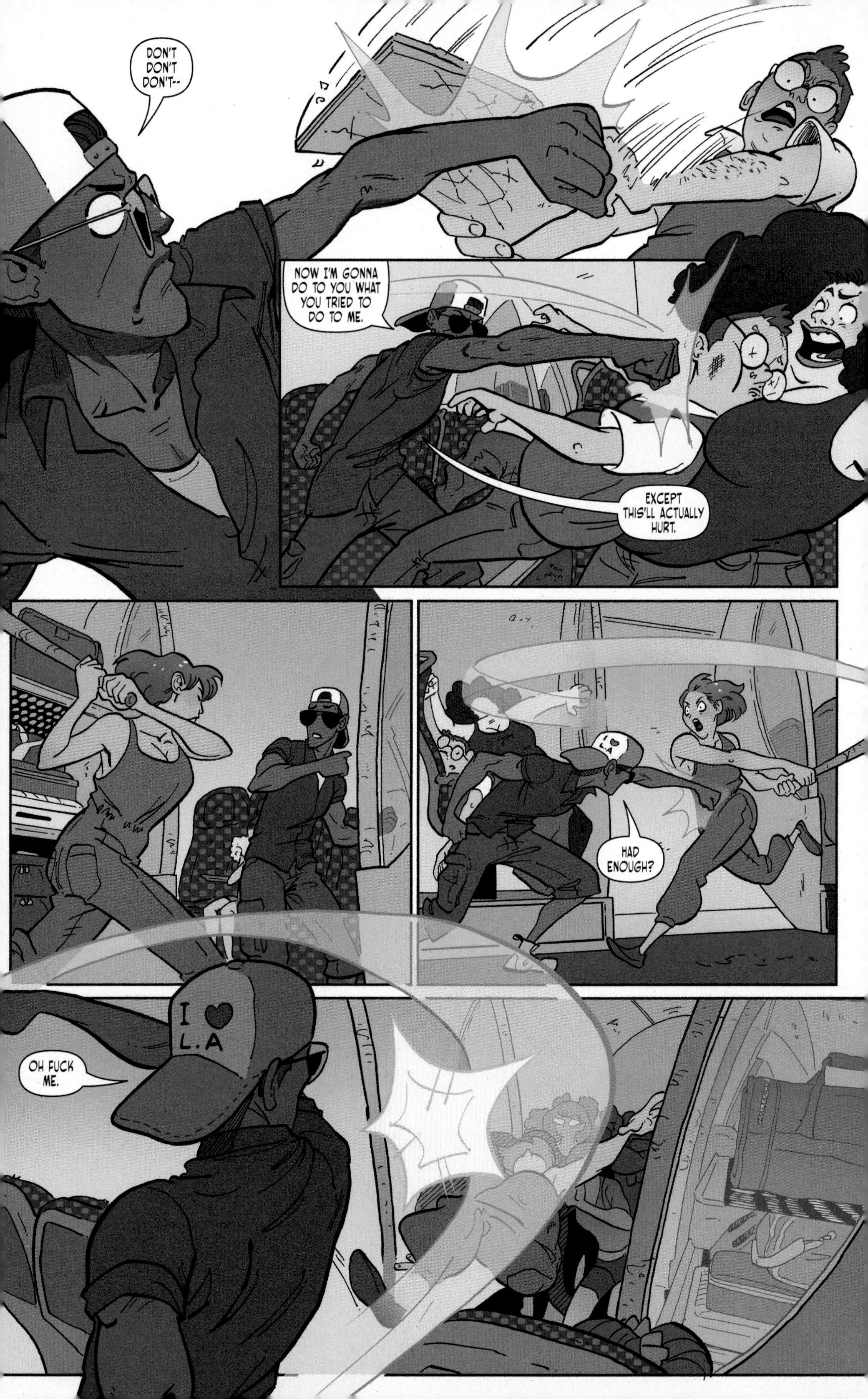
DON'T DON'T DON'T--
NOW I'M GONNA DO TO YOU WHAT YOU TRIED TO DO TO ME.
EXCEPT THIS'LL ACTUALLY HURT.
HAD ENOUGH?
I ♥ L.A
OH FUCK ME.

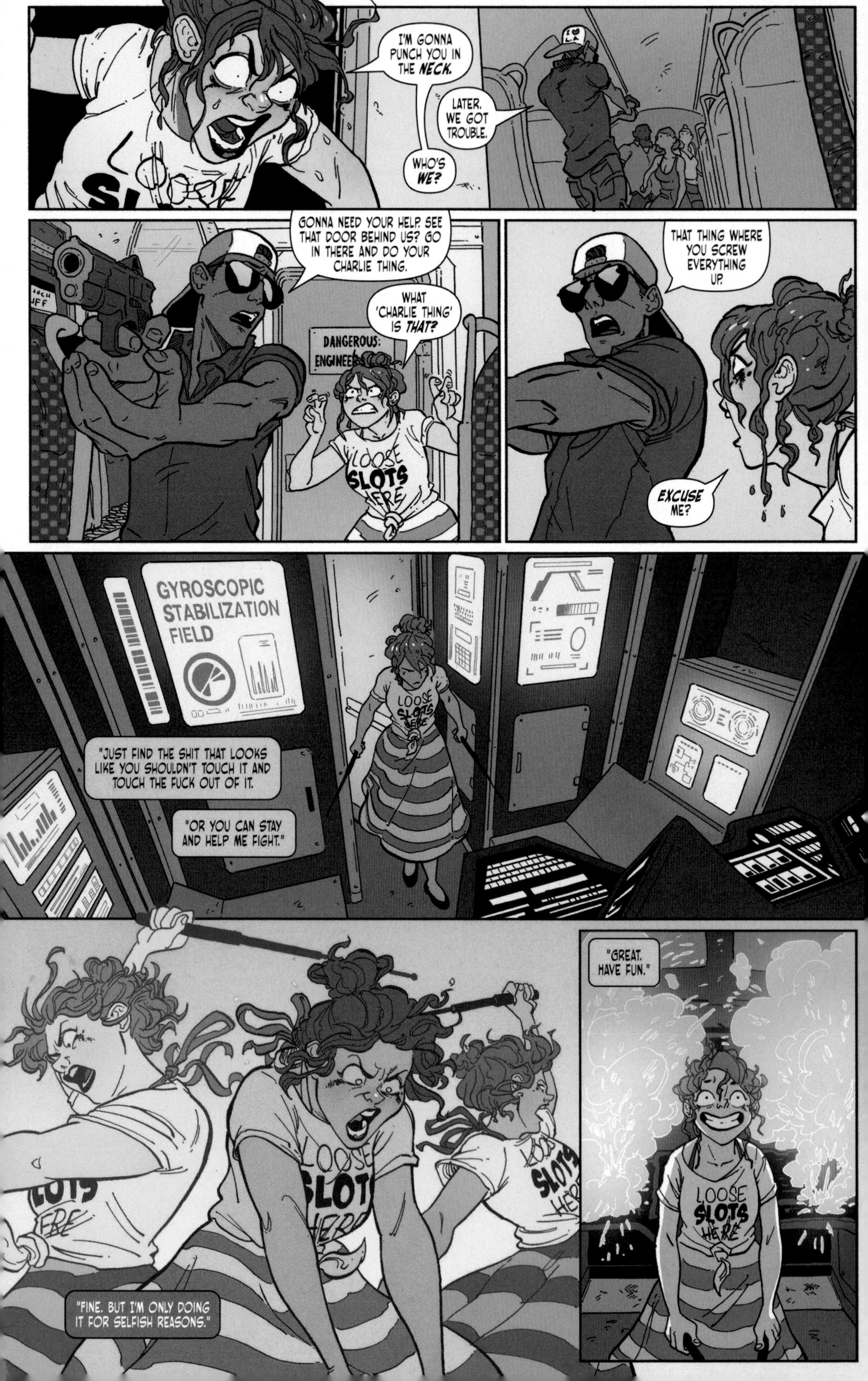
I'M GONNA PUNCH YOU IN THE NECK.
LATER, WE GOT TROUBLE.
WHO'S WE?
GONNA NEED YOUR HELP. SEE THAT DOOR BEHIND US? GO IN THERE AND DO YOUR CHARLIE THING.
DANGEROUS: ENGINEE
WHAT 'CHARLIE THING' IS THAT?
THAT THING WHERE YOU SCREW EVERYTHING UP.
EXCUSE ME?
GYROSCOPIC STABILIZATION FIELD
"JUST FIND THE SHIT THAT LOOKS LIKE YOU SHOULDN'T TOUCH IT AND TOUCH THE FUCK OUT OF IT.
"OR YOU CAN STAY AND HELP ME FIGHT."
"FINE. BUT I'M ONLY DOING IT FOR SELFISH REASONS."
"GREAT. HAVE FUN."
LOOSE SLOTS HERE

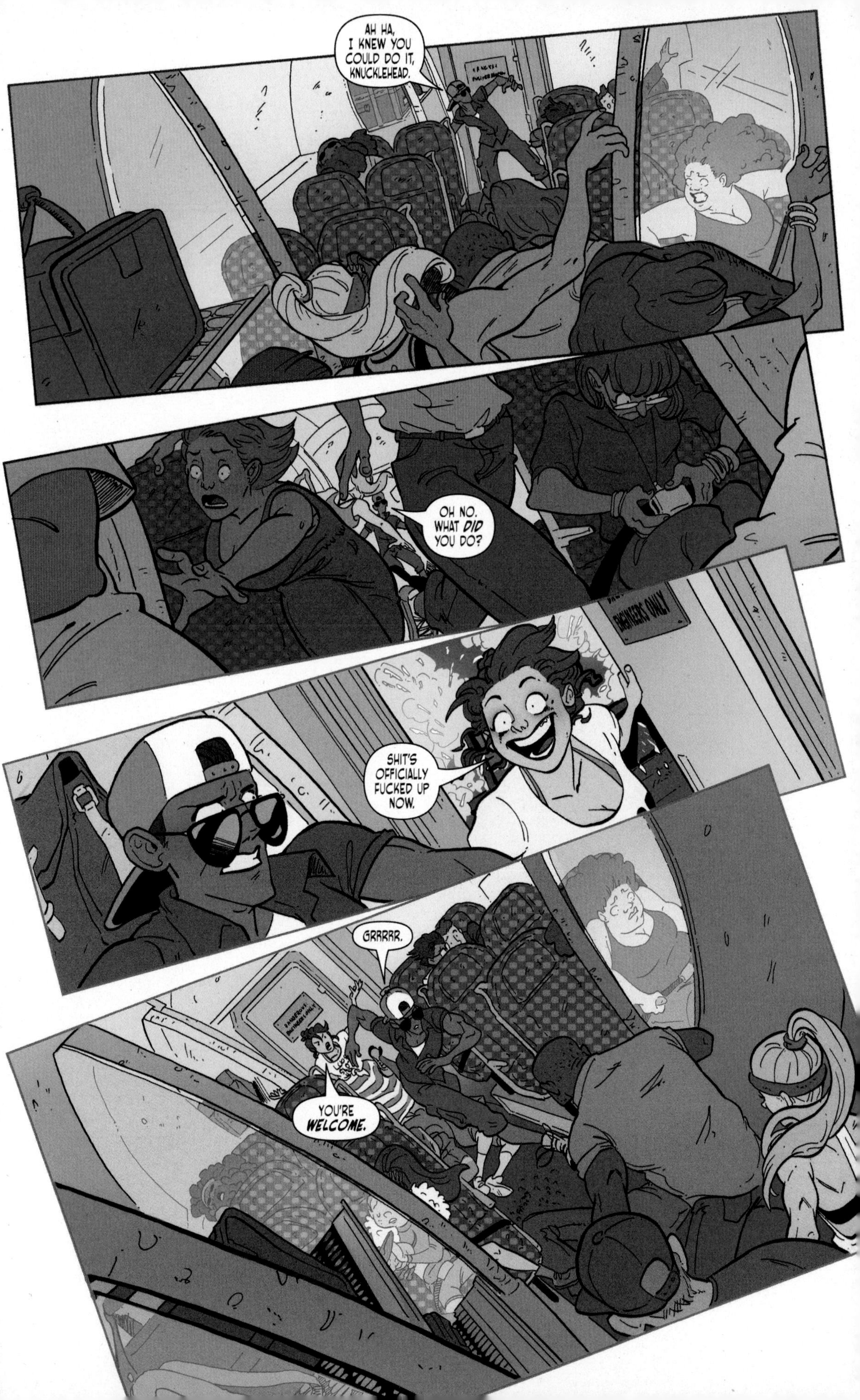
AH HA, I KNEW YOU COULD DO IT, KNUCKLEHEAD.
OH NO. WHAT *DID* YOU DO?
ENGINEERS ONLY
SHIT'S OFFICIALLY FUCKED UP NOW.
GRRRRR.
YOU'RE ***WELCOME.***

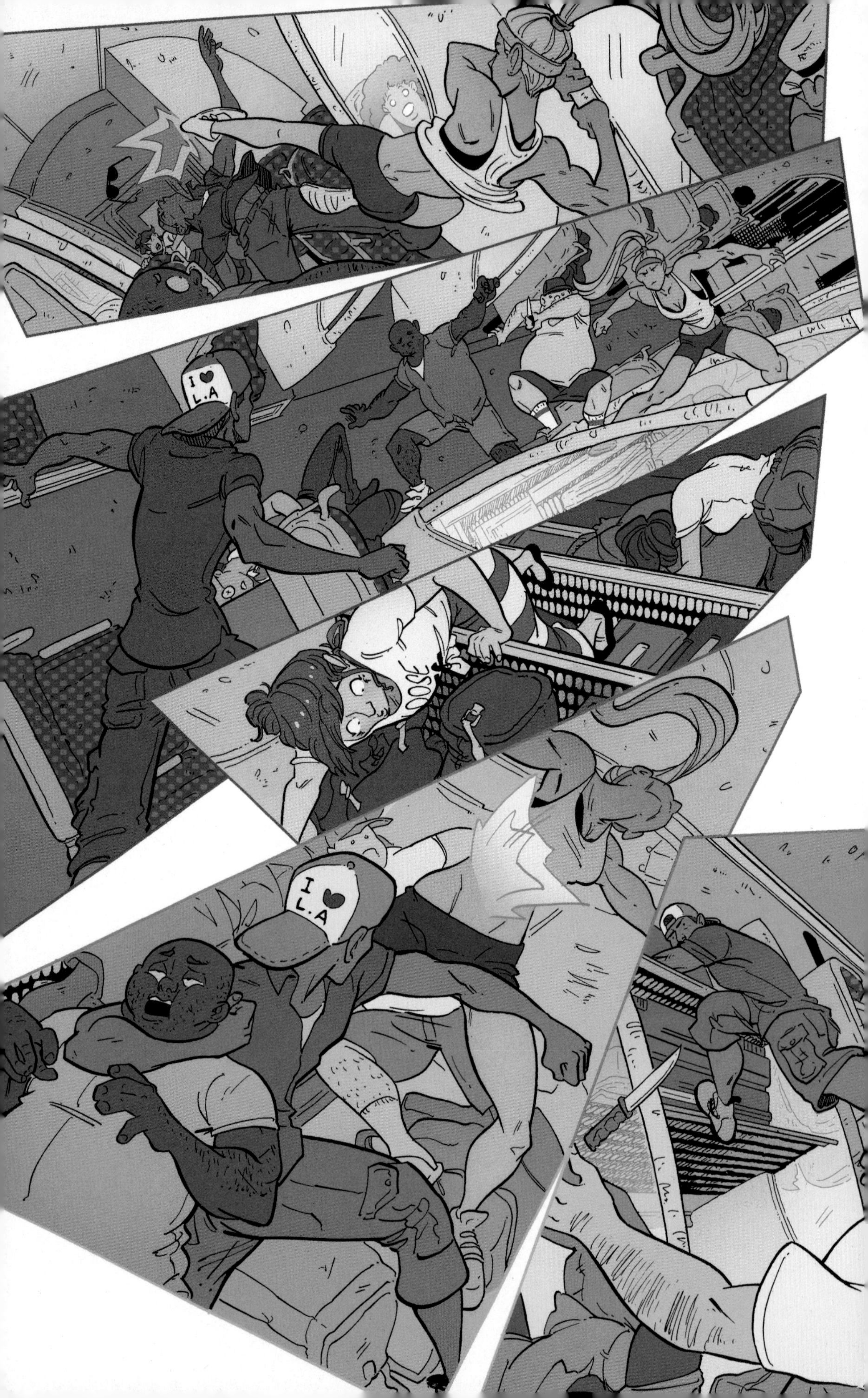

I ♥ L.A
I ♥ L.A

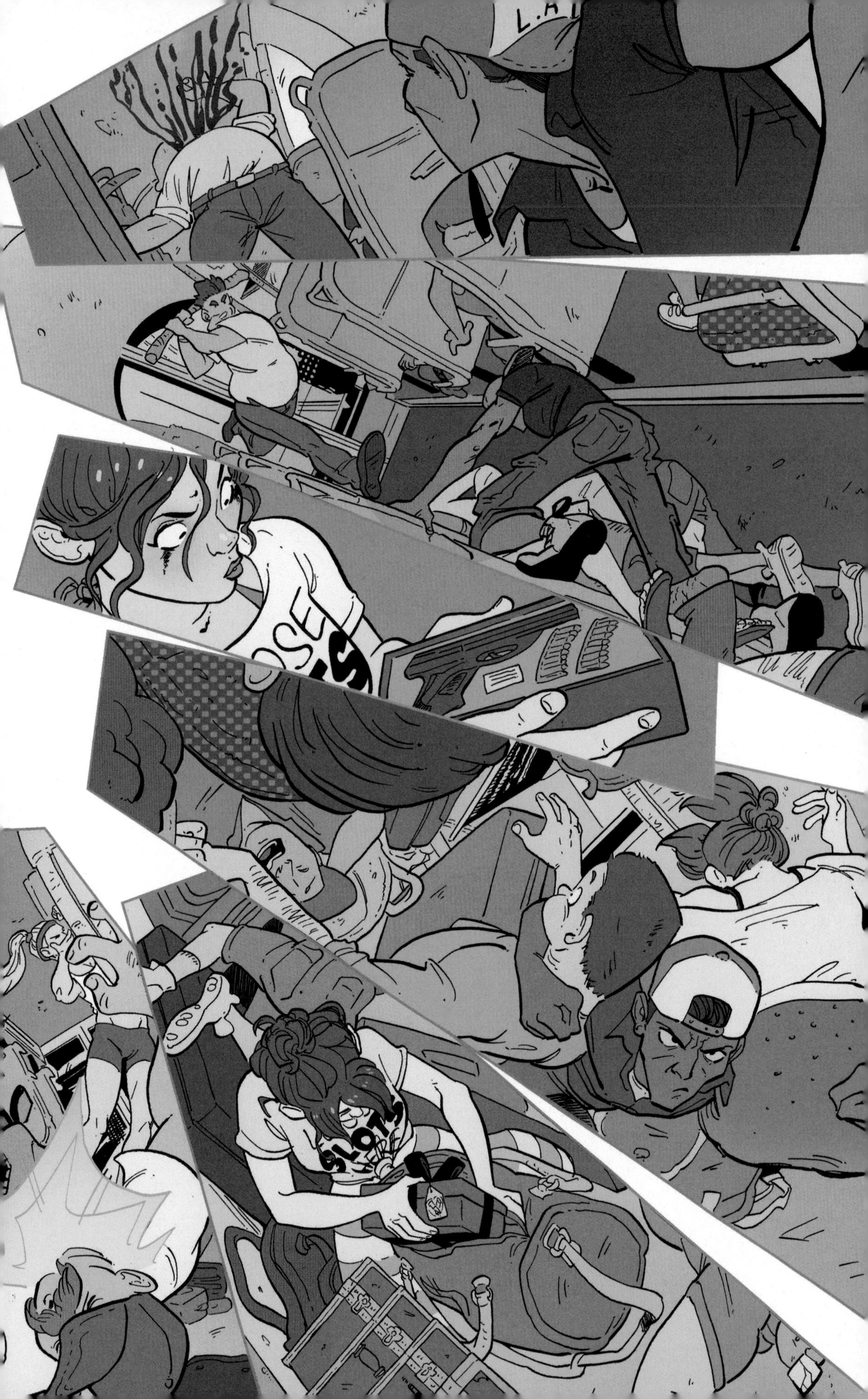

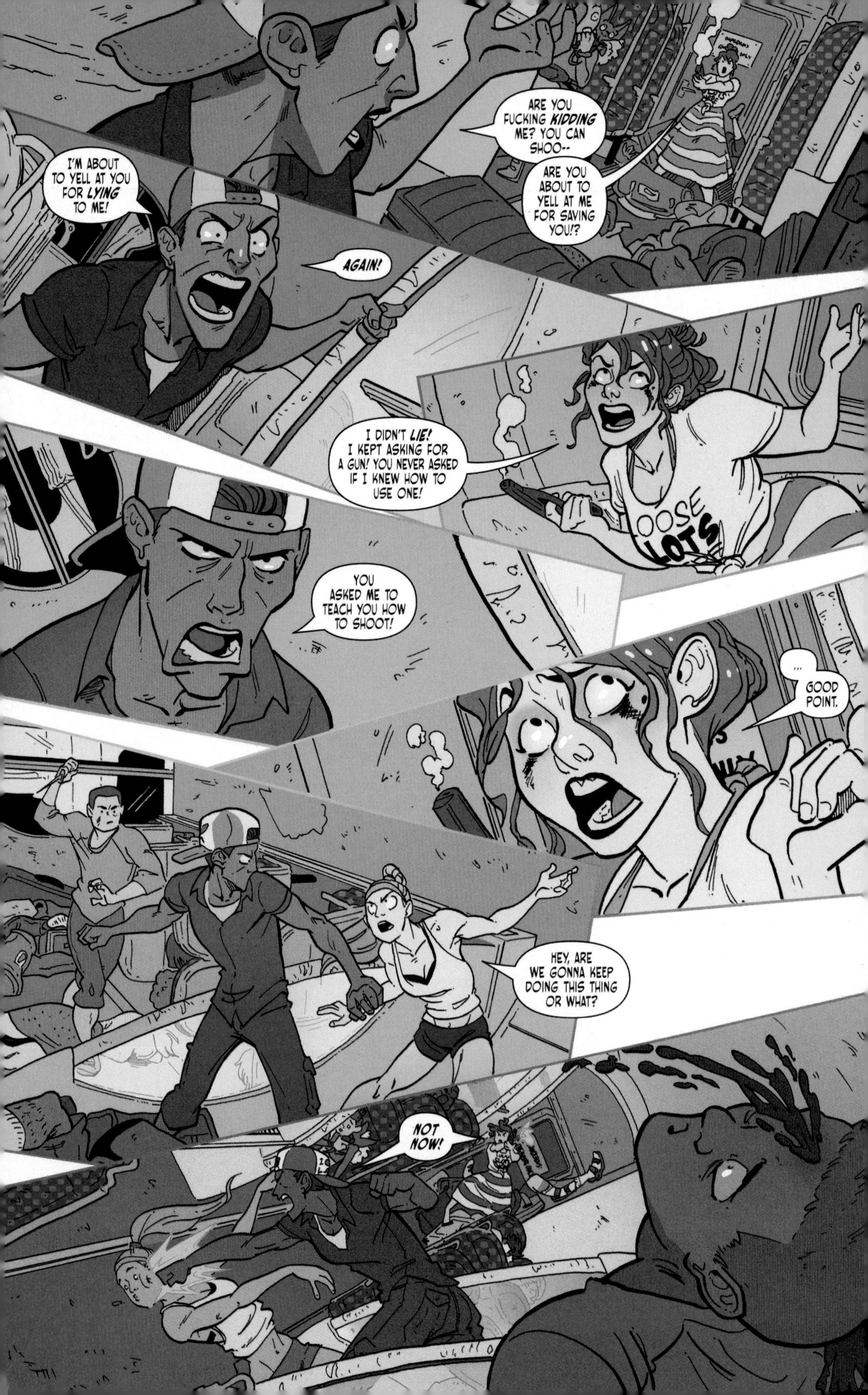

ARE YOU FUCKING *KIDDING* ME? YOU CAN SHOO--
ARE YOU ABOUT TO YELL AT ME FOR SAVING YOU!?
I'M ABOUT TO YELL AT YOU FOR *LYING* TO ME!
AGAIN!
I DIDN'T *LIE!* I KEPT ASKING FOR A GUN! YOU NEVER ASKED IF I KNEW HOW TO USE ONE!
LOOSE LOTS
YOU ASKED ME TO TEACH YOU HOW TO SHOOT!
... GOOD POINT.
HEY, ARE WE GONNA KEEP DOING THIS THING OR WHAT?
NOT NOW!

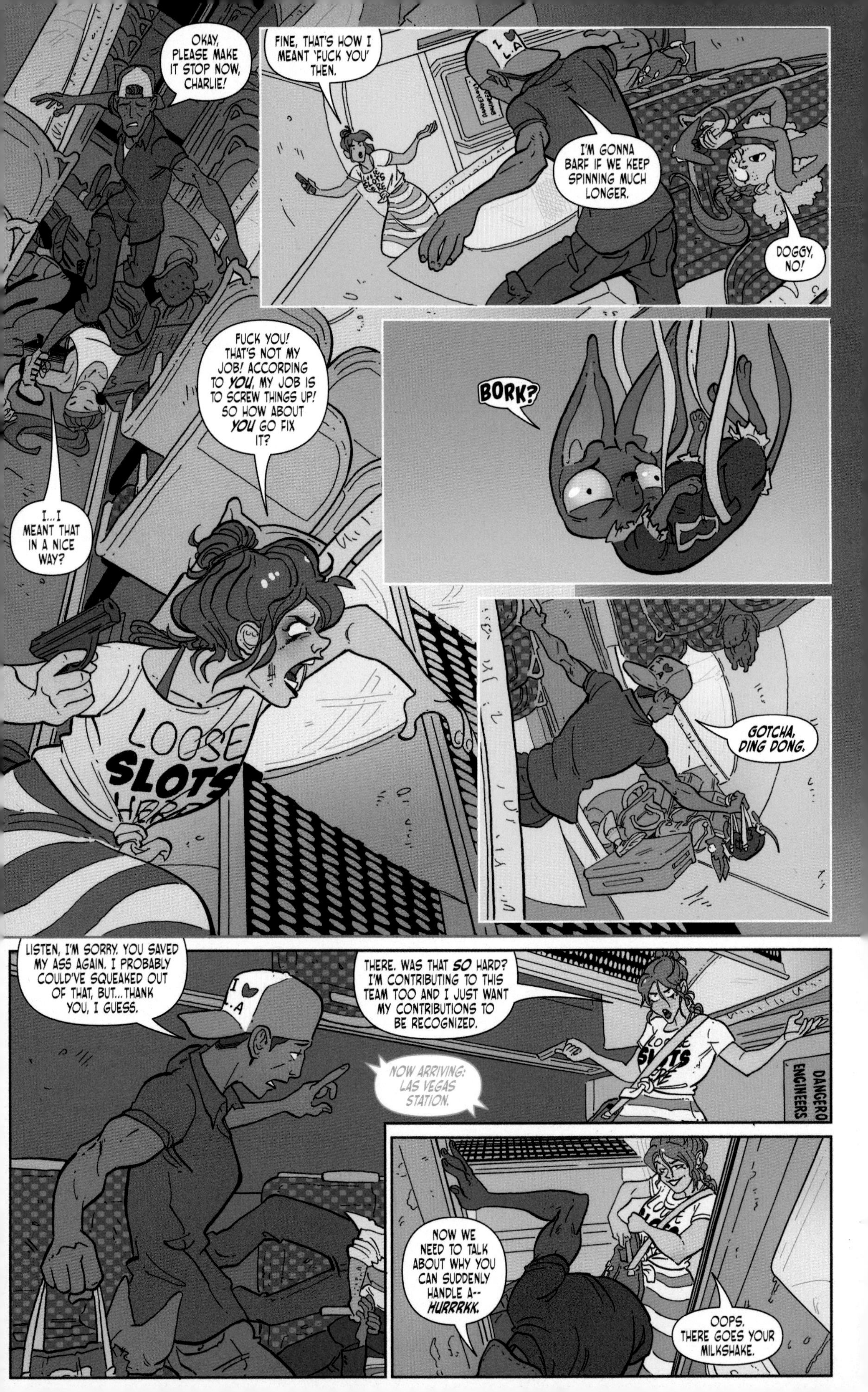

OKAY, PLEASE MAKE IT STOP NOW, CHARLIE!
FINE, THAT'S HOW I MEANT 'FUCK YOU' THEN.
I'M GONNA BARF IF WE KEEP SPINNING MUCH LONGER.
DOGGY, NO!
FUCK YOU! THAT'S NOT MY JOB! ACCORDING TO YOU, MY JOB IS TO SCREW THINGS UP! SO HOW ABOUT YOU GO FIX IT?
I...I MEANT THAT IN A NICE WAY?
LOOSE SLOTS
BORK?
GOTCHA, DING DONG.
LISTEN, I'M SORRY. YOU SAVED MY ASS AGAIN. I PROBABLY COULD'VE SQUEAKED OUT OF THAT, BUT...THANK YOU, I GUESS.
I ♥ L.A
THERE. WAS THAT SO HARD? I'M CONTRIBUTING TO THIS TEAM TOO AND I JUST WANT MY CONTRIBUTIONS TO BE RECOGNIZED.
NOW ARRIVING: LAS VEGAS STATION.
DANGERO ENGINEERS
NOW WE NEED TO TALK ABOUT WHY YOU CAN SUDDENLY HANDLE A-- HURRRKK.
OOPS. THERE GOES YOUR MILKSHAKE.

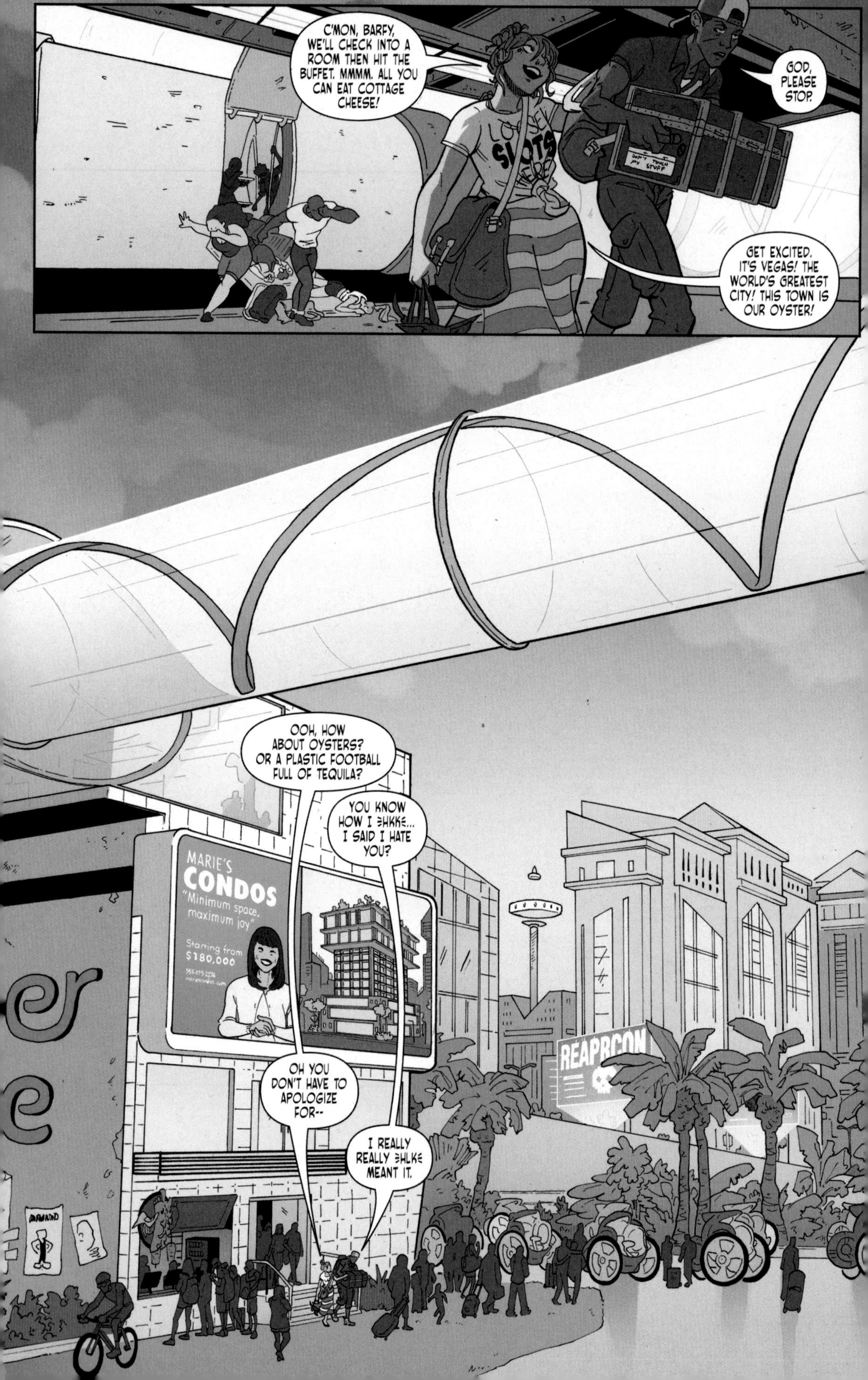
C'MON, BARFY, WE'LL CHECK INTO A ROOM THEN HIT THE BUFFET. MMMM. ALL YOU CAN EAT COTTAGE CHEESE!
GOD, PLEASE STOP.
GET EXCITED. IT'S VEGAS! THE WORLD'S GREATEST CITY! THIS TOWN IS OUR OYSTER!
OOH, HOW ABOUT OYSTERS? OR A PLASTIC FOOTBALL FULL OF TEQUILA?
YOU KNOW HOW I ƎHKKƎ... I SAID I HATE YOU?
MARIE'S CONDOS
"Minimum space, maximum joy"
Starting from $180,000
OH YOU DON'T HAVE TO APOLOGIZE FOR--
I REALLY REALLY ƎHLKƎ MEANT IT.
REAPRCON

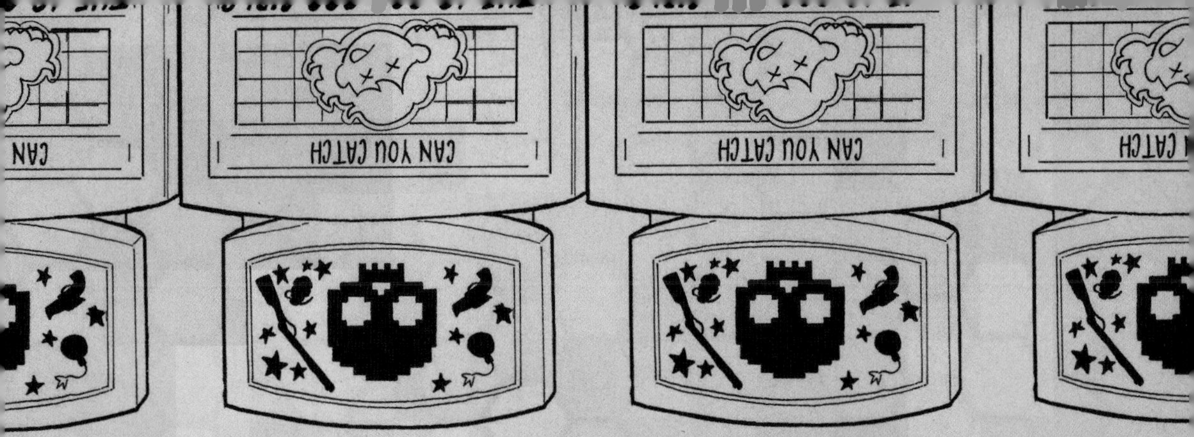
CAN YOU CATCH

CHAPTER EIGHT

JUMP INTO THE FIRE

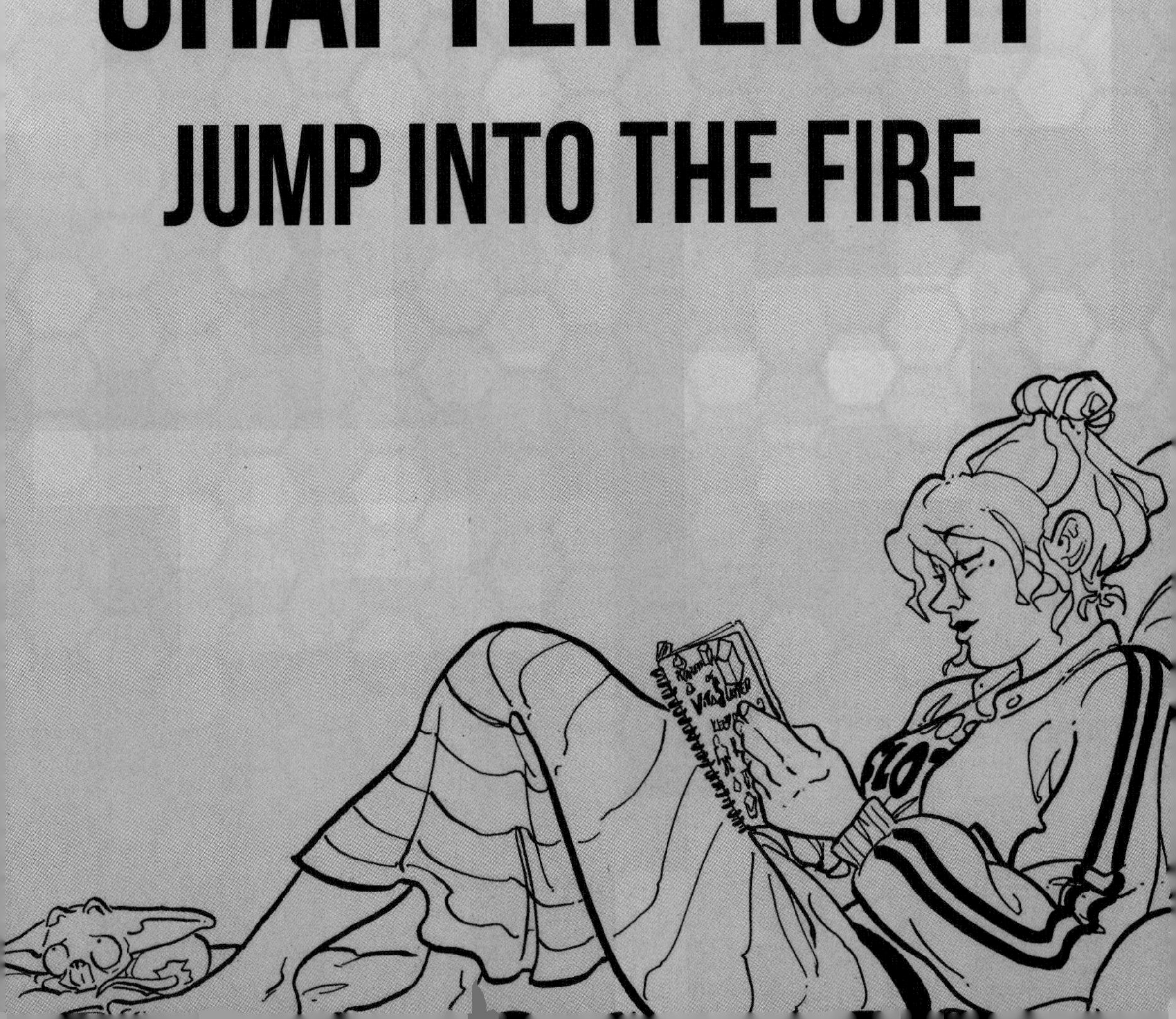

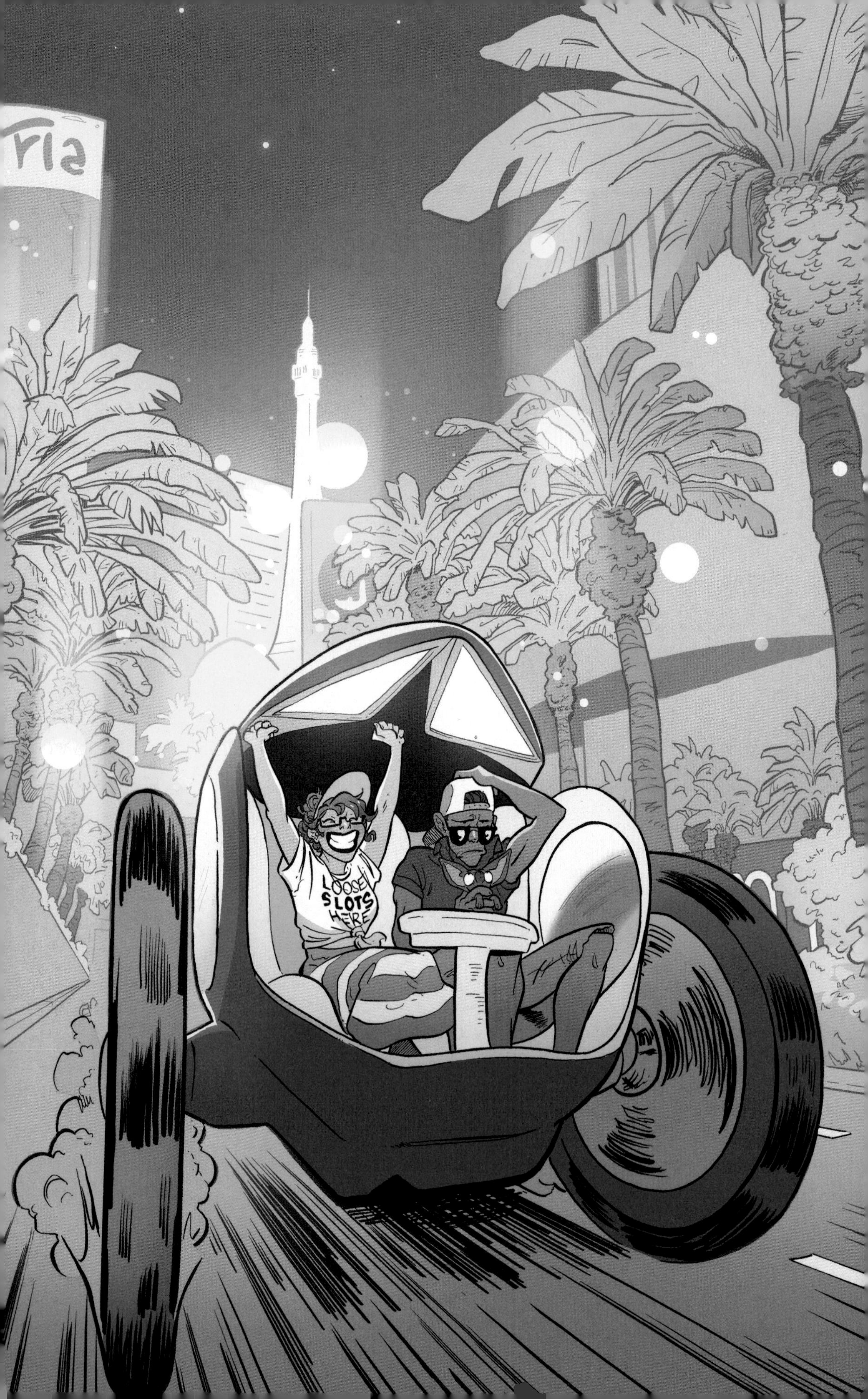
LOOSE SLOTS HERE

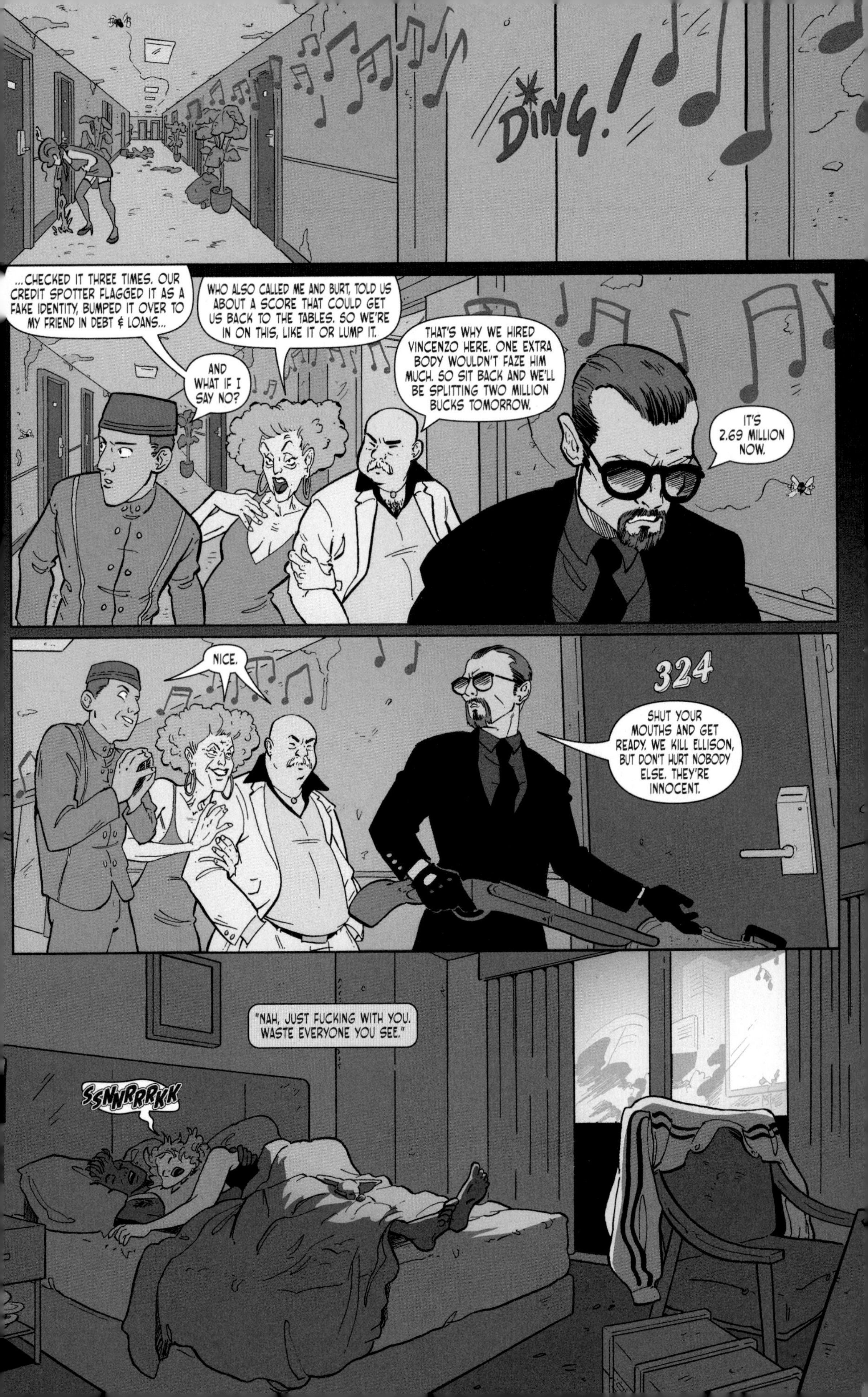
DING!
...CHECKED IT THREE TIMES. OUR CREDIT SPOTTER FLAGGED IT AS A FAKE IDENTITY, BUMPED IT OVER TO MY FRIEND IN DEBT & LOANS...
WHO ALSO CALLED ME AND BURT, TOLD US ABOUT A SCORE THAT COULD GET US BACK TO THE TABLES. SO WE'RE IN ON THIS, LIKE IT OR LUMP IT.
AND WHAT IF I SAY NO?
THAT'S WHY WE HIRED VINCENZO HERE. ONE EXTRA BODY WOULDN'T FAZE HIM MUCH. SO SIT BACK AND WE'LL BE SPLITTING TWO MILLION BUCKS TOMORROW.
IT'S 2.69 MILLION NOW.
NICE.
324
SHUT YOUR MOUTHS AND GET READY. WE KILL ELLISON, BUT DON'T HURT NOBODY ELSE. THEY'RE INNOCENT.
"NAH, JUST FUCKING WITH YOU. WASTE EVERYONE YOU SEE."
SSNNRRRKK

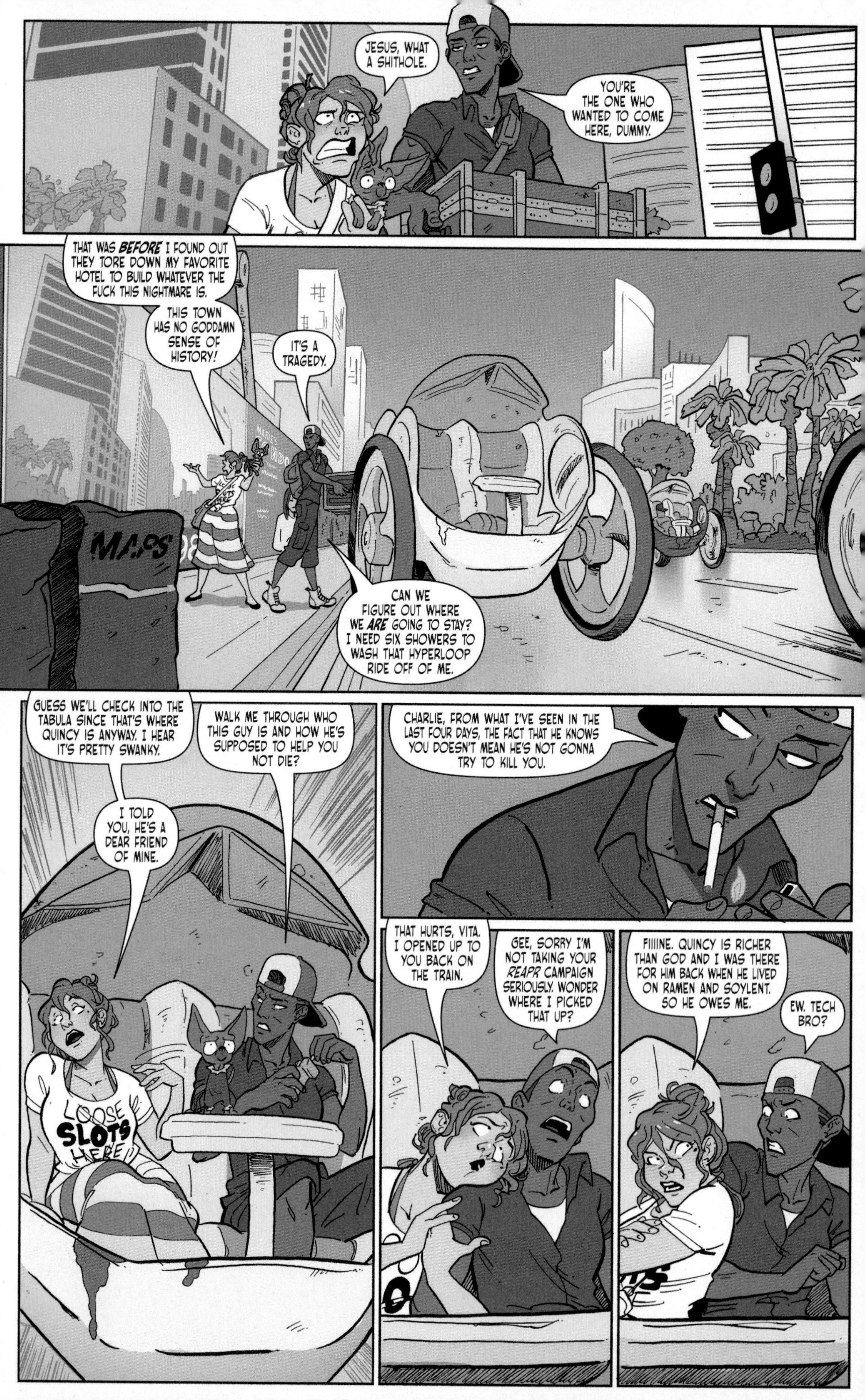

JESUS, WHAT A SHITHOLE.
YOU'RE THE ONE WHO WANTED TO COME HERE, DUMMY.
THAT WAS *BEFORE* I FOUND OUT THEY TORE DOWN MY FAVORITE HOTEL TO BUILD WHATEVER THE FUCK THIS NIGHTMARE IS.
THIS TOWN HAS NO GODDAMN SENSE OF HISTORY!
IT'S A TRAGEDY.
CAN WE FIGURE OUT WHERE WE *ARE* GOING TO STAY? I NEED SIX SHOWERS TO WASH THAT HYPERLOOP RIDE OFF OF ME.
MARS
GUESS WE'LL CHECK INTO THE TABULA SINCE THAT'S WHERE QUINCY IS ANYWAY. I HEAR IT'S PRETTY SWANKY.
WALK ME THROUGH WHO THIS GUY IS AND HOW HE'S SUPPOSED TO HELP YOU NOT DIE?
I TOLD YOU, HE'S A DEAR FRIEND OF MINE.
LOOSE SLOTS HERE
CHARLIE, FROM WHAT I'VE SEEN IN THE LAST FOUR DAYS, THE FACT THAT HE KNOWS YOU DOESN'T MEAN HE'S NOT GONNA TRY TO KILL YOU.
THAT HURTS, VITA. I OPENED UP TO YOU BACK ON THE TRAIN.
GEE, SORRY I'M NOT TAKING YOUR *REAPR* CAMPAIGN SERIOUSLY. WONDER WHERE I PICKED THAT UP?
FIIIINE. QUINCY IS RICHER THAN GOD AND I WAS THERE FOR HIM BACK WHEN HE LIVED ON RAMEN AND SOYLENT. SO HE OWES ME.
EW. TECH BRO?

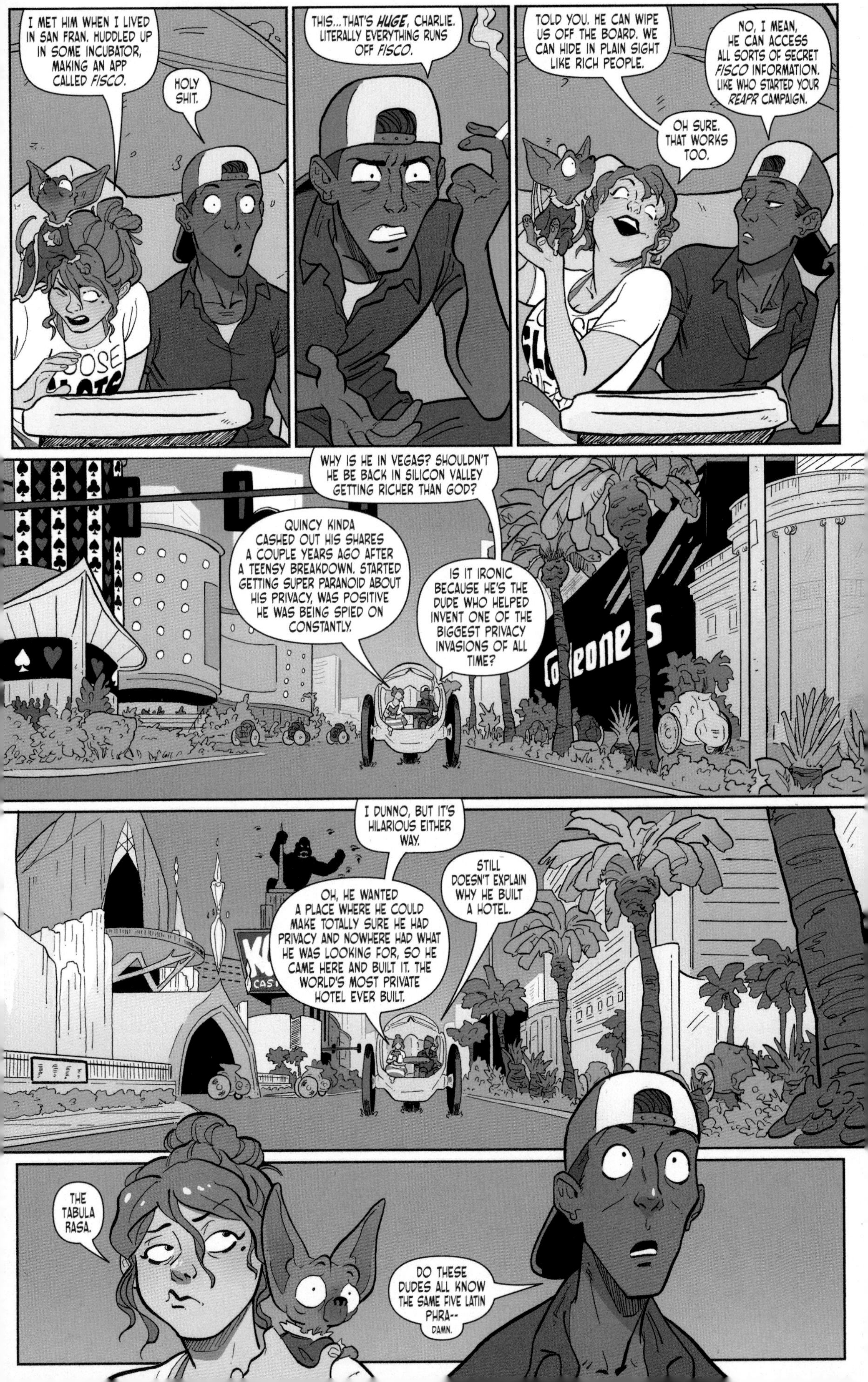
I MET HIM WHEN I LIVED IN SAN FRAN. HUDDLED UP IN SOME INCUBATOR, MAKING AN APP CALLED *FISCO*.
HOLY SHIT.
THIS...THAT'S *HUGE*, CHARLIE. LITERALLY EVERYTHING RUNS OFF *FISCO*.
TOLD YOU. HE CAN WIPE US OFF THE BOARD. WE CAN HIDE IN PLAIN SIGHT LIKE RICH PEOPLE.
NO, I MEAN, HE CAN ACCESS ALL SORTS OF SECRET *FISCO* INFORMATION. LIKE WHO STARTED YOUR *REAPR* CAMPAIGN.
OH SURE. THAT WORKS TOO.
WHY IS HE IN VEGAS? SHOULDN'T HE BE BACK IN SILICON VALLEY GETTING RICHER THAN GOD?
QUINCY KINDA CASHED OUT HIS SHARES A COUPLE YEARS AGO AFTER A TEENSY BREAKDOWN. STARTED GETTING SUPER PARANOID ABOUT HIS PRIVACY, WAS POSITIVE HE WAS BEING SPIED ON CONSTANTLY.
IS IT IRONIC BECAUSE HE'S THE DUDE WHO HELPED INVENT ONE OF THE BIGGEST PRIVACY INVASIONS OF ALL TIME?
Corleone's
I DUNNO, BUT IT'S HILARIOUS EITHER WAY.
STILL DOESN'T EXPLAIN WHY HE BUILT A HOTEL.
OH, HE WANTED A PLACE WHERE HE COULD MAKE TOTALLY SURE HE HAD PRIVACY AND NOWHERE HAD WHAT HE WAS LOOKING FOR, SO HE CAME HERE AND BUILT IT. THE WORLD'S MOST PRIVATE HOTEL EVER BUILT.
THE TABULA RASA.
DO THESE DUDES ALL KNOW THE SAME FIVE LATIN PHRA--
DAMN.

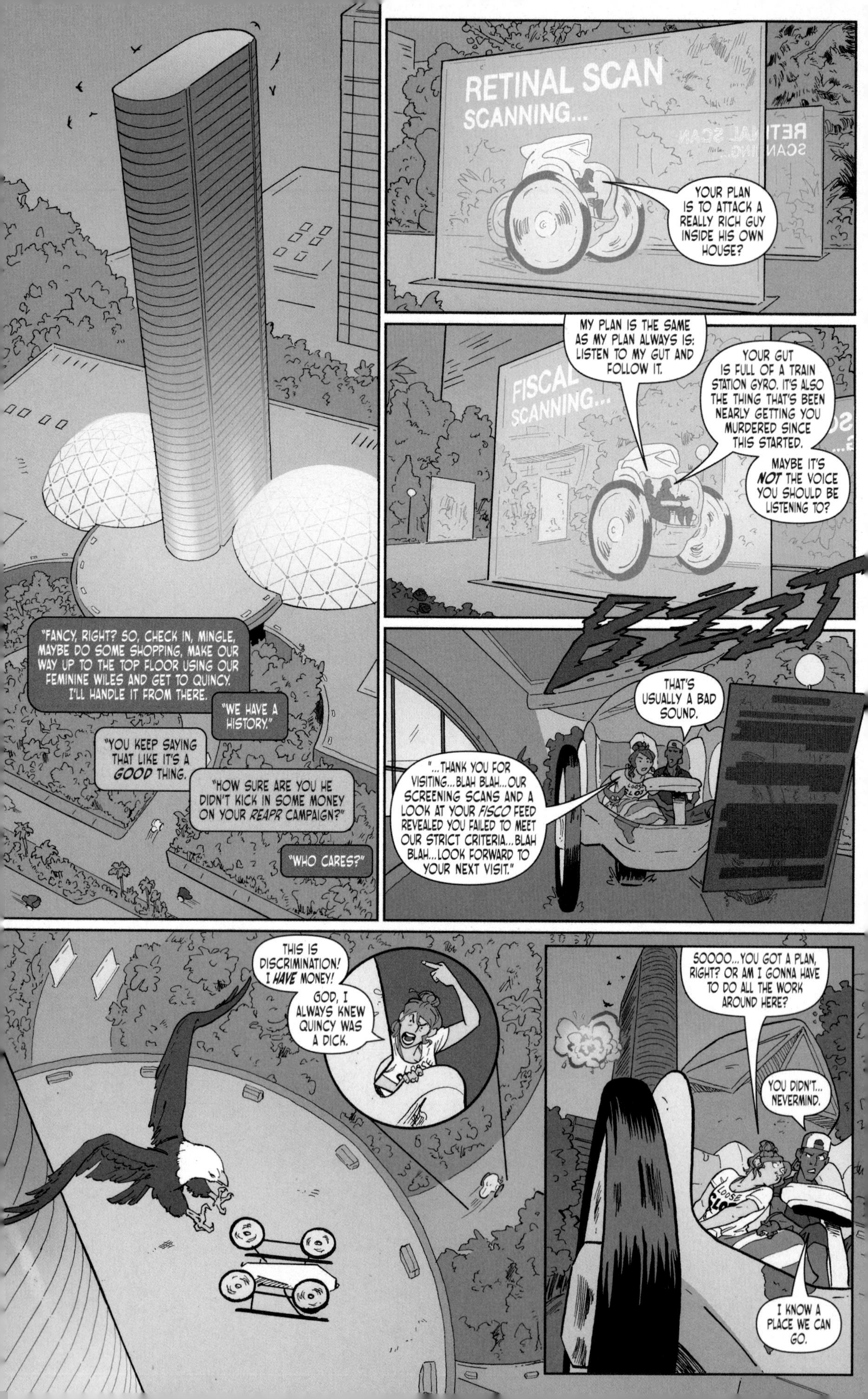
"FANCY, RIGHT? SO, CHECK IN, MINGLE, MAYBE DO SOME SHOPPING, MAKE OUR WAY UP TO THE TOP FLOOR USING OUR FEMININE WILES AND GET TO QUINCY. I'LL HANDLE IT FROM THERE.
"WE HAVE A HISTORY."
"YOU KEEP SAYING THAT LIKE IT'S A *GOOD* THING.
"HOW SURE ARE YOU HE DIDN'T KICK IN SOME MONEY ON YOUR *REAPR* CAMPAIGN?"
"WHO CARES?"
RETINAL SCAN
SCANNING...
YOUR PLAN IS TO ATTACK A REALLY RICH GUY INSIDE HIS OWN HOUSE?
MY PLAN IS THE SAME AS MY PLAN ALWAYS IS: LISTEN TO MY GUT AND FOLLOW IT.
FISCAL SCANNING...
YOUR GUT IS FULL OF A TRAIN STATION GYRO. IT'S ALSO THE THING THAT'S BEEN NEARLY GETTING YOU MURDERED SINCE THIS STARTED.
MAYBE IT'S *NOT* THE VOICE YOU SHOULD BE LISTENING TO?
BZZZT
THAT'S USUALLY A BAD SOUND.
"...THANK YOU FOR VISITING...BLAH BLAH...OUR SCREENING SCANS AND A LOOK AT YOUR *FISCO* FEED REVEALED YOU FAILED TO MEET OUR STRICT CRITERIA...BLAH BLAH...LOOK FORWARD TO YOUR NEXT VISIT."
THIS IS DISCRIMINATION! I *HAVE* MONEY!
GOD, I ALWAYS KNEW QUINCY WAS A DICK.
SOOOO...YOU GOT A PLAN, RIGHT? OR AM I GONNA HAVE TO DO ALL THE WORK AROUND HERE?
YOU DIDN'T... NEVERMIND.
I KNOW A PLACE WE CAN GO.

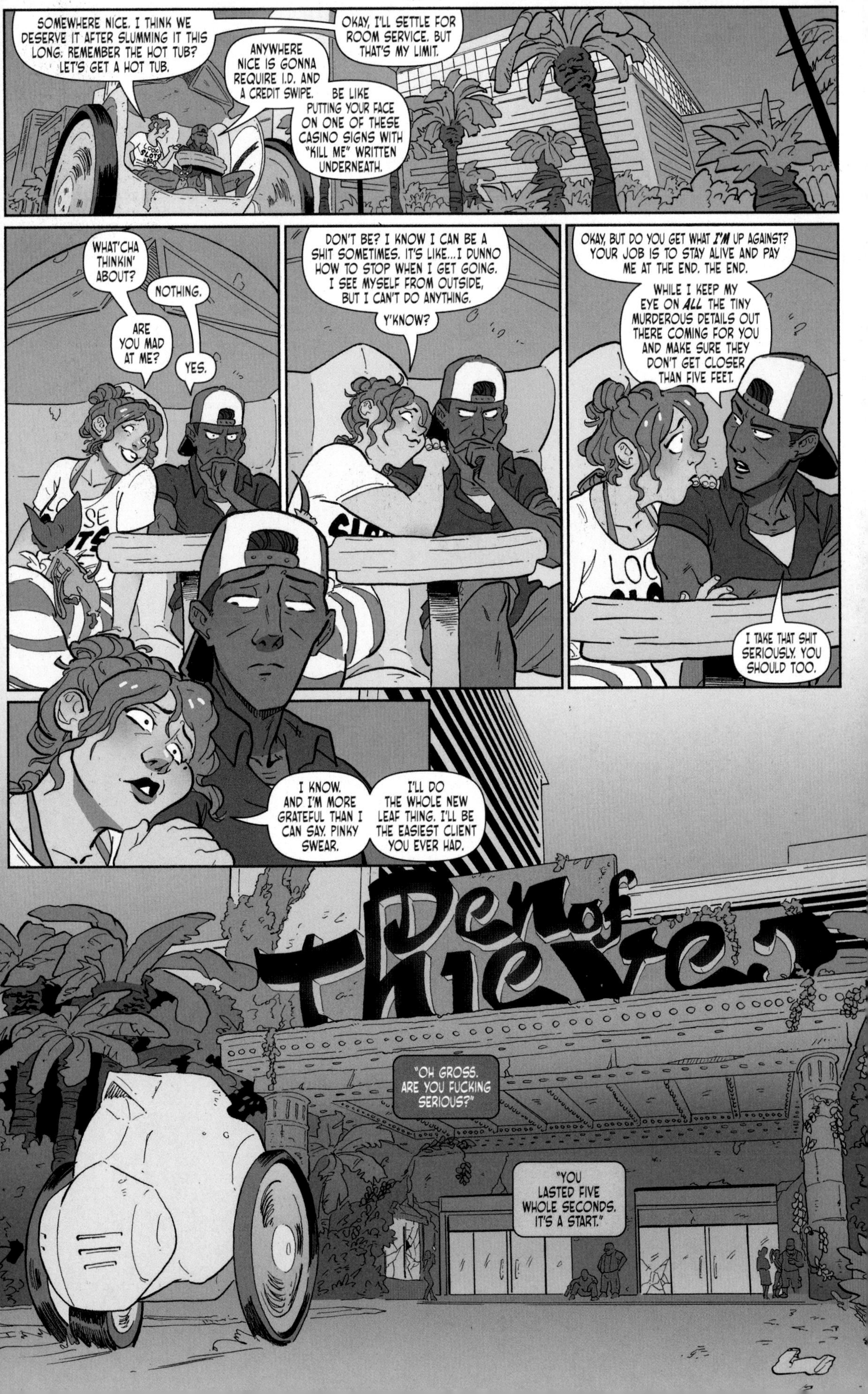
SOMEWHERE NICE. I THINK WE DESERVE IT AFTER SLUMMING IT THIS LONG. REMEMBER THE HOT TUB? LET'S GET A HOT TUB.
ANYWHERE NICE IS GONNA REQUIRE I.D. AND A CREDIT SWIPE.
BE LIKE PUTTING YOUR FACE ON ONE OF THESE CASINO SIGNS WITH "KILL ME" WRITTEN UNDERNEATH.
OKAY, I'LL SETTLE FOR ROOM SERVICE. BUT THAT'S MY LIMIT.
WHAT'CHA THINKIN' ABOUT?
NOTHING.
ARE YOU MAD AT ME?
YES.
DON'T BE? I KNOW I CAN BE A SHIT SOMETIMES. IT'S LIKE...I DUNNO HOW TO STOP WHEN I GET GOING. I SEE MYSELF FROM OUTSIDE, BUT I CAN'T DO ANYTHING.
Y'KNOW?
OKAY, BUT DO YOU GET WHAT I'M UP AGAINST? YOUR JOB IS TO STAY ALIVE AND PAY ME AT THE END. THE END.
WHILE I KEEP MY EYE ON ALL THE TINY MURDEROUS DETAILS OUT THERE COMING FOR YOU AND MAKE SURE THEY DON'T GET CLOSER THAN FIVE FEET.
I TAKE THAT SHIT SERIOUSLY. YOU SHOULD TOO.
I KNOW. AND I'M MORE GRATEFUL THAN I CAN SAY. PINKY SWEAR.
I'LL DO THE WHOLE NEW LEAF THING. I'LL BE THE EASIEST CLIENT YOU EVER HAD.
Den of Thieves
"OH GROSS. ARE YOU FUCKING SERIOUS?"
"YOU LASTED FIVE WHOLE SECONDS. IT'S A START."

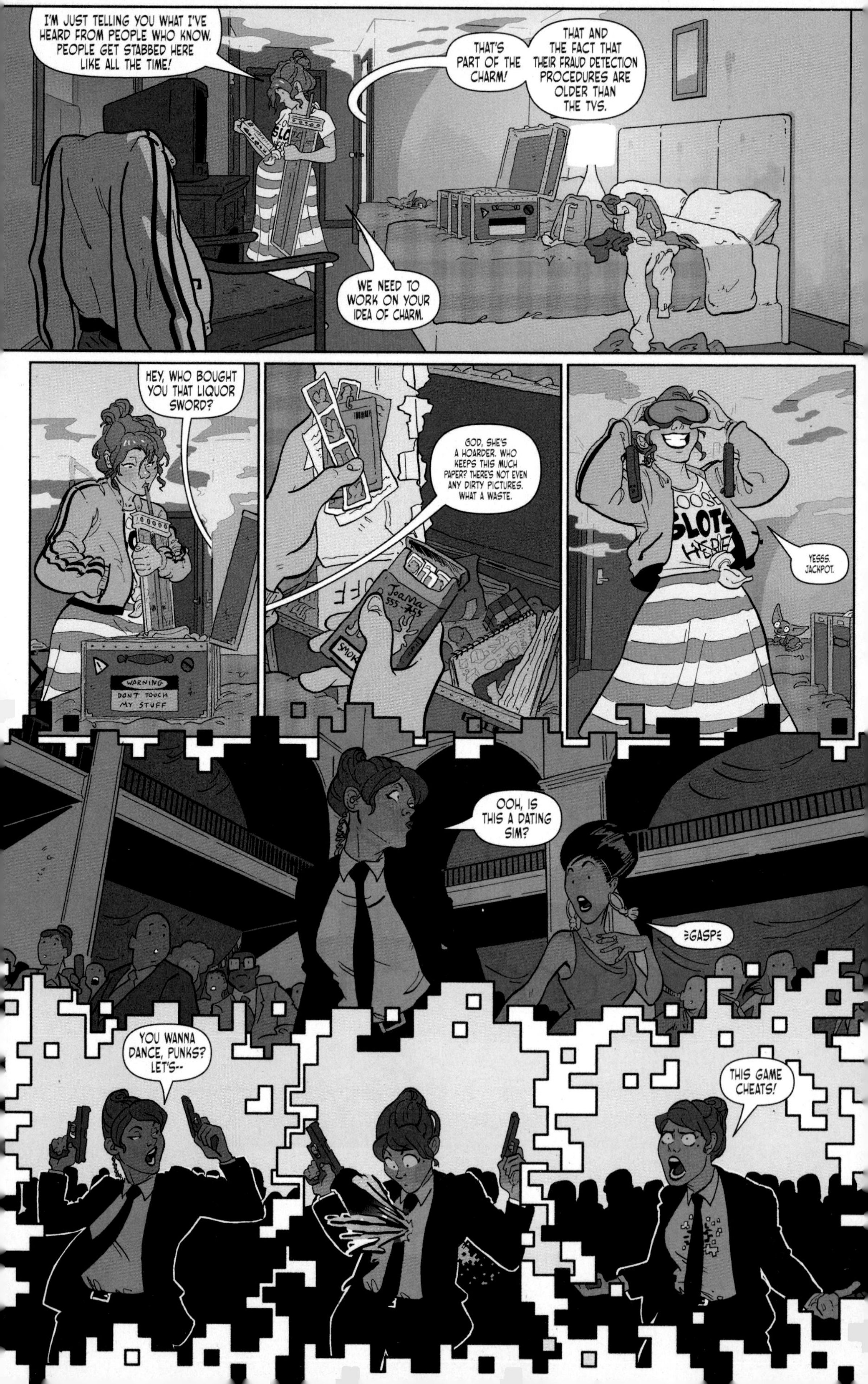
I'M JUST TELLING YOU WHAT I'VE HEARD FROM PEOPLE WHO KNOW. PEOPLE GET STABBED HERE LIKE ALL THE TIME!
THAT'S PART OF THE CHARM!
THAT AND THE FACT THAT THEIR FRAUD DETECTION PROCEDURES ARE OLDER THAN THE TVS.
WE NEED TO WORK ON YOUR IDEA OF CHARM.
HEY, WHO BOUGHT YOU THAT LIQUOR SWORD?
WARNING DON'T TOUCH MY STUFF
GOD, SHE'S A HOARDER. WHO KEEPS THIS MUCH PAPER? THERE'S NOT EVEN ANY DIRTY PICTURES. WHAT A WASTE.
Joanna 555-7755
LOOSE SLOTS HERE
YESSS. JACKPOT.
OOH, IS THIS A DATING SIM?
GASP
YOU WANNA DANCE, PUNKS? LET'S--
THIS GAME CHEATS!

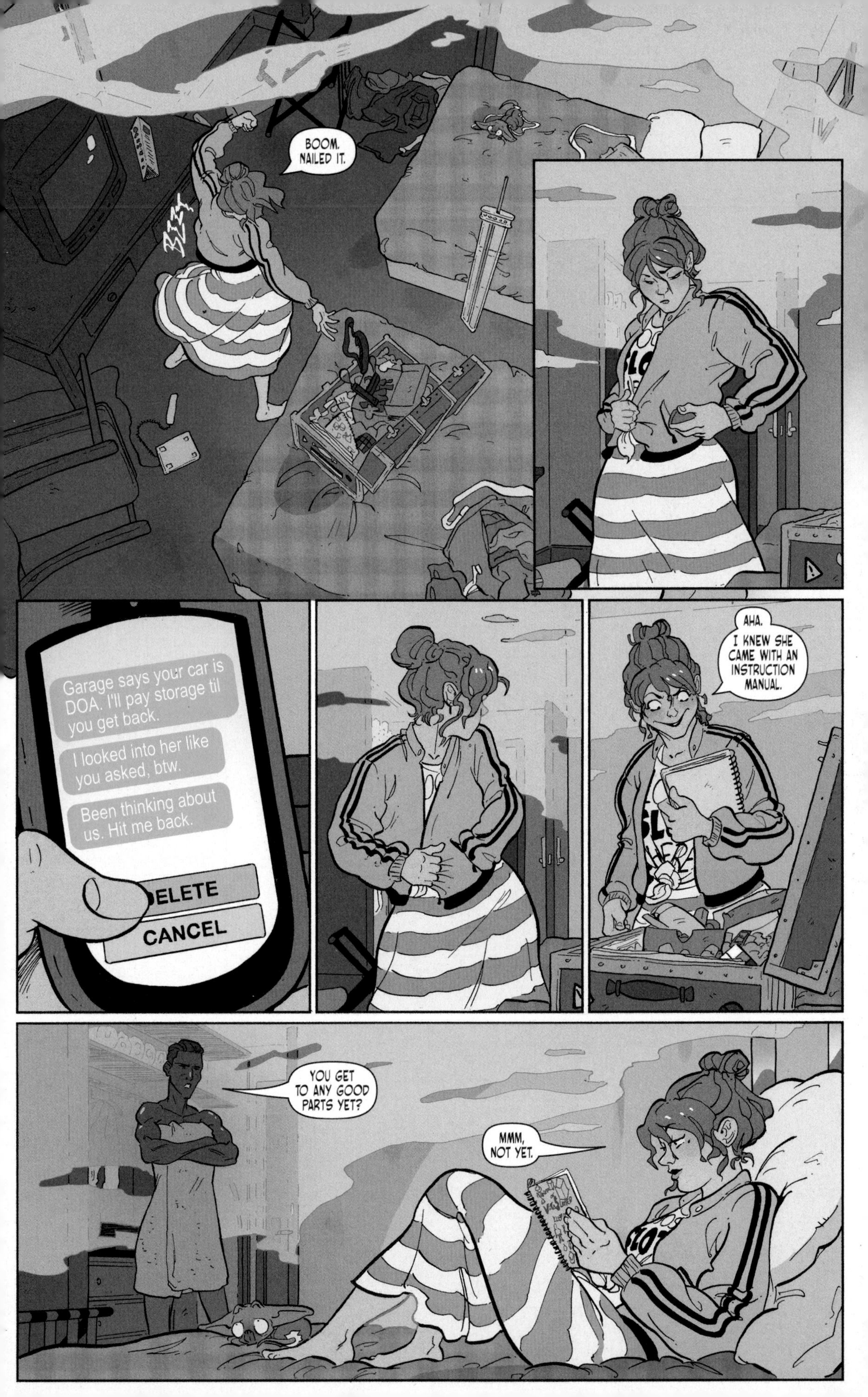
BOOM. NAILED IT.
BZZT
Garage says your car is DOA. I'll pay storage til you get back.
I looked into her like you asked, btw.
Been thinking about us. Hit me back.
DELETE
CANCEL
AHA. I KNEW SHE CAME WITH AN INSTRUCTION MANUAL.
YOU GET TO ANY GOOD PARTS YET?
MMM, NOT YET.

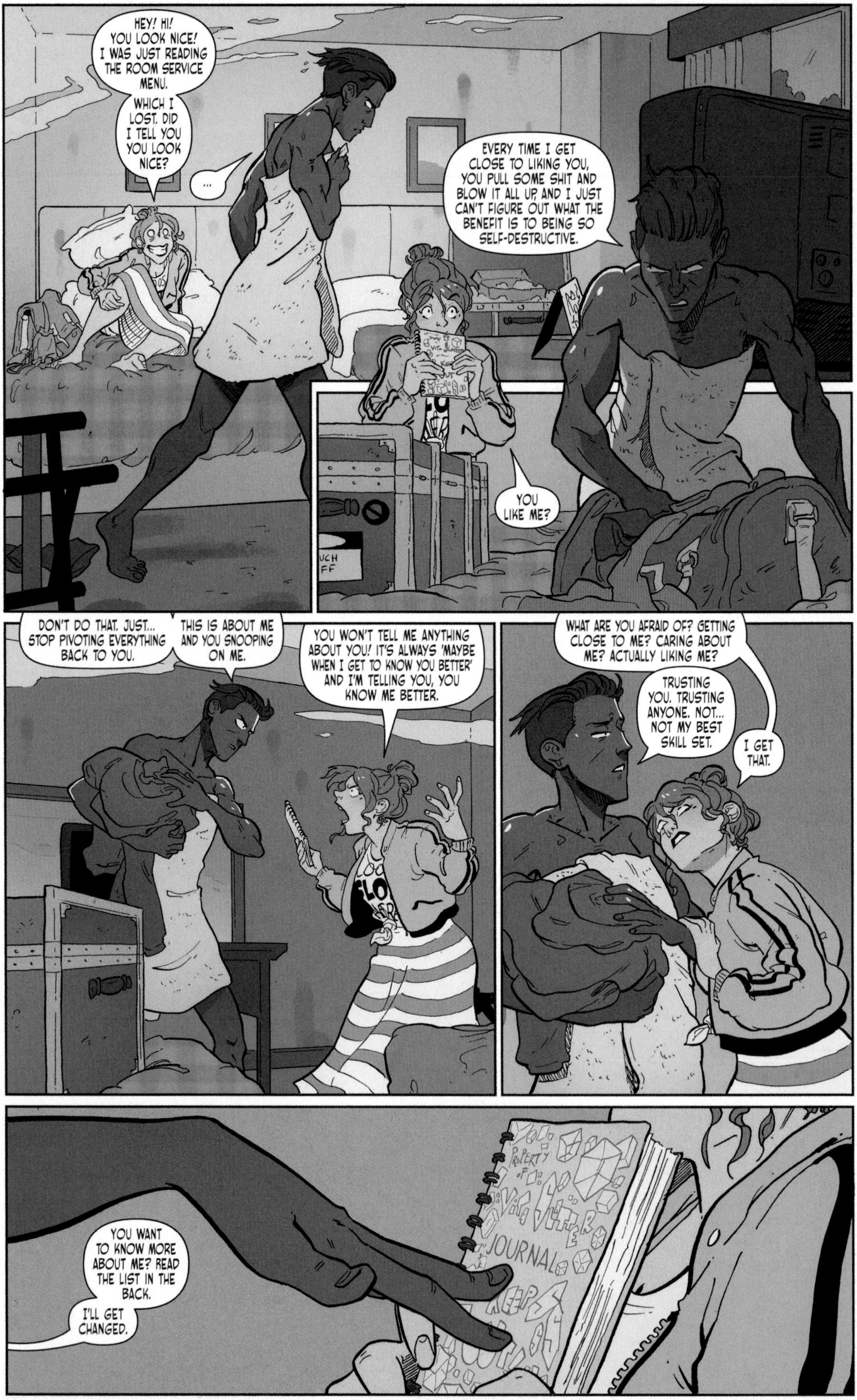
HEY! HI! YOU LOOK NICE! I WAS JUST READING THE ROOM SERVICE MENU.
WHICH I LOST. DID I TELL YOU YOU LOOK NICE?
...
EVERY TIME I GET CLOSE TO LIKING YOU, YOU PULL SOME SHIT AND BLOW IT ALL UP, AND I JUST CAN'T FIGURE OUT WHAT THE BENEFIT IS TO BEING SO SELF-DESTRUCTIVE.
YOU LIKE ME?
DON'T DO THAT. JUST... STOP PIVOTING EVERYTHING BACK TO YOU.
THIS IS ABOUT ME AND YOU SNOOPING ON ME.
YOU WON'T TELL ME ANYTHING ABOUT YOU! IT'S ALWAYS 'MAYBE WHEN I GET TO KNOW YOU BETTER' AND I'M TELLING YOU, YOU KNOW ME BETTER.
WHAT ARE YOU AFRAID OF? GETTING CLOSE TO ME? CARING ABOUT ME? ACTUALLY LIKING ME?
TRUSTING YOU. TRUSTING ANYONE. NOT... NOT MY BEST SKILL SET.
I GET THAT.
YOU WANT TO KNOW MORE ABOUT ME? READ THE LIST IN THE BACK.
I'LL GET CHANGED.
JOURNAL

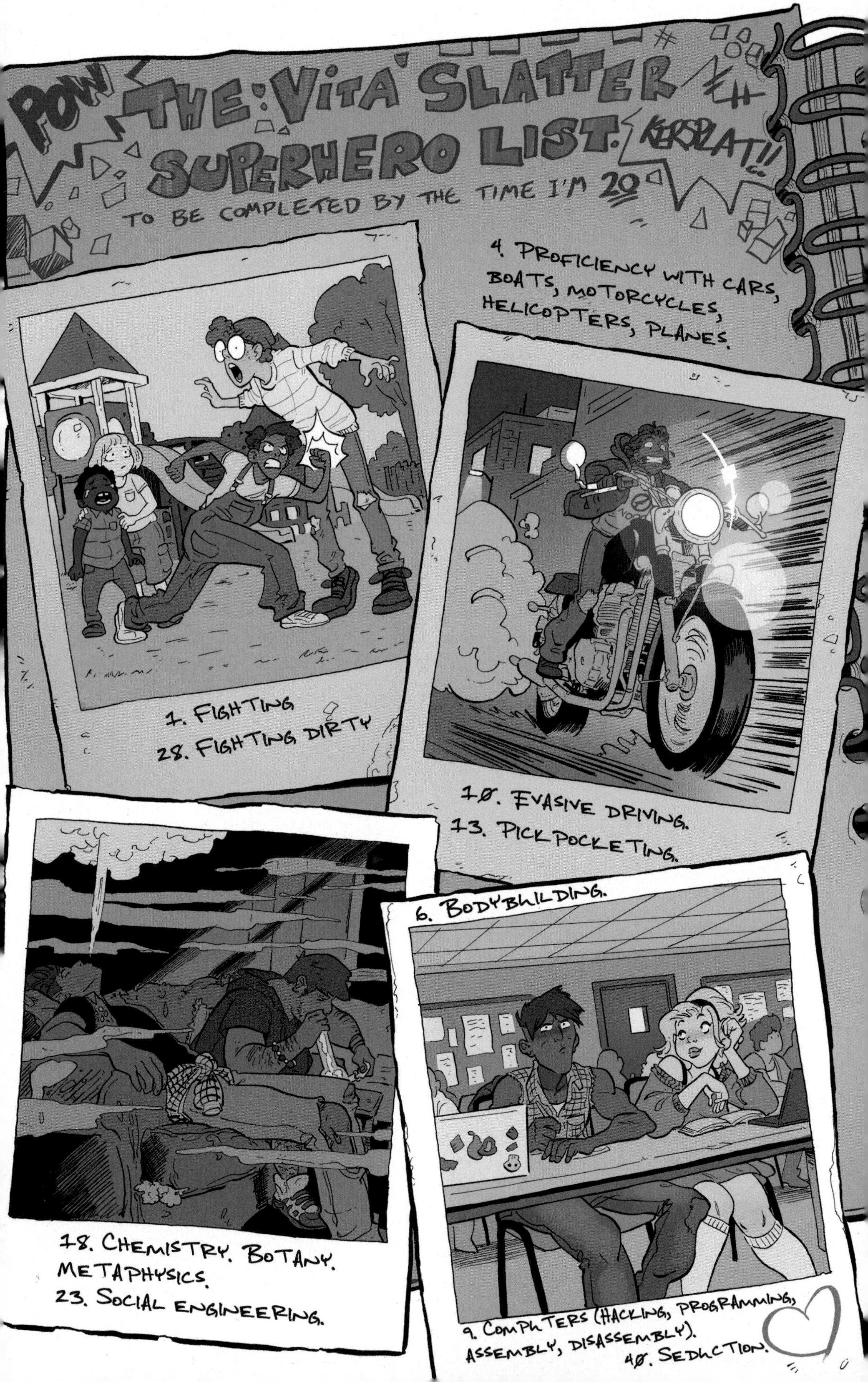
POW
THE VITA SLATTER SUPERHERO LIST.
KERSPLAT!!
TO BE COMPLETED BY THE TIME I'M 20
4. PROFICIENCY WITH CARS, BOATS, MOTORCYCLES, HELICOPTERS, PLANES.
1. FIGHTING
28. FIGHTING DIRTY
10. EVASIVE DRIVING.
13. PICKPOCKETING.
6. BODYBUILDING.
18. CHEMISTRY. BOTANY. METAPHYSICS.
23. SOCIAL ENGINEERING.
9. COMPUTERS (HACKING, PROGRAMMING, ASSEMBLY, DISASSEMBLY).
40. SEDUCTION.

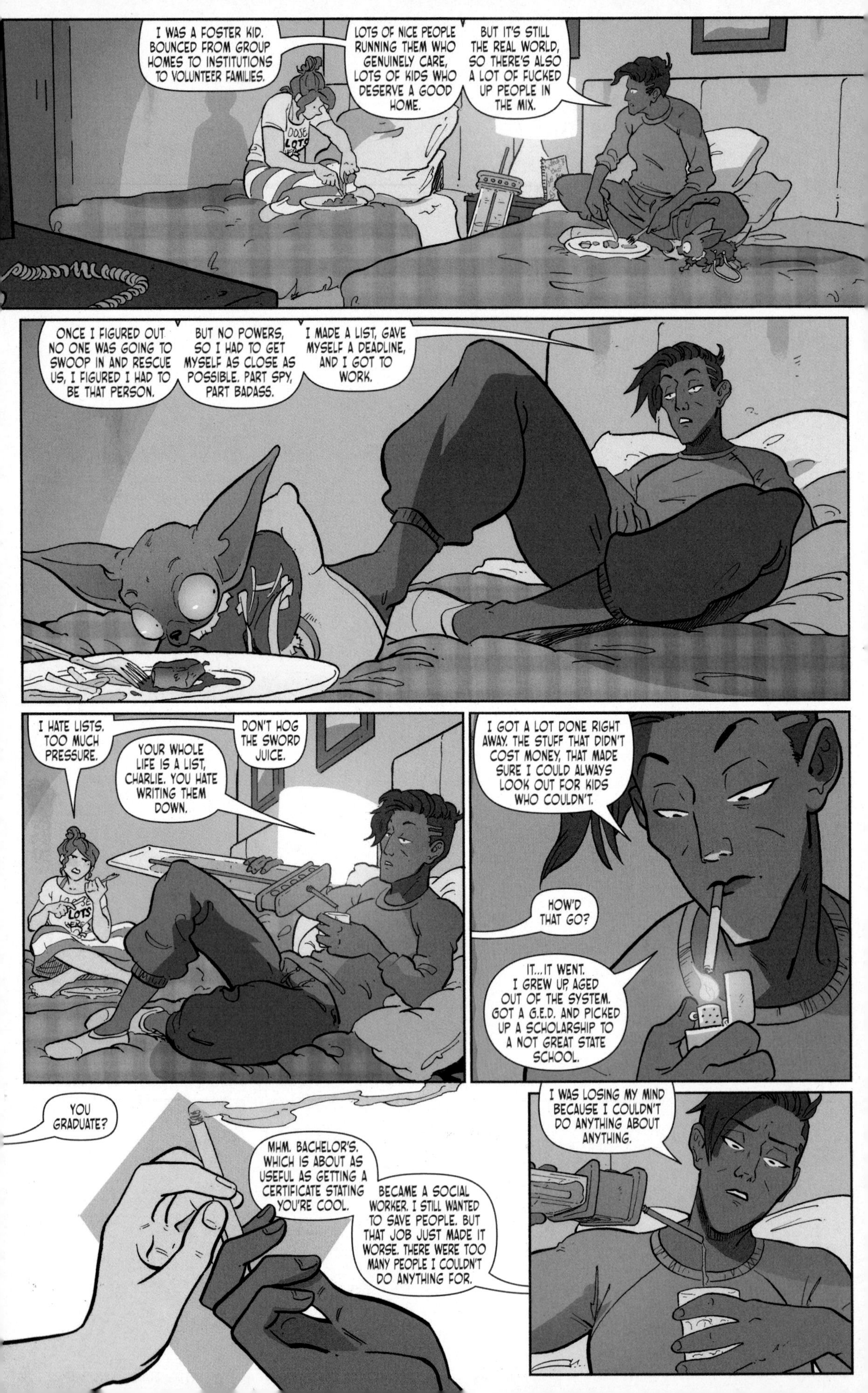

I WAS A FOSTER KID. BOUNCED FROM GROUP HOMES TO INSTITUTIONS TO VOLUNTEER FAMILIES.
LOTS OF NICE PEOPLE RUNNING THEM WHO GENUINELY CARE, LOTS OF KIDS WHO DESERVE A GOOD HOME.
BUT IT'S STILL THE REAL WORLD, SO THERE'S ALSO A LOT OF FUCKED UP PEOPLE IN THE MIX.
ONCE I FIGURED OUT NO ONE WAS GOING TO SWOOP IN AND RESCUE US, I FIGURED I HAD TO BE THAT PERSON.
BUT NO POWERS, SO I HAD TO GET MYSELF AS CLOSE AS POSSIBLE. PART SPY, PART BADASS.
I MADE A LIST, GAVE MYSELF A DEADLINE, AND I GOT TO WORK.
I HATE LISTS. TOO MUCH PRESSURE.
YOUR WHOLE LIFE IS A LIST, CHARLIE. YOU HATE WRITING THEM DOWN.
DON'T HOG THE SWORD JUICE.
I GOT A LOT DONE RIGHT AWAY. THE STUFF THAT DIDN'T COST MONEY, THAT MADE SURE I COULD ALWAYS LOOK OUT FOR KIDS WHO COULDN'T.
HOW'D THAT GO?
IT... IT WENT. I GREW UP, AGED OUT OF THE SYSTEM. GOT A G.E.D. AND PICKED UP A SCHOLARSHIP TO A NOT GREAT STATE SCHOOL.
YOU GRADUATE?
MHM. BACHELOR'S. WHICH IS ABOUT AS USEFUL AS GETTING A CERTIFICATE STATING YOU'RE COOL.
BECAME A SOCIAL WORKER. I STILL WANTED TO SAVE PEOPLE. BUT THAT JOB JUST MADE IT WORSE. THERE WERE TOO MANY PEOPLE I COULDN'T DO ANYTHING FOR.
I WAS LOSING MY MIND BECAUSE I COULDN'T DO ANYTHING ABOUT ANYTHING.

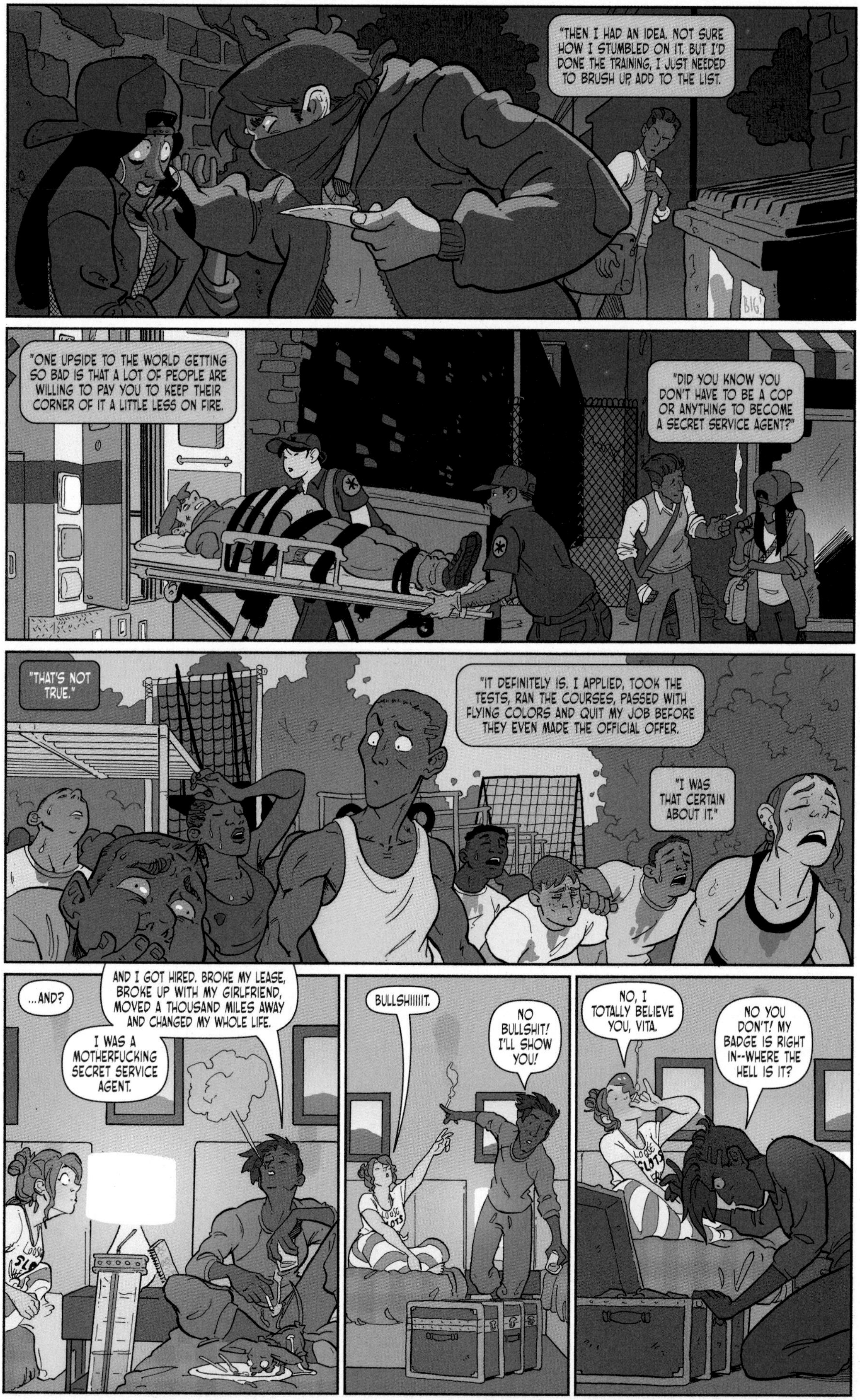
"THEN I HAD AN IDEA. NOT SURE HOW I STUMBLED ON IT. BUT I'D DONE THE TRAINING, I JUST NEEDED TO BRUSH UP, ADD TO THE LIST.
BIG
"ONE UPSIDE TO THE WORLD GETTING SO BAD IS THAT A LOT OF PEOPLE ARE WILLING TO PAY YOU TO KEEP THEIR CORNER OF IT A LITTLE LESS ON FIRE.
"DID YOU KNOW YOU DON'T HAVE TO BE A COP OR ANYTHING TO BECOME A SECRET SERVICE AGENT?"
"THAT'S NOT TRUE."
"IT DEFINITELY IS. I APPLIED, TOOK THE TESTS, RAN THE COURSES, PASSED WITH FLYING COLORS AND QUIT MY JOB BEFORE THEY EVEN MADE THE OFFICIAL OFFER.
"I WAS THAT CERTAIN ABOUT IT."
...AND?
AND I GOT HIRED. BROKE MY LEASE, BROKE UP WITH MY GIRLFRIEND, MOVED A THOUSAND MILES AWAY AND CHANGED MY WHOLE LIFE.
I WAS A MOTHERFUCKING SECRET SERVICE AGENT.
BULLSHIIIIIT.
NO BULLSHIT! I'LL SHOW YOU!
NO, I TOTALLY BELIEVE YOU, VITA.
NO YOU DON'T! MY BADGE IS RIGHT IN--WHERE THE HELL IS IT?

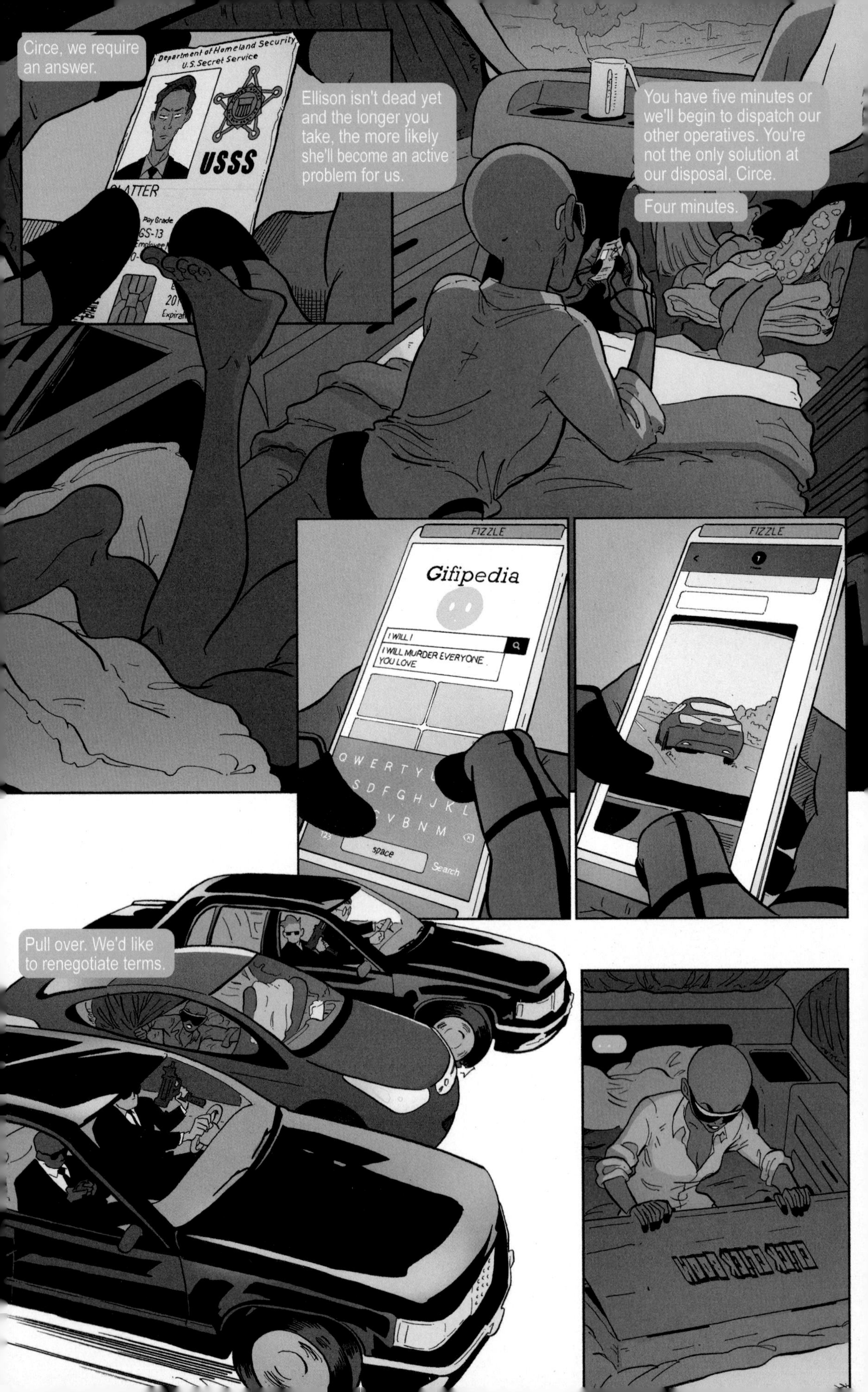

Circe, we require an answer.
Department of Homeland Security
U.S. Secret Service
USSS
Pay Grade
GS-13
Ellison isn't dead yet and the longer you take, the more likely she'll become an active problem for us.
You have five minutes or we'll begin to dispatch our other operatives. You're not the only solution at our disposal, Circe.
Four minutes.
FIZZLE
Gifipedia
I WILL I
I WILL MURDER EVERYONE YOU LOVE
space
Search
FIZZLE
Pull over. We'd like to renegotiate terms.

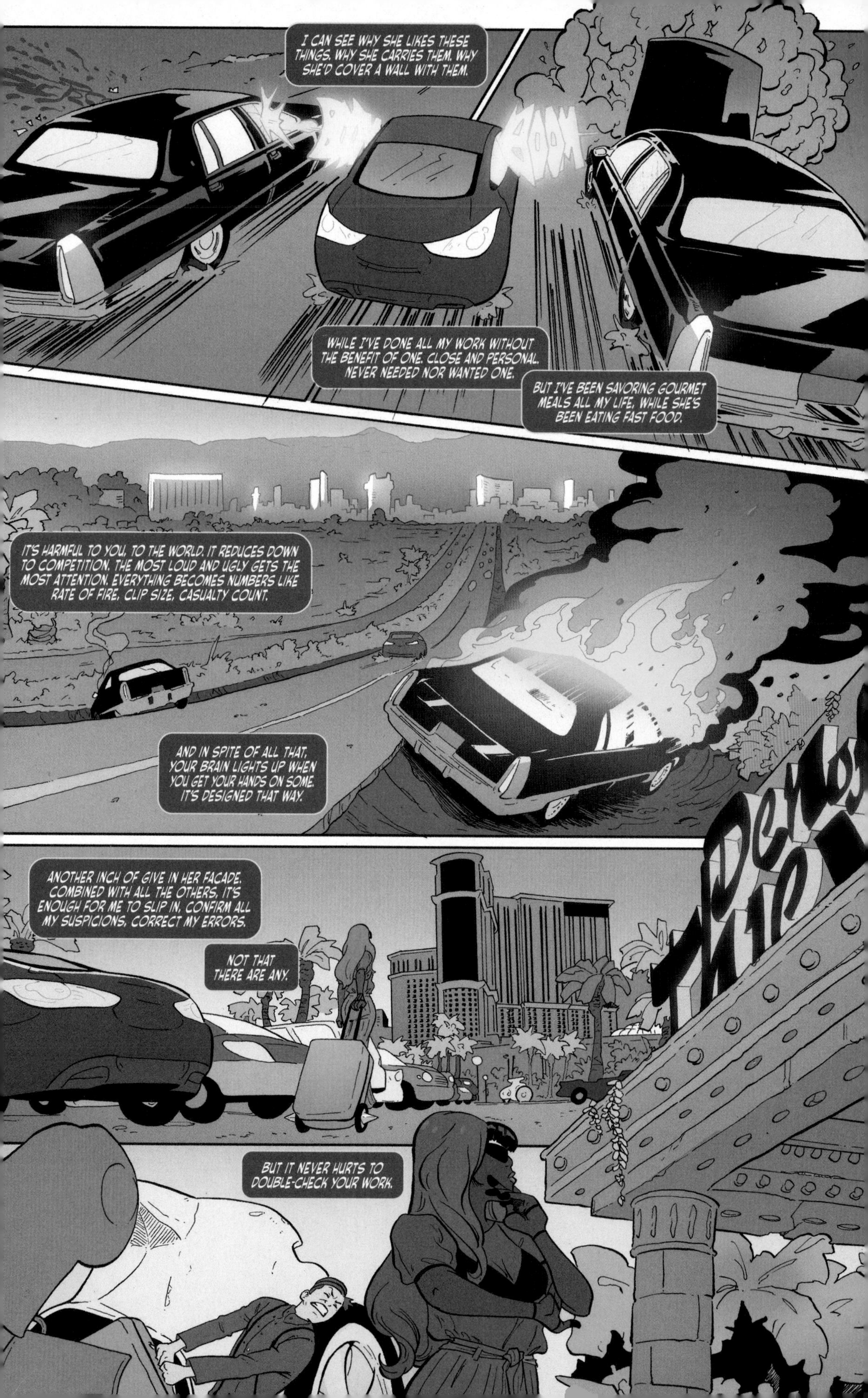
I CAN SEE WHY SHE LIKES THESE THINGS. WHY SHE CARRIES THEM. WHY SHE'D COVER A WALL WITH THEM.
BOOM
WHILE I'VE DONE ALL MY WORK WITHOUT THE BENEFIT OF ONE. CLOSE AND PERSONAL. NEVER NEEDED NOR WANTED ONE.
BUT I'VE BEEN SAVORING GOURMET MEALS ALL MY LIFE, WHILE SHE'S BEEN EATING FAST FOOD.
IT'S HARMFUL TO YOU, TO THE WORLD. IT REDUCES DOWN TO COMPETITION. THE MOST LOUD AND UGLY GETS THE MOST ATTENTION. EVERYTHING BECOMES NUMBERS LIKE RATE OF FIRE, CLIP SIZE, CASUALTY COUNT.
AND IN SPITE OF ALL THAT, YOUR BRAIN LIGHTS UP WHEN YOU GET YOUR HANDS ON SOME. IT'S DESIGNED THAT WAY.
ANOTHER INCH OF GIVE IN HER FACADE. COMBINED WITH ALL THE OTHERS, IT'S ENOUGH FOR ME TO SLIP IN, CONFIRM ALL MY SUSPICIONS, CORRECT MY ERRORS.
NOT THAT THERE ARE ANY.
BUT IT NEVER HURTS TO DOUBLE-CHECK YOUR WORK.

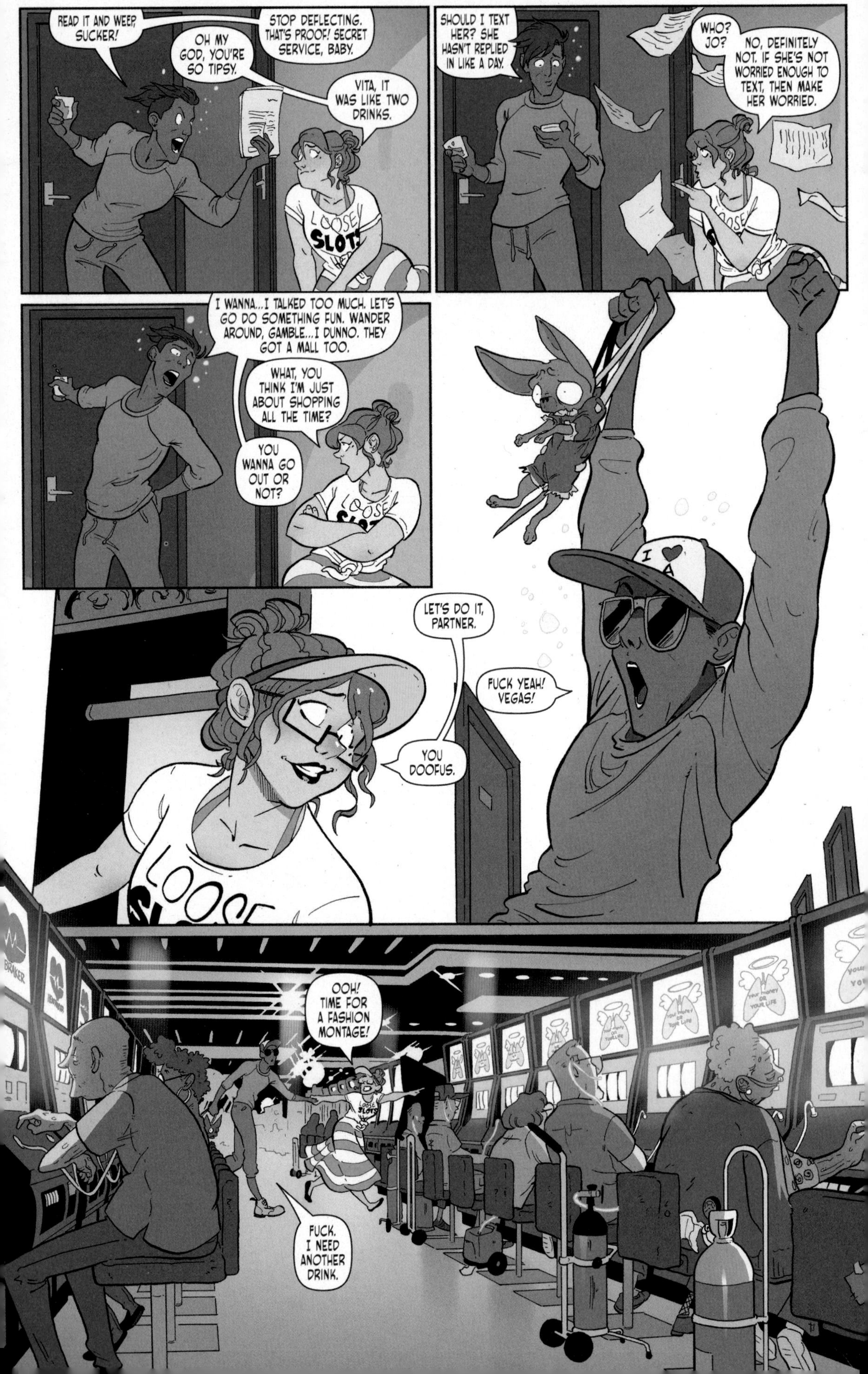
READ IT AND WEEP, SUCKER!
OH MY GOD, YOU'RE SO TIPSY.
STOP DEFLECTING. THAT'S PROOF! SECRET SERVICE, BABY.
VITA, IT WAS LIKE TWO DRINKS.
LOOSE SLOTS
SHOULD I TEXT HER? SHE HASN'T REPLIED IN LIKE A DAY.
WHO? JO?
NO, DEFINITELY NOT. IF SHE'S NOT WORRIED ENOUGH TO TEXT, THEN MAKE HER WORRIED.
I WANNA...I TALKED TOO MUCH. LET'S GO DO SOMETHING FUN. WANDER AROUND, GAMBLE...I DUNNO. THEY GOT A MALL TOO.
WHAT, YOU THINK I'M JUST ABOUT SHOPPING ALL THE TIME?
YOU WANNA GO OUT OR NOT?
LET'S DO IT, PARTNER.
FUCK YEAH! VEGAS!
YOU DOOFUS.
LOOSE
OOH! TIME FOR A FASHION MONTAGE!
FUCK. I NEED ANOTHER DRINK.

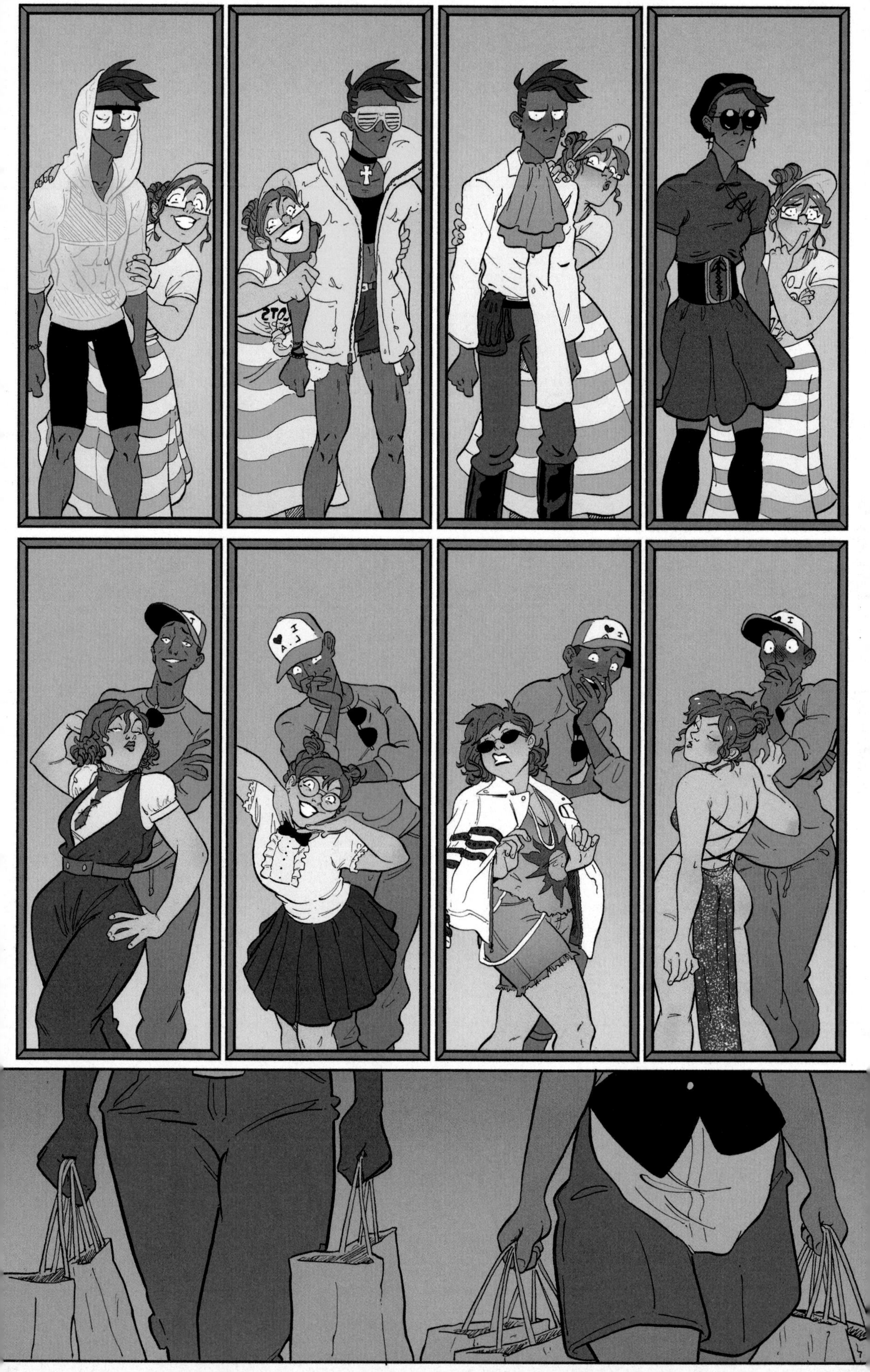

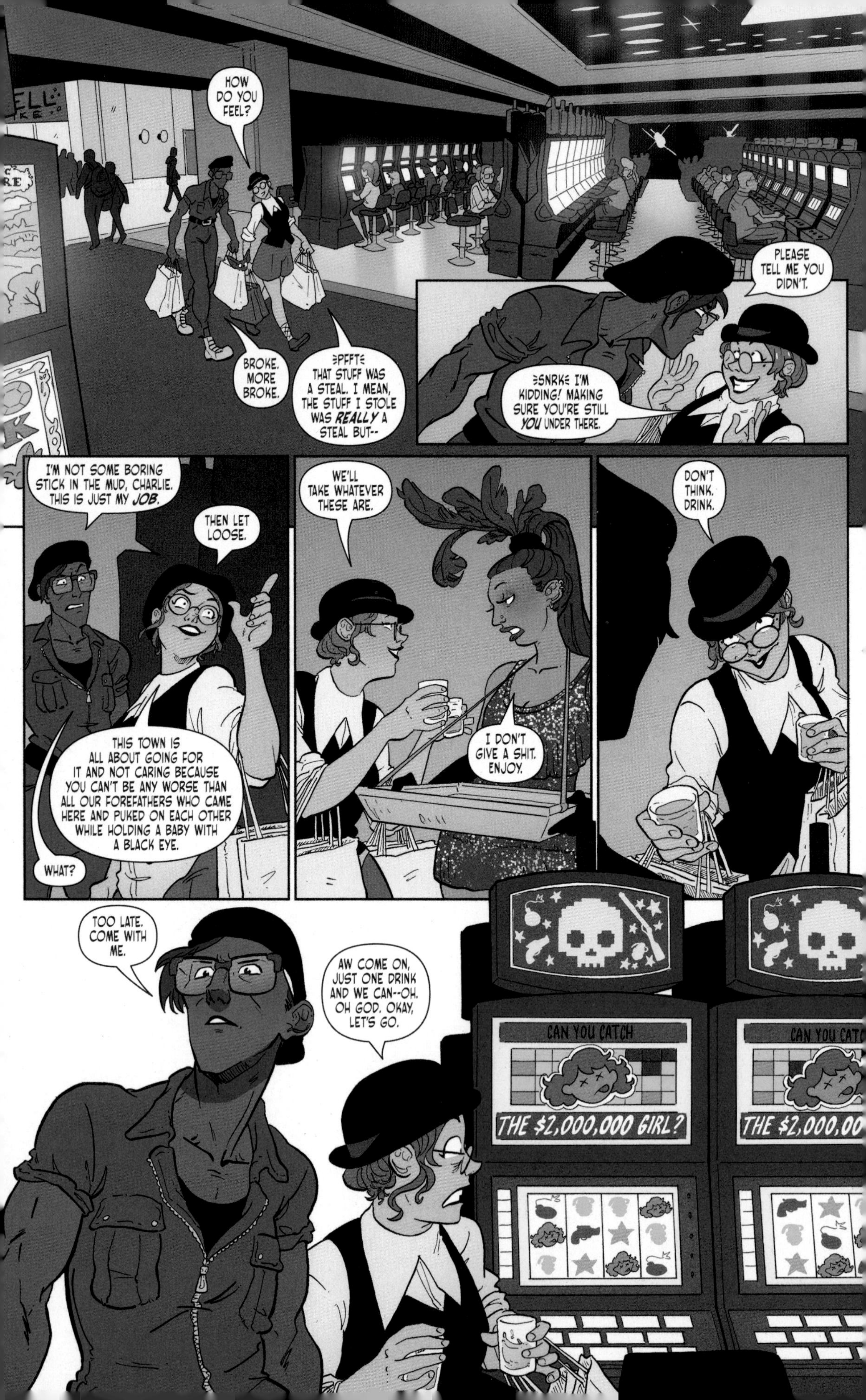
HOW DO YOU FEEL?
BROKE. MORE BROKE.
≡PFFT≡ THAT STUFF WAS A STEAL. I MEAN, THE STUFF I STOLE WAS *REALLY* A STEAL BUT--
PLEASE TELL ME YOU DIDN'T.
≡SNRK≡ I'M KIDDING! MAKING SURE YOU'RE STILL *YOU* UNDER THERE.
I'M NOT SOME BORING STICK IN THE MUD, CHARLIE. THIS IS JUST MY *JOB*.
THEN LET LOOSE.
THIS TOWN IS ALL ABOUT GOING FOR IT AND NOT CARING BECAUSE YOU CAN'T BE ANY WORSE THAN ALL OUR FOREFATHERS WHO CAME HERE AND PUKED ON EACH OTHER WHILE HOLDING A BABY WITH A BLACK EYE.
WHAT?
WE'LL TAKE WHATEVER THESE ARE.
I DON'T GIVE A SHIT. ENJOY.
DON'T THINK. DRINK.
TOO LATE. COME WITH ME.
AW COME ON, JUST ONE DRINK AND WE CAN--OH. OH GOD. OKAY, LET'S GO.
CAN YOU CATCH
THE $2,000,000 GIRL?

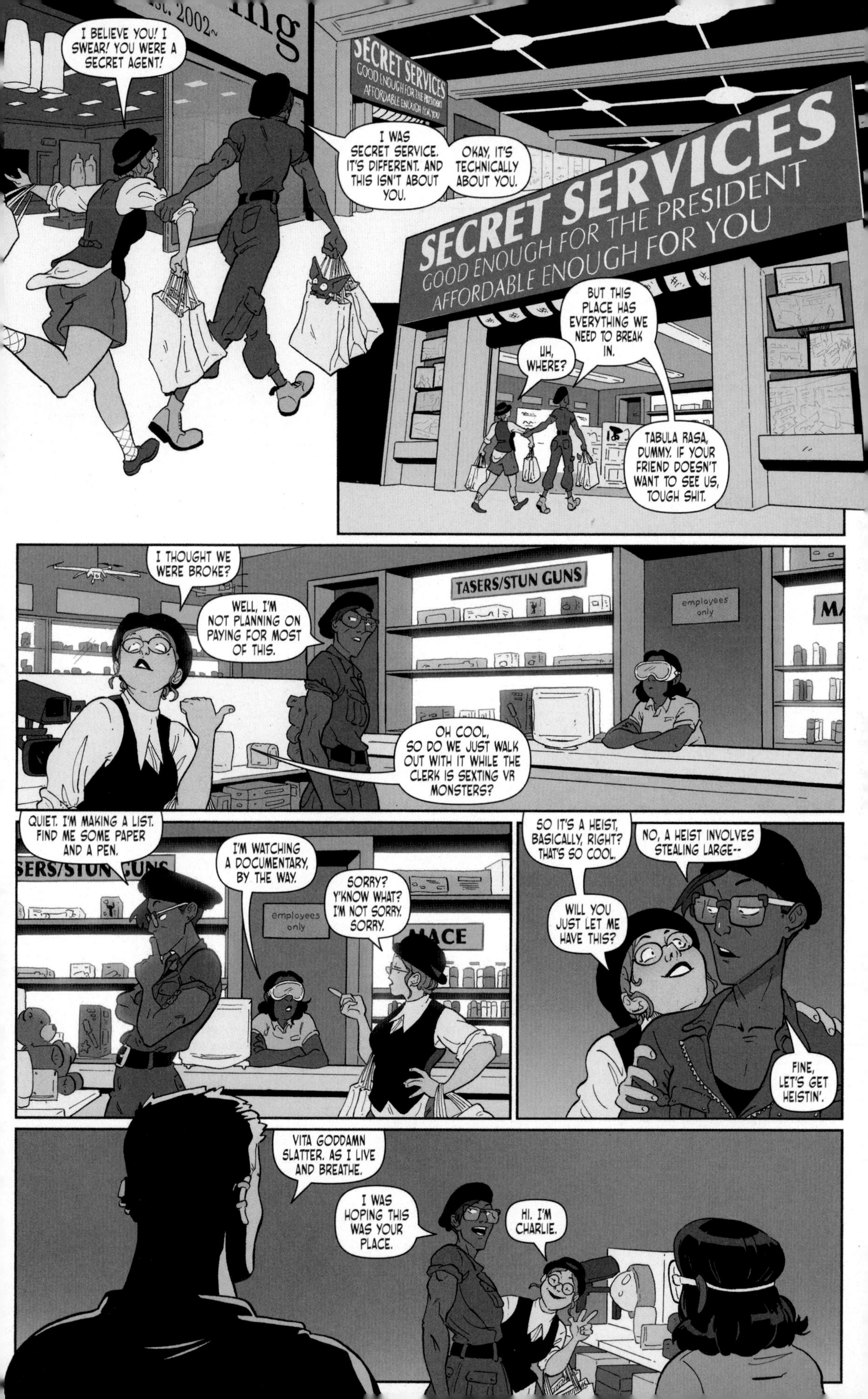

I BELIEVE YOU! I SWEAR! YOU WERE A SECRET AGENT!
I WAS SECRET SERVICE. IT'S DIFFERENT. AND THIS ISN'T ABOUT YOU.
OKAY, IT'S TECHNICALLY ABOUT YOU.
SECRET SERVICES GOOD ENOUGH FOR THE PRESIDENT AFFORDABLE ENOUGH FOR YOU
UH, WHERE?
BUT THIS PLACE HAS EVERYTHING WE NEED TO BREAK IN.
TABULA RASA, DUMMY. IF YOUR FRIEND DOESN'T WANT TO SEE US, TOUGH SHIT.
I THOUGHT WE WERE BROKE?
WELL, I'M NOT PLANNING ON PAYING FOR MOST OF THIS.
TASERS/STUN GUNS
employees only
OH COOL, SO DO WE JUST WALK OUT WITH IT WHILE THE CLERK IS SEXTING VR MONSTERS?
QUIET. I'M MAKING A LIST. FIND ME SOME PAPER AND A PEN.
I'M WATCHING A DOCUMENTARY, BY THE WAY.
SORRY? Y'KNOW WHAT? I'M NOT SORRY. SORRY.
MACE
SO IT'S A HEIST, BASICALLY, RIGHT? THAT'S SO COOL.
NO, A HEIST INVOLVES STEALING LARGE--
WILL YOU JUST LET ME HAVE THIS?
FINE, LET'S GET HEISTIN'.
VITA GODDAMN SLATTER. AS I LIVE AND BREATHE.
I WAS HOPING THIS WAS YOUR PLACE.
HI. I'M CHARLIE.

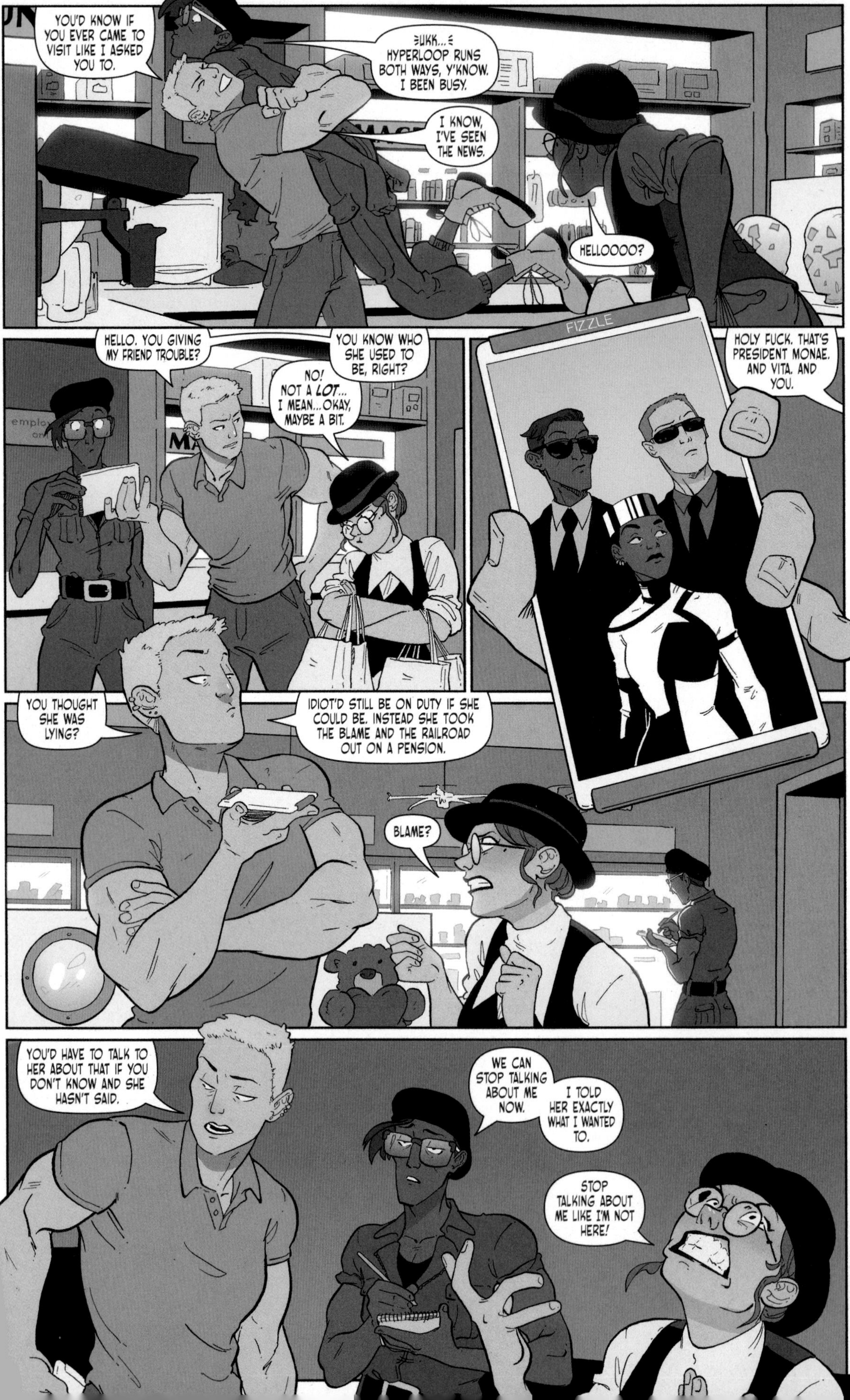
YOU'D KNOW IF YOU EVER CAME TO VISIT LIKE I ASKED YOU TO.
ƎUKK...Ǝ HYPERLOOP RUNS BOTH WAYS, Y'KNOW. I BEEN BUSY.
I KNOW, I'VE SEEN THE NEWS.
HELLOOOO?
HELLO. YOU GIVING MY FRIEND TROUBLE?
YOU KNOW WHO SHE USED TO BE, RIGHT?
NO! NOT A *LOT*... I MEAN...OKAY, MAYBE A BIT.
FIZZLE
HOLY FUCK. THAT'S PRESIDENT MONAE. AND VITA. AND YOU.
YOU THOUGHT SHE WAS LYING?
IDIOT'D STILL BE ON DUTY IF SHE COULD BE. INSTEAD SHE TOOK THE BLAME AND THE RAILROAD OUT ON A PENSION.
BLAME?
YOU'D HAVE TO TALK TO HER ABOUT THAT IF YOU DON'T KNOW AND SHE HASN'T SAID.
WE CAN STOP TALKING ABOUT ME NOW.
I TOLD HER EXACTLY WHAT I WANTED TO.
STOP TALKING ABOUT ME LIKE I'M NOT HERE!

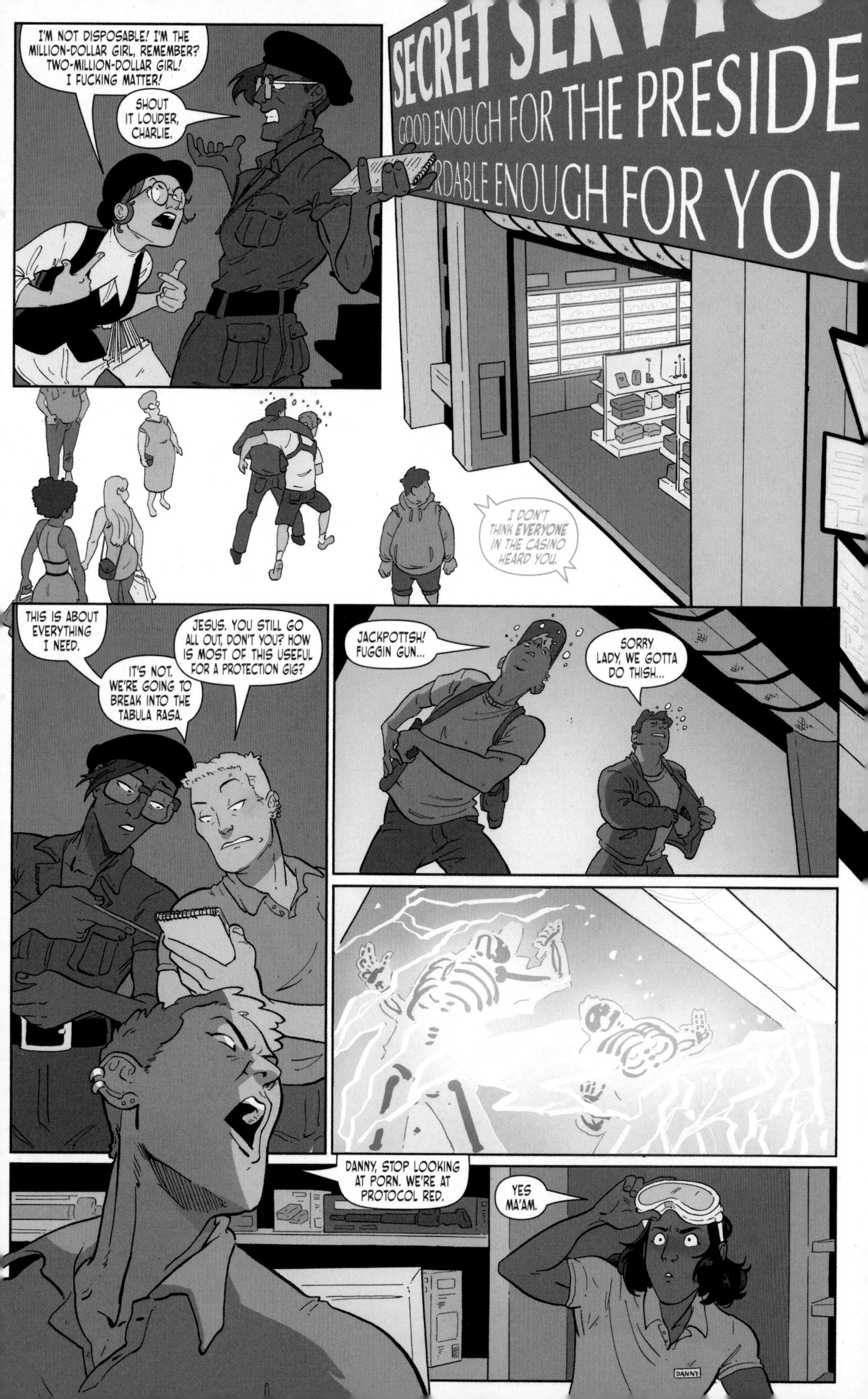

I'M NOT DISPOSABLE! I'M THE MILLION-DOLLAR GIRL, REMEMBER? TWO-MILLION-DOLLAR GIRL! I FUCKING MATTER!
SHOUT IT LOUDER, CHARLIE.
SECRET SERV
GOOD ENOUGH FOR THE PRESIDE
RDABLE ENOUGH FOR YOU
I DON'T THINK EVERYONE IN THE CASINO HEARD YOU.
THIS IS ABOUT EVERYTHING I NEED.
JESUS. YOU STILL GO ALL OUT, DON'T YOU? HOW IS MOST OF THIS USEFUL FOR A PROTECTION GIG?
IT'S NOT. WE'RE GOING TO BREAK INTO THE TABULA RASA.
JACKPOTTSH! FUGGIN GUN...
SORRY LADY, WE GOTTA DO THISH...
DANNY, STOP LOOKING AT PORN. WE'RE AT PROTOCOL RED.
YES MA'AM.
DANNY

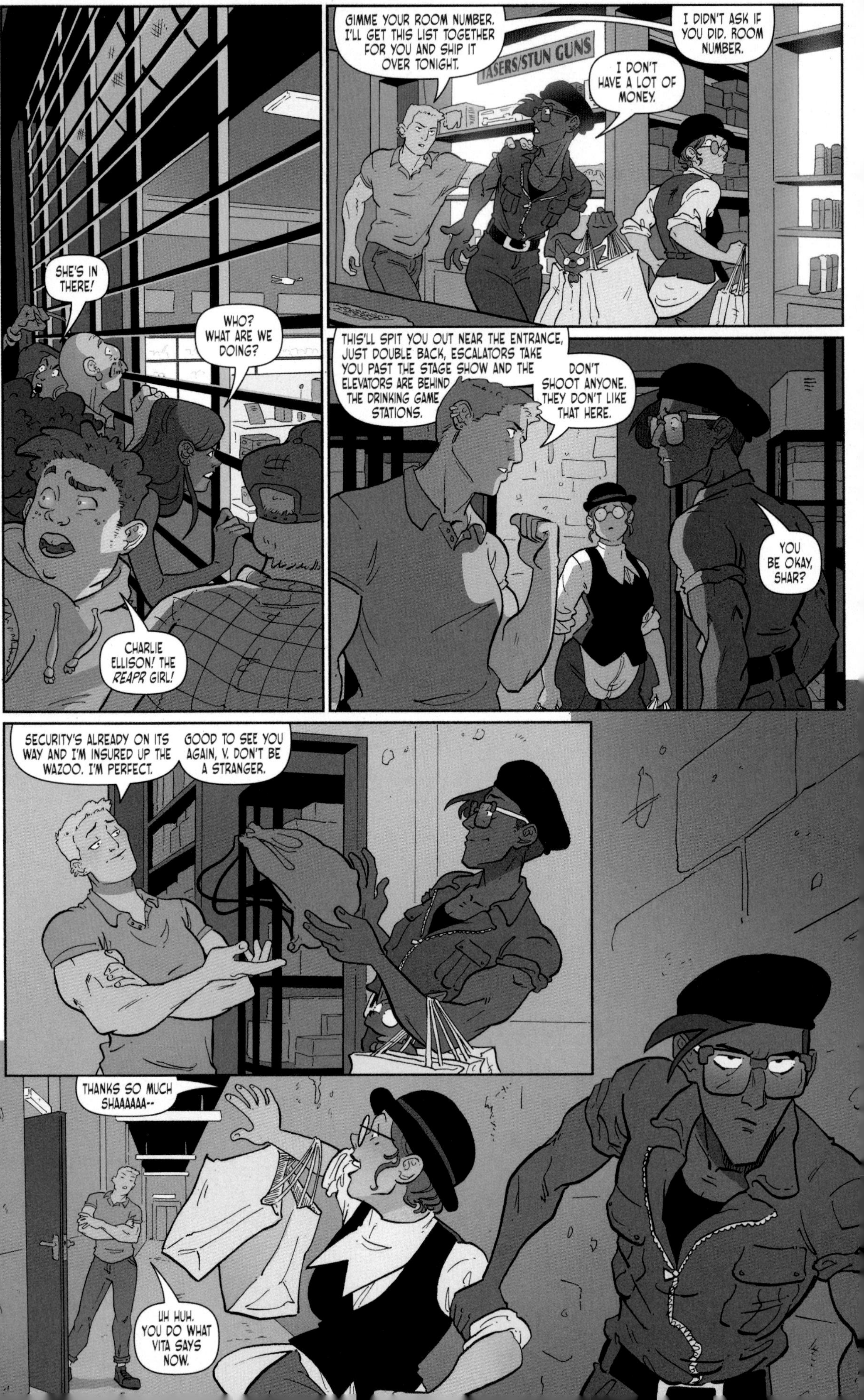
SHE'S IN THERE!
WHO? WHAT ARE WE DOING?
CHARLIE ELLISON! THE *REAPR* GIRL!
GIMME YOUR ROOM NUMBER. I'LL GET THIS LIST TOGETHER FOR YOU AND SHIP IT OVER TONIGHT.
TASERS/STUN GUNS
I DON'T HAVE A LOT OF MONEY.
I DIDN'T ASK IF YOU DID. ROOM NUMBER.
THIS'LL SPIT YOU OUT NEAR THE ENTRANCE, JUST DOUBLE BACK, ESCALATORS TAKE YOU PAST THE STAGE SHOW AND THE ELEVATORS ARE BEHIND THE DRINKING GAME STATIONS.
DON'T SHOOT ANYONE. THEY DON'T LIKE THAT HERE.
YOU BE OKAY, SHAR?
SECURITY'S ALREADY ON ITS WAY AND I'M INSURED UP THE WAZOO. I'M PERFECT.
GOOD TO SEE YOU AGAIN, V. DON'T BE A STRANGER.
THANKS SO MUCH SHAAAAAA--
UH HUH. YOU DO WHAT VITA SAYS NOW.

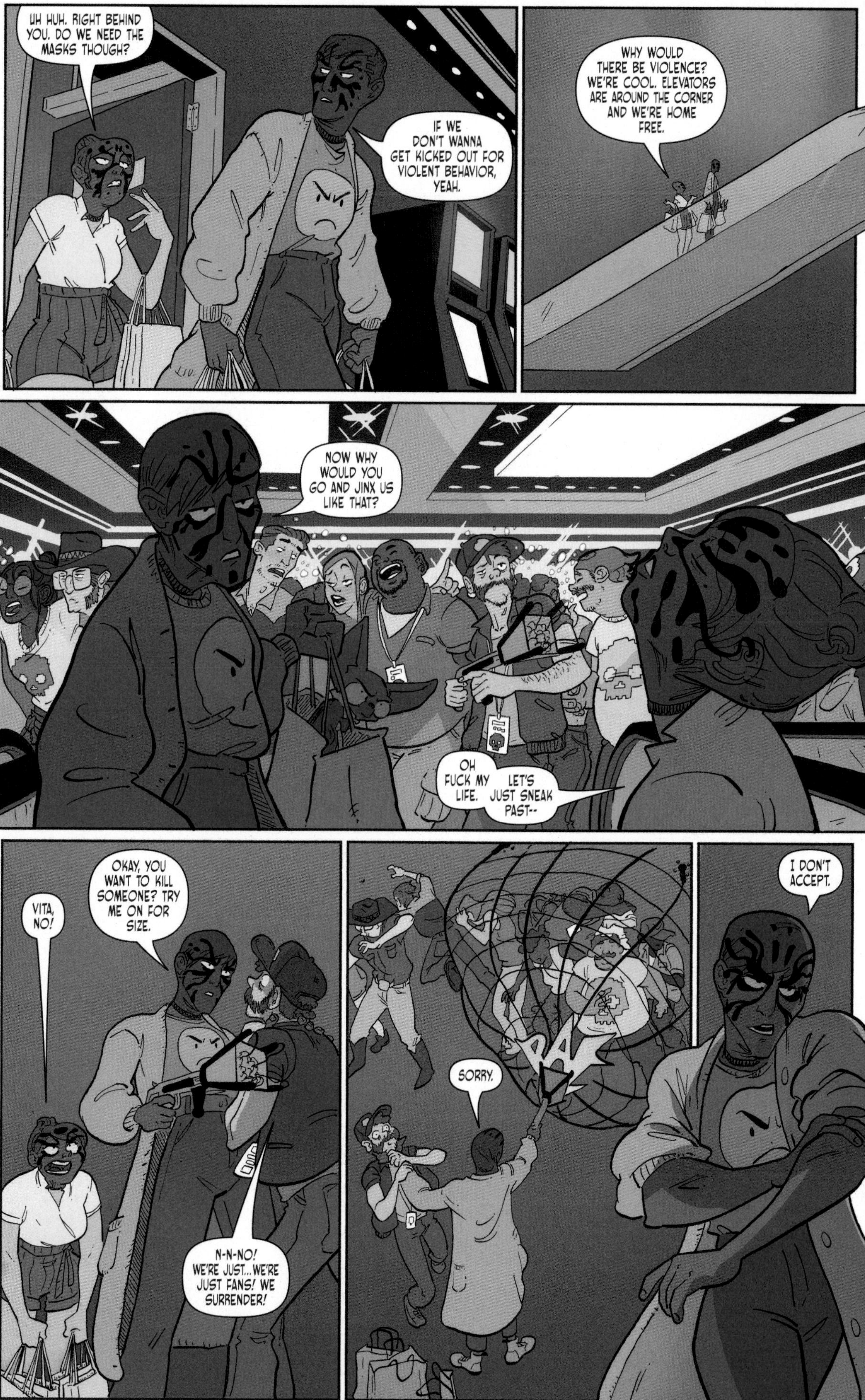
UH HUH. RIGHT BEHIND YOU. DO WE NEED THE MASKS THOUGH?
IF WE DON'T WANNA GET KICKED OUT FOR VIOLENT BEHAVIOR, YEAH.
WHY WOULD THERE BE VIOLENCE? WE'RE COOL. ELEVATORS ARE AROUND THE CORNER AND WE'RE HOME FREE.
NOW WHY WOULD YOU GO AND JINX US LIKE THAT?
OH FUCK MY LIFE.
LET'S JUST SNEAK PAST--
VITA, NO!
OKAY, YOU WANT TO KILL SOMEONE? TRY ME ON FOR SIZE.
N-N-NO! WE'RE JUST...WE'RE JUST FANS! WE SURRENDER!
SORRY.
I DON'T ACCEPT.

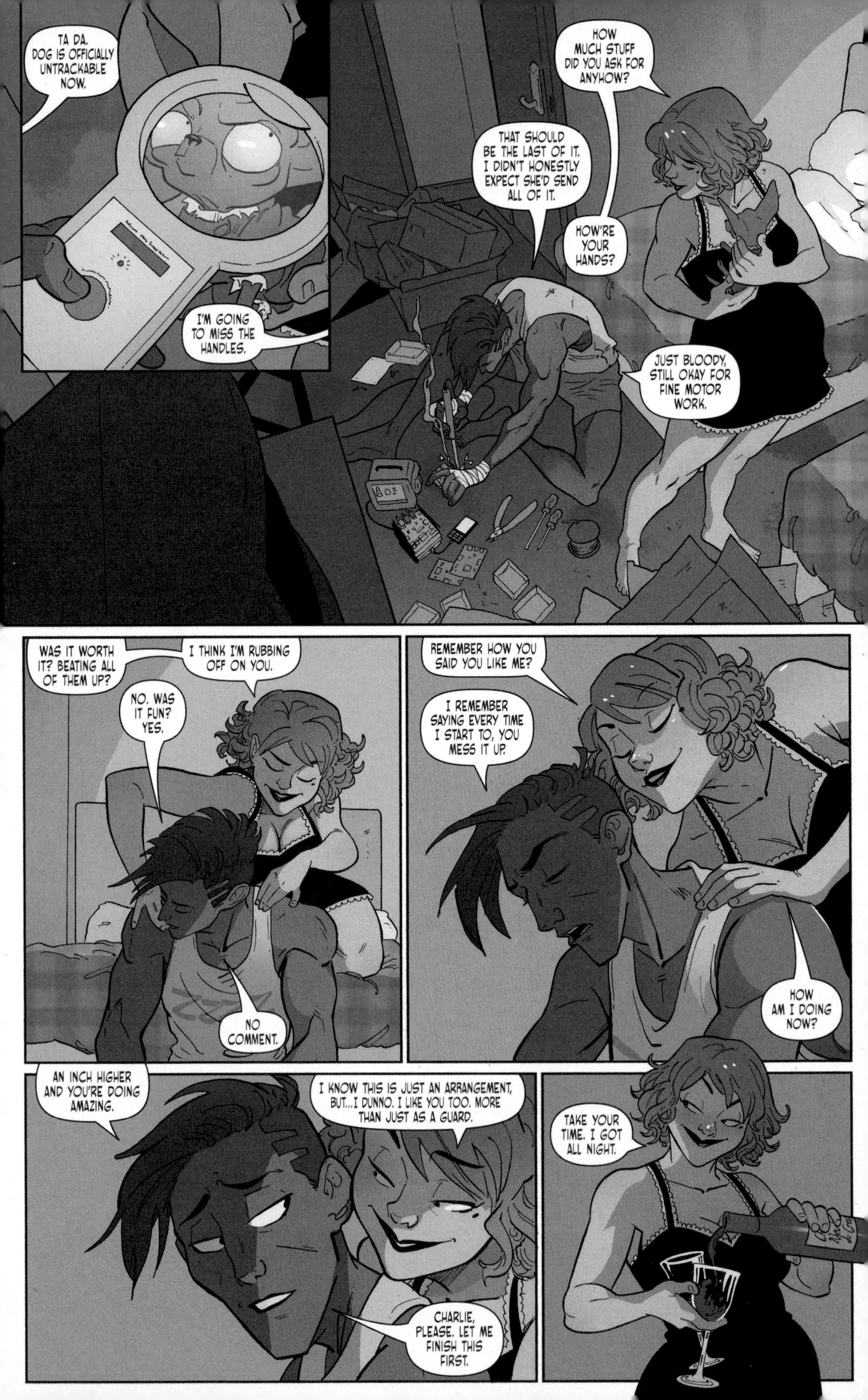
TA DA. DOG IS OFFICIALLY UNTRACKABLE NOW.
I'M GOING TO MISS THE HANDLES.
HOW MUCH STUFF DID YOU ASK FOR ANYHOW?
THAT SHOULD BE THE LAST OF IT. I DIDN'T HONESTLY EXPECT SHE'D SEND ALL OF IT.
HOW'RE YOUR HANDS?
JUST BLOODY, STILL OKAY FOR FINE MOTOR WORK.
WAS IT WORTH IT? BEATING ALL OF THEM UP?
NO. WAS IT FUN? YES.
I THINK I'M RUBBING OFF ON YOU.
NO COMMENT.
REMEMBER HOW YOU SAID YOU LIKE ME?
I REMEMBER SAYING EVERY TIME I START TO, YOU MESS IT UP.
HOW AM I DOING NOW?
AN INCH HIGHER AND YOU'RE DOING AMAZING.
I KNOW THIS IS JUST AN ARRANGEMENT, BUT...I DUNNO. I LIKE YOU TOO. MORE THAN JUST AS A GUARD.
CHARLIE, PLEASE. LET ME FINISH THIS FIRST.
TAKE YOUR TIME. I GOT ALL NIGHT.

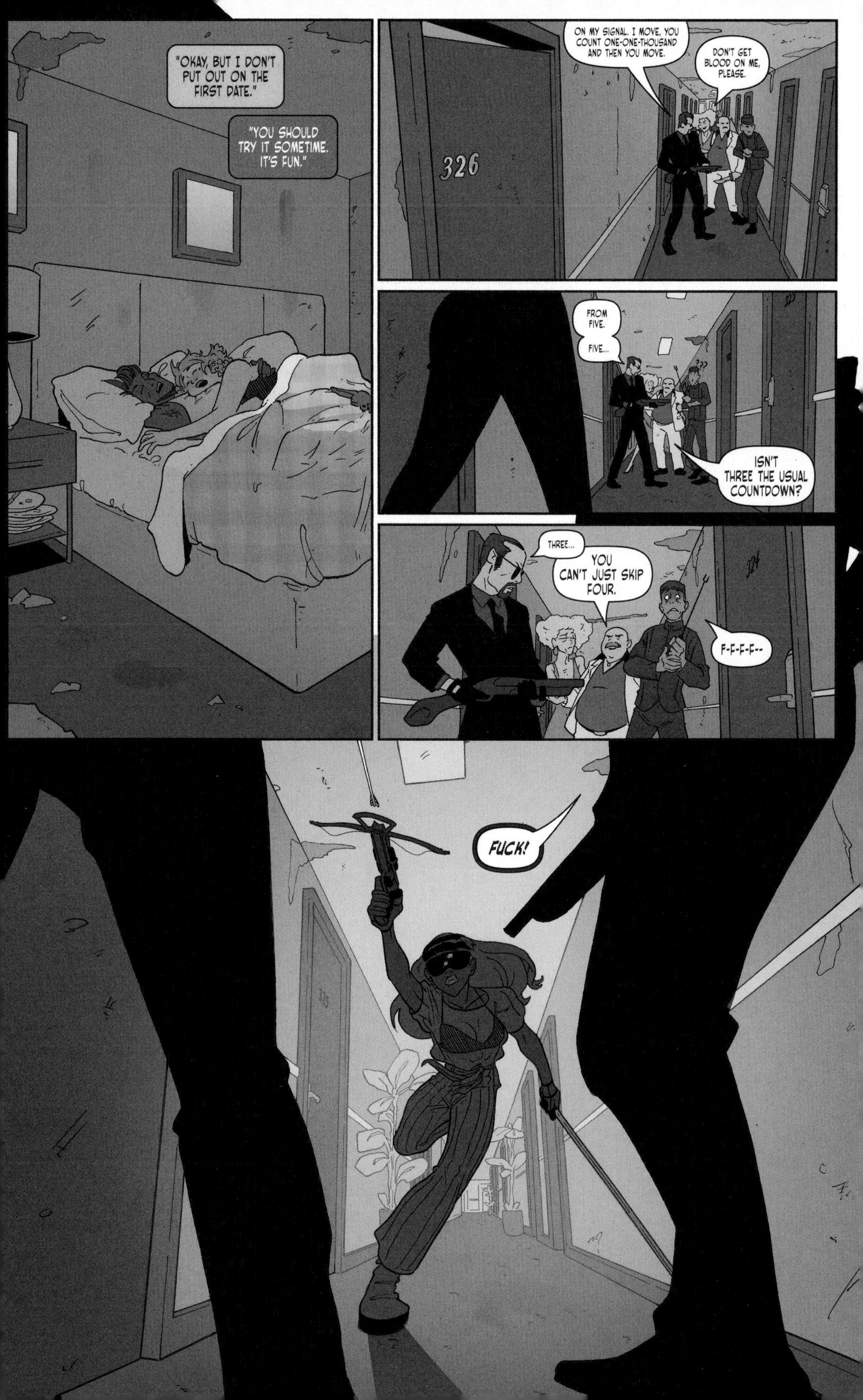
"OKAY, BUT I DON'T PUT OUT ON THE FIRST DATE."
"YOU SHOULD TRY IT SOMETIME. IT'S FUN."
ON MY SIGNAL. I MOVE, YOU COUNT ONE-ONE-THOUSAND AND THEN YOU MOVE.
DON'T GET BLOOD ON ME, PLEASE.
326
FROM FIVE.
FIVE...
ISN'T THREE THE USUAL COUNTDOWN?
THREE...
YOU CAN'T JUST SKIP FOUR.
F-F-F-F--
FUCK!

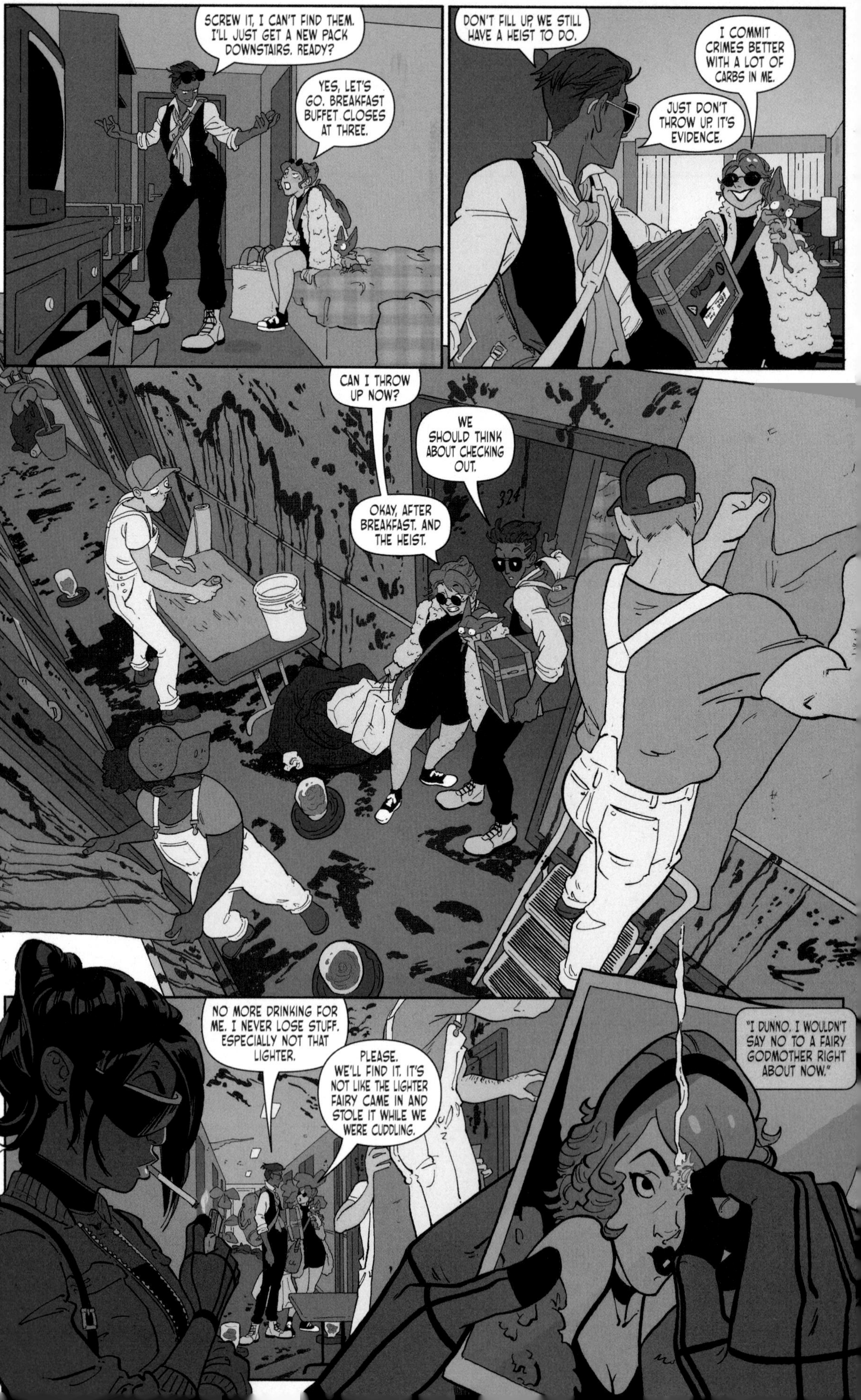
SCREW IT, I CAN'T FIND THEM. I'LL JUST GET A NEW PACK DOWNSTAIRS. READY?
YES, LET'S GO. BREAKFAST BUFFET CLOSES AT THREE.
DON'T FILL UP, WE STILL HAVE A HEIST TO DO.
I COMMIT CRIMES BETTER WITH A LOT OF CARBS IN ME.
JUST DON'T THROW UP. IT'S EVIDENCE.
CAN I THROW UP NOW?
WE SHOULD THINK ABOUT CHECKING OUT.
OKAY, AFTER BREAKFAST. AND THE HEIST.
324
NO MORE DRINKING FOR ME. I NEVER LOSE STUFF. ESPECIALLY NOT THAT LIGHTER.
PLEASE. WE'LL FIND IT. IT'S NOT LIKE THE LIGHTER FAIRY CAME IN AND STOLE IT WHILE WE WERE CUDDLING.
"I DUNNO. I WOULDN'T SAY NO TO A FAIRY GODMOTHER RIGHT ABOUT NOW."

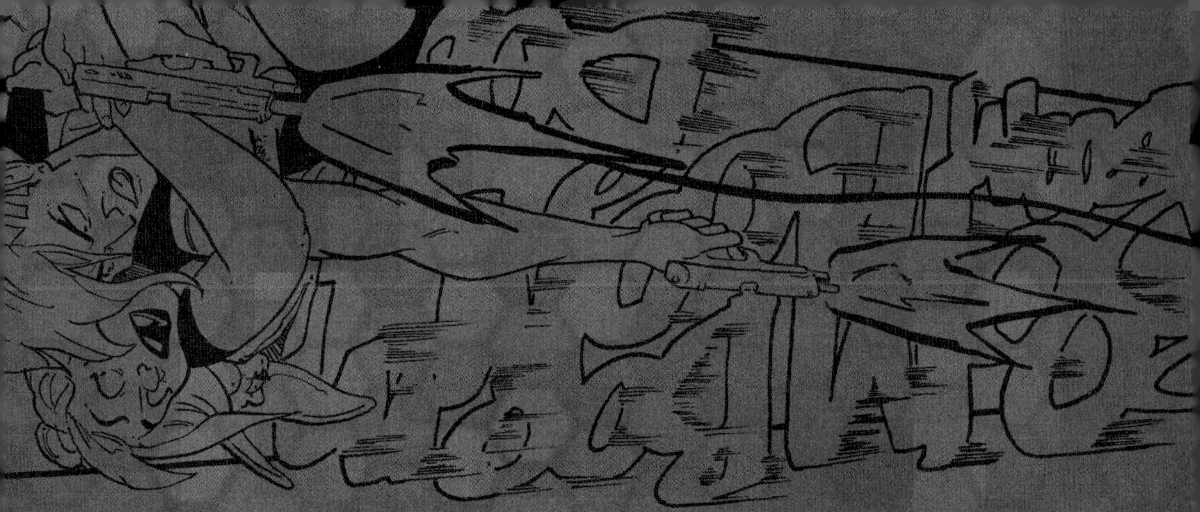

CHAPTER NINE

BABES NEVER DIE

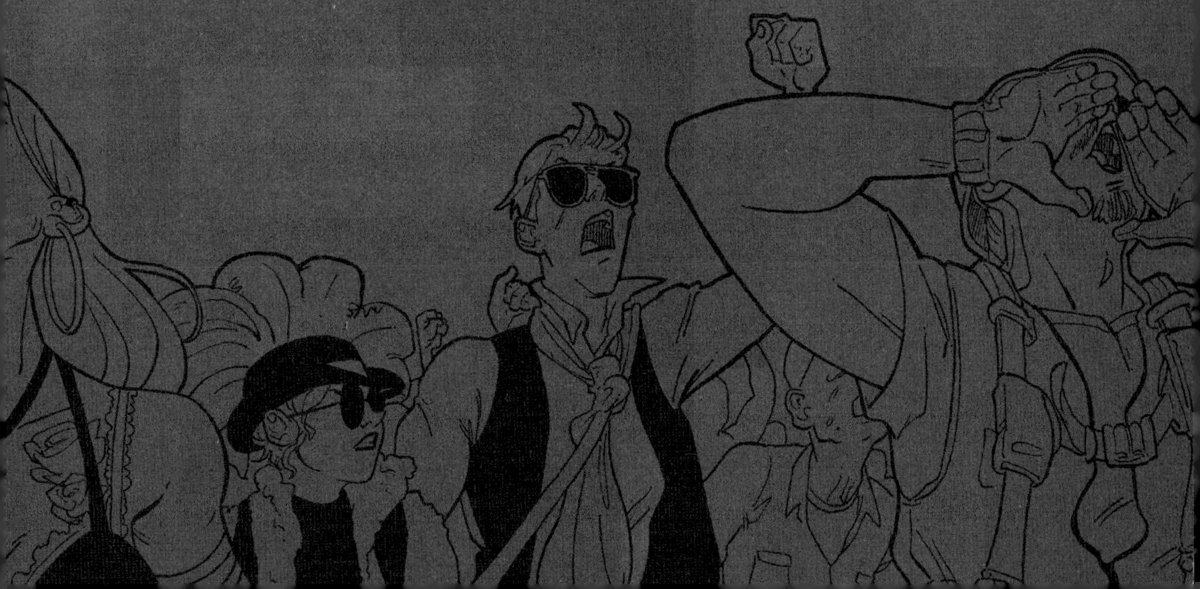

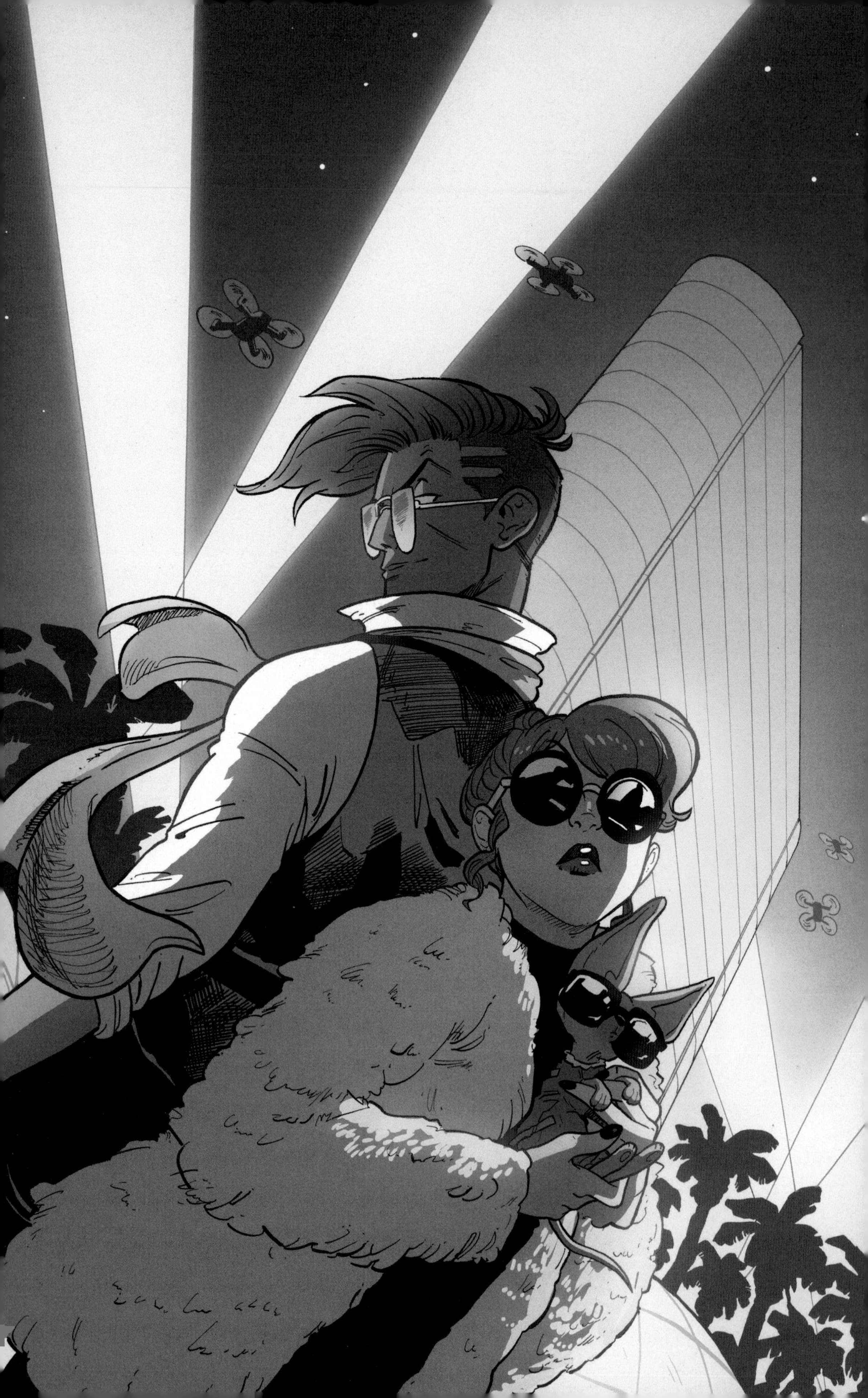

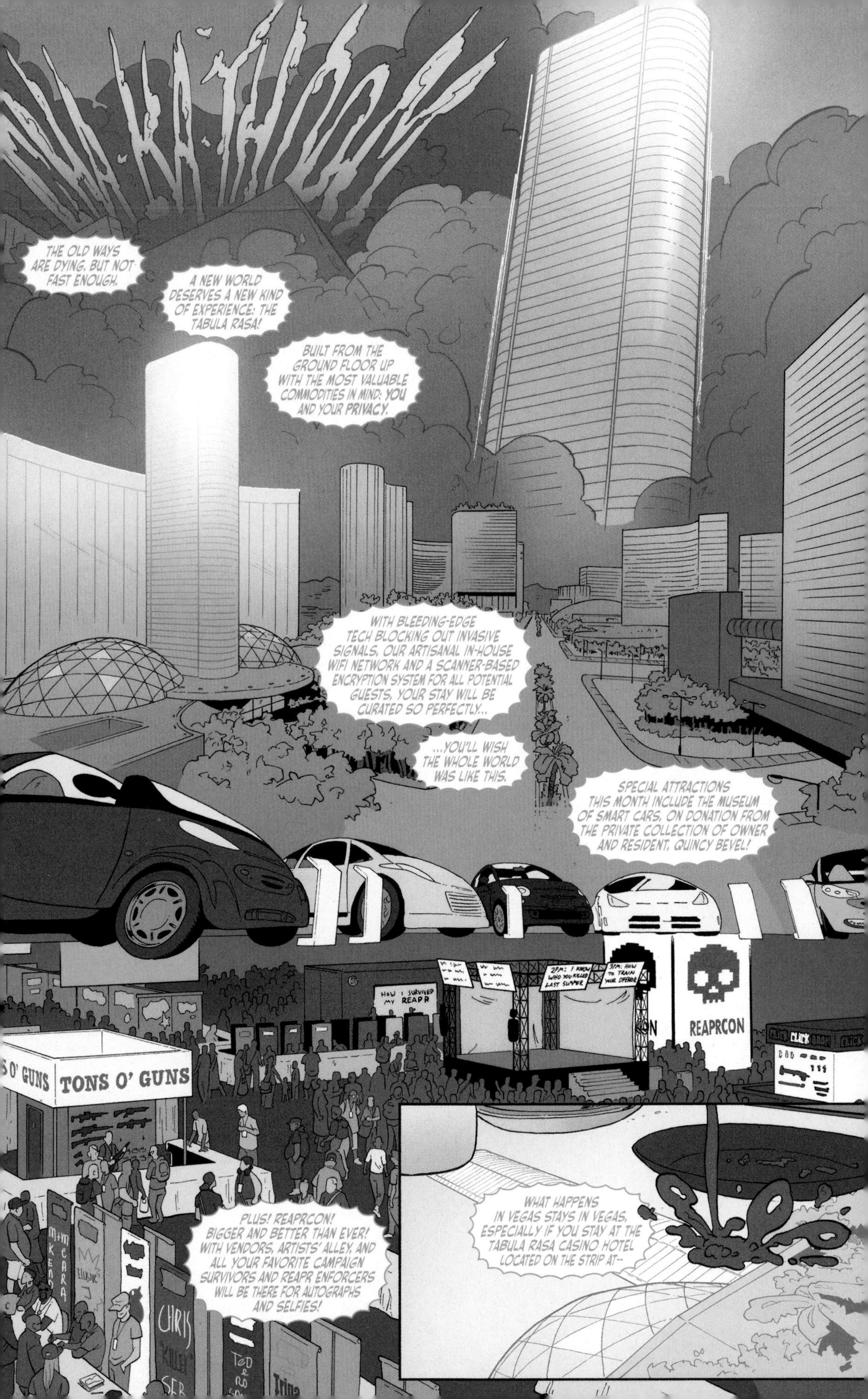
THE OLD WAYS ARE DYING. BUT NOT FAST ENOUGH.
A NEW WORLD DESERVES A NEW KIND OF EXPERIENCE: THE TABULA RASA!
BUILT FROM THE GROUND FLOOR UP WITH THE MOST VALUABLE COMMODITIES IN MIND: YOU AND YOUR PRIVACY.
WITH BLEEDING-EDGE TECH BLOCKING OUT INVASIVE SIGNALS, OUR ARTISANAL IN-HOUSE WIFI NETWORK AND A SCANNER-BASED ENCRYPTION SYSTEM FOR ALL POTENTIAL GUESTS, YOUR STAY WILL BE CURATED SO PERFECTLY...
...YOU'LL WISH THE WHOLE WORLD WAS LIKE THIS.
SPECIAL ATTRACTIONS THIS MONTH INCLUDE THE MUSEUM OF SMART CARS, ON DONATION FROM THE PRIVATE COLLECTION OF OWNER AND RESIDENT, QUINCY BEVEL!
HOW I SURVIVED MY REAPR
2PM: I KNOW WHO YOU KILLED LAST SUMMER
3PM: HOW TO TRAIN YOUR DFENDR
REAPRCON
TONS O' GUNS
PLUS! REAPRCON! BIGGER AND BETTER THAN EVER! WITH VENDORS, ARTISTS' ALLEY, AND ALL YOUR FAVORITE CAMPAIGN SURVIVORS AND REAPR ENFORCERS WILL BE THERE FOR AUTOGRAPHS AND SELFIES!
WHAT HAPPENS IN VEGAS STAYS IN VEGAS, ESPECIALLY IF YOU STAY AT THE TABULA RASA CASINO HOTEL LOCATED ON THE STRIP AT--

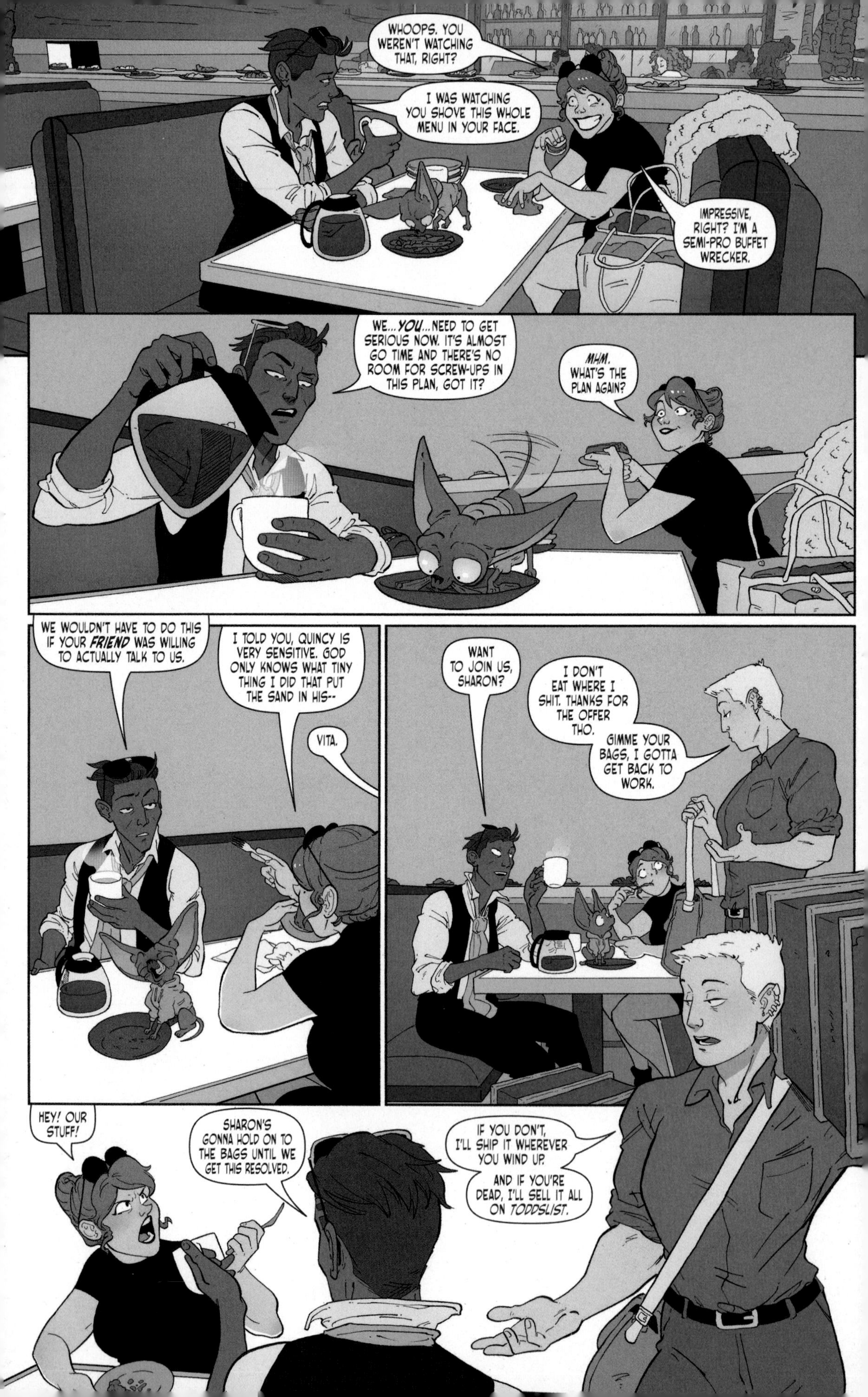
WHOOPS. YOU WEREN'T WATCHING THAT, RIGHT?
I WAS WATCHING YOU SHOVE THIS WHOLE MENU IN YOUR FACE.
IMPRESSIVE, RIGHT? I'M A SEMI-PRO BUFFET WRECKER.
WE... *YOU*... NEED TO GET SERIOUS NOW. IT'S ALMOST GO TIME AND THERE'S NO ROOM FOR SCREW-UPS IN THIS PLAN, GOT IT?
MHM. WHAT'S THE PLAN AGAIN?
WE WOULDN'T HAVE TO DO THIS IF YOUR *FRIEND* WAS WILLING TO ACTUALLY TALK TO US.
I TOLD YOU, QUINCY IS VERY SENSITIVE. GOD ONLY KNOWS WHAT TINY THING I DID THAT PUT THE SAND IN HIS--
VITA.
WANT TO JOIN US, SHARON?
I DON'T EAT WHERE I SHIT. THANKS FOR THE OFFER THO.
GIMME YOUR BAGS, I GOTTA GET BACK TO WORK.
HEY! OUR STUFF!
SHARON'S GONNA HOLD ON TO THE BAGS UNTIL WE GET THIS RESOLVED.
IF YOU DON'T, I'LL SHIP IT WHEREVER YOU WIND UP.
AND IF YOU'RE DEAD, I'LL SELL IT ALL ON *TODDSLIST*.

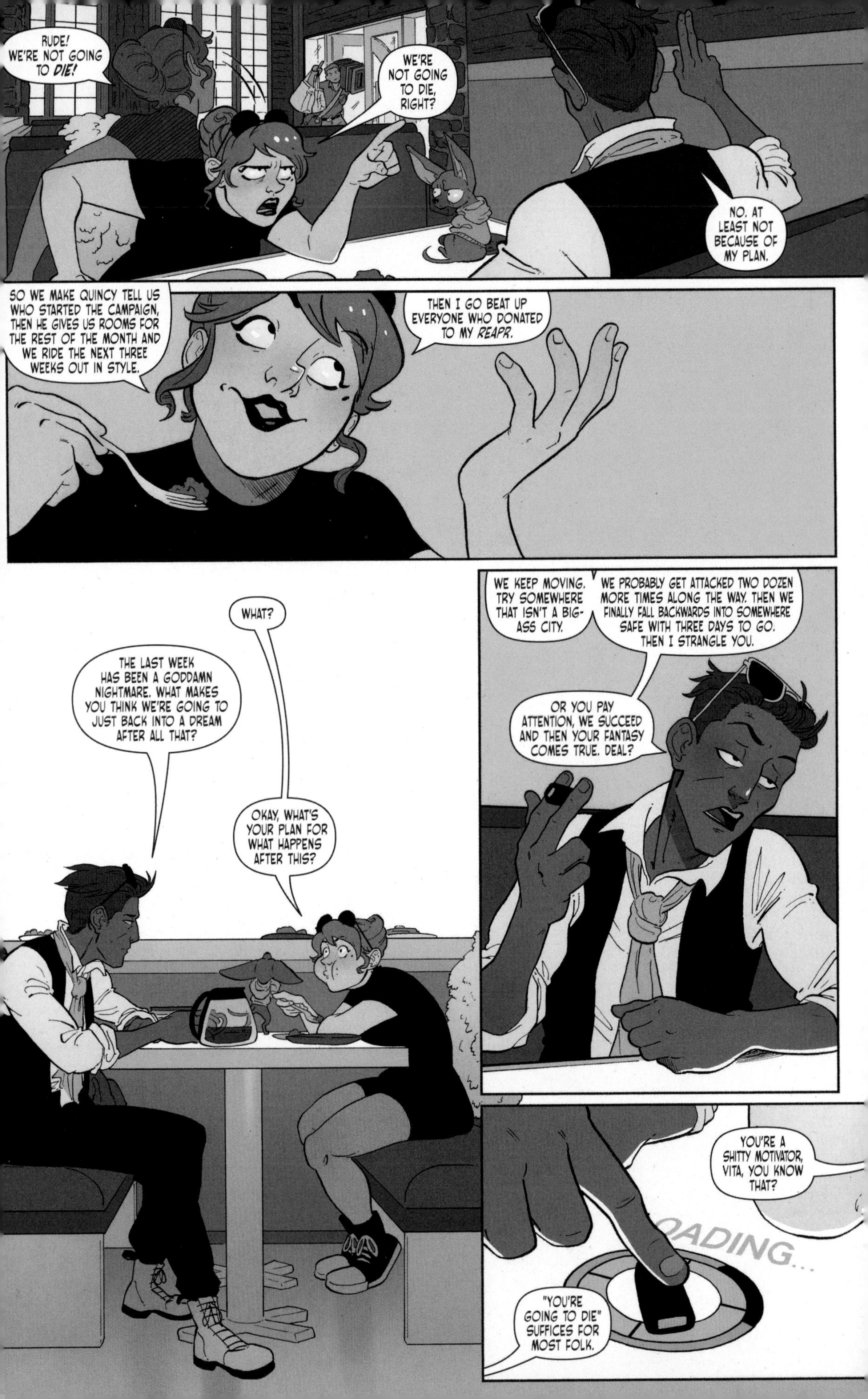
RUDE! WE'RE NOT GOING TO DIE!
WE'RE NOT GOING TO DIE, RIGHT?
NO. AT LEAST NOT BECAUSE OF MY PLAN.
SO WE MAKE QUINCY TELL US WHO STARTED THE CAMPAIGN, THEN HE GIVES US ROOMS FOR THE REST OF THE MONTH AND WE RIDE THE NEXT THREE WEEKS OUT IN STYLE.
THEN I GO BEAT UP EVERYONE WHO DONATED TO MY REAPR.
THE LAST WEEK HAS BEEN A GODDAMN NIGHTMARE. WHAT MAKES YOU THINK WE'RE GOING TO JUST BACK INTO A DREAM AFTER ALL THAT?
WHAT?
OKAY, WHAT'S YOUR PLAN FOR WHAT HAPPENS AFTER THIS?
WE KEEP MOVING. TRY SOMEWHERE THAT ISN'T A BIG-ASS CITY.
WE PROBABLY GET ATTACKED TWO DOZEN MORE TIMES ALONG THE WAY. THEN WE FINALLY FALL BACKWARDS INTO SOMEWHERE SAFE WITH THREE DAYS TO GO. THEN I STRANGLE YOU.
OR YOU PAY ATTENTION, WE SUCCEED AND THEN YOUR FANTASY COMES TRUE. DEAL?
YOU'RE A SHITTY MOTIVATOR, VITA, YOU KNOW THAT?
LOADING...
"YOU'RE GOING TO DIE" SUFFICES FOR MOST FOLK.

VITA'S PLAN

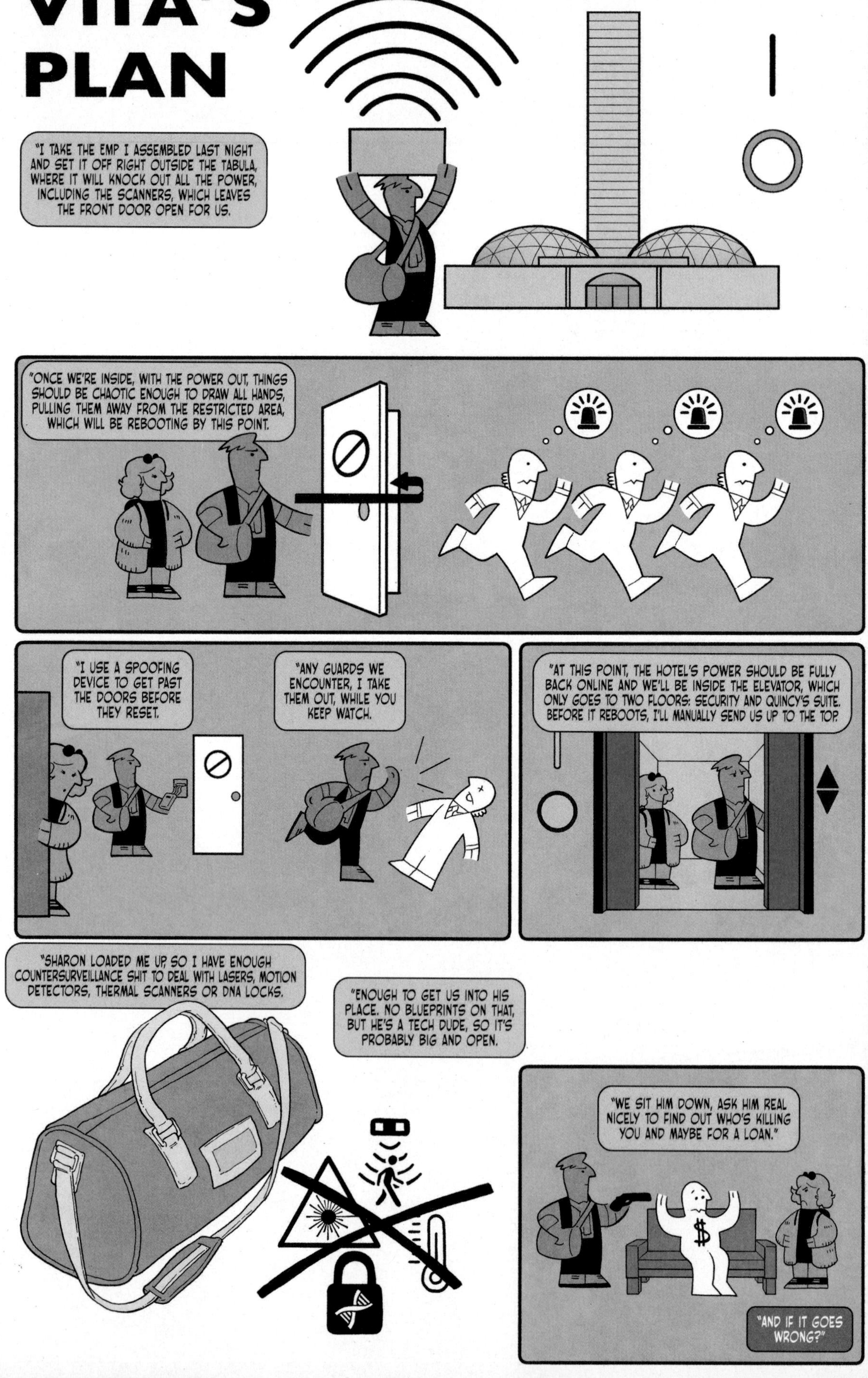
"I TAKE THE EMP I ASSEMBLED LAST NIGHT AND SET IT OFF RIGHT OUTSIDE THE TABULA, WHERE IT WILL KNOCK OUT ALL THE POWER, INCLUDING THE SCANNERS, WHICH LEAVES THE FRONT DOOR OPEN FOR US.
"ONCE WE'RE INSIDE, WITH THE POWER OUT, THINGS SHOULD BE CHAOTIC ENOUGH TO DRAW ALL HANDS, PULLING THEM AWAY FROM THE RESTRICTED AREA, WHICH WILL BE REBOOTING BY THIS POINT.
"I USE A SPOOFING DEVICE TO GET PAST THE DOORS BEFORE THEY RESET.
"ANY GUARDS WE ENCOUNTER, I TAKE THEM OUT, WHILE YOU KEEP WATCH.
"AT THIS POINT, THE HOTEL'S POWER SHOULD BE FULLY BACK ONLINE AND WE'LL BE INSIDE THE ELEVATOR, WHICH ONLY GOES TO TWO FLOORS: SECURITY AND QUINCY'S SUITE. BEFORE IT REBOOTS, I'LL MANUALLY SEND US UP TO THE TOP.
"SHARON LOADED ME UP, SO I HAVE ENOUGH COUNTERSURVEILLANCE SHIT TO DEAL WITH LASERS, MOTION DETECTORS, THERMAL SCANNERS OR DNA LOCKS.
"ENOUGH TO GET US INTO HIS PLACE. NO BLUEPRINTS ON THAT, BUT HE'S A TECH DUDE, SO IT'S PROBABLY BIG AND OPEN.
"WE SIT HIM DOWN, ASK HIM REAL NICELY TO FIND OUT WHO'S KILLING YOU AND MAYBE FOR A LOAN."
"AND IF IT GOES WRONG?"

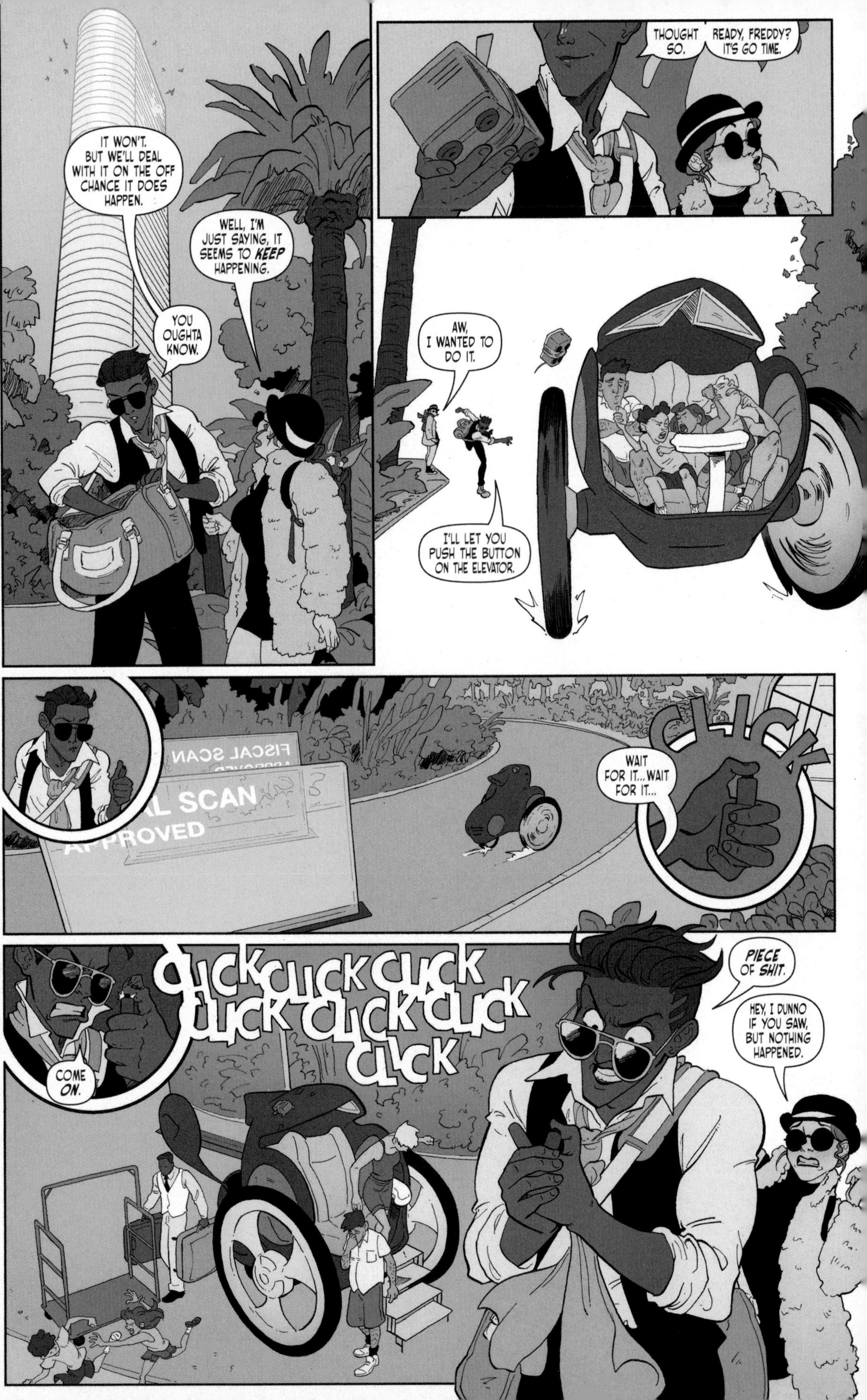
IT WON'T. BUT WE'LL DEAL WITH IT ON THE OFF CHANCE IT DOES HAPPEN.
WELL, I'M JUST SAYING, IT SEEMS TO *KEEP* HAPPENING.
YOU OUGHTA KNOW.
THOUGHT SO.
READY, FREDDY? IT'S GO TIME.
AW, I WANTED TO DO IT.
I'LL LET YOU PUSH THE BUTTON ON THE ELEVATOR.
FISCAL SCAN APPROVED
AL SCAN APPROVED
WAIT FOR IT...WAIT FOR IT...
CLICK
CLICK CLICK CLICK CLICK CLICK CLICK CLICK
COME *ON*.
PIECE OF *SHIT*.
HEY, I DUNNO IF YOU SAW, BUT NOTHING HAPPENED.

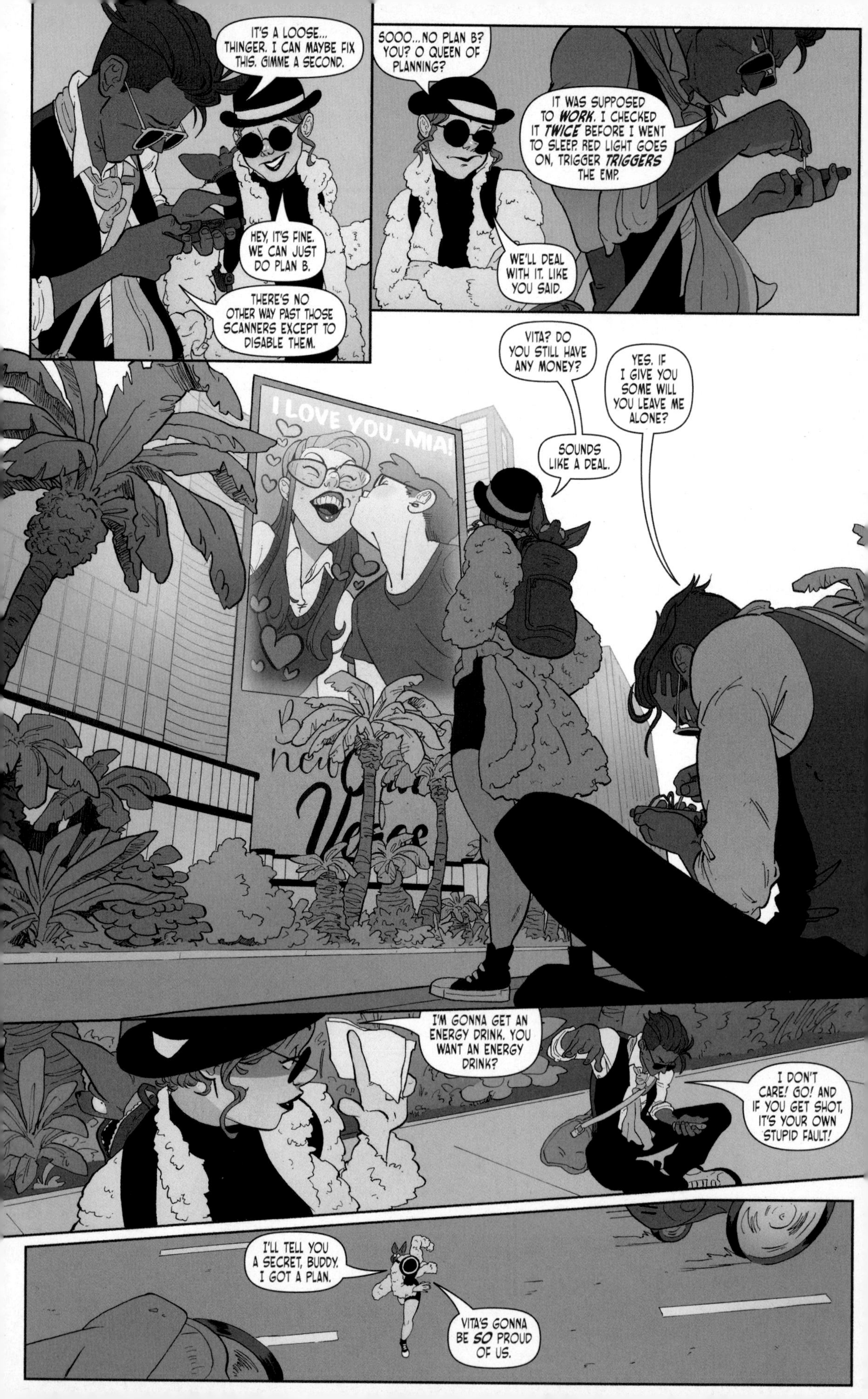
IT'S A LOOSE... THINGER. I CAN MAYBE FIX THIS. GIMME A SECOND.
HEY, IT'S FINE. WE CAN JUST DO PLAN B.
THERE'S NO OTHER WAY PAST THOSE SCANNERS EXCEPT TO DISABLE THEM.
SOOO...NO PLAN B? YOU? O QUEEN OF PLANNING?
IT WAS SUPPOSED TO WORK. I CHECKED IT TWICE BEFORE I WENT TO SLEEP. RED LIGHT GOES ON, TRIGGER TRIGGERS THE EMP.
WE'LL DEAL WITH IT. LIKE YOU SAID.
I LOVE YOU, MIA!
VITA? DO YOU STILL HAVE ANY MONEY?
YES. IF I GIVE YOU SOME WILL YOU LEAVE ME ALONE?
SOUNDS LIKE A DEAL.
I'M GONNA GET AN ENERGY DRINK. YOU WANT AN ENERGY DRINK?
I DON'T CARE! GO! AND IF YOU GET SHOT, IT'S YOUR OWN STUPID FAULT!
I'LL TELL YOU A SECRET, BUDDY. I GOT A PLAN.
VITA'S GONNA BE SO PROUD OF US.

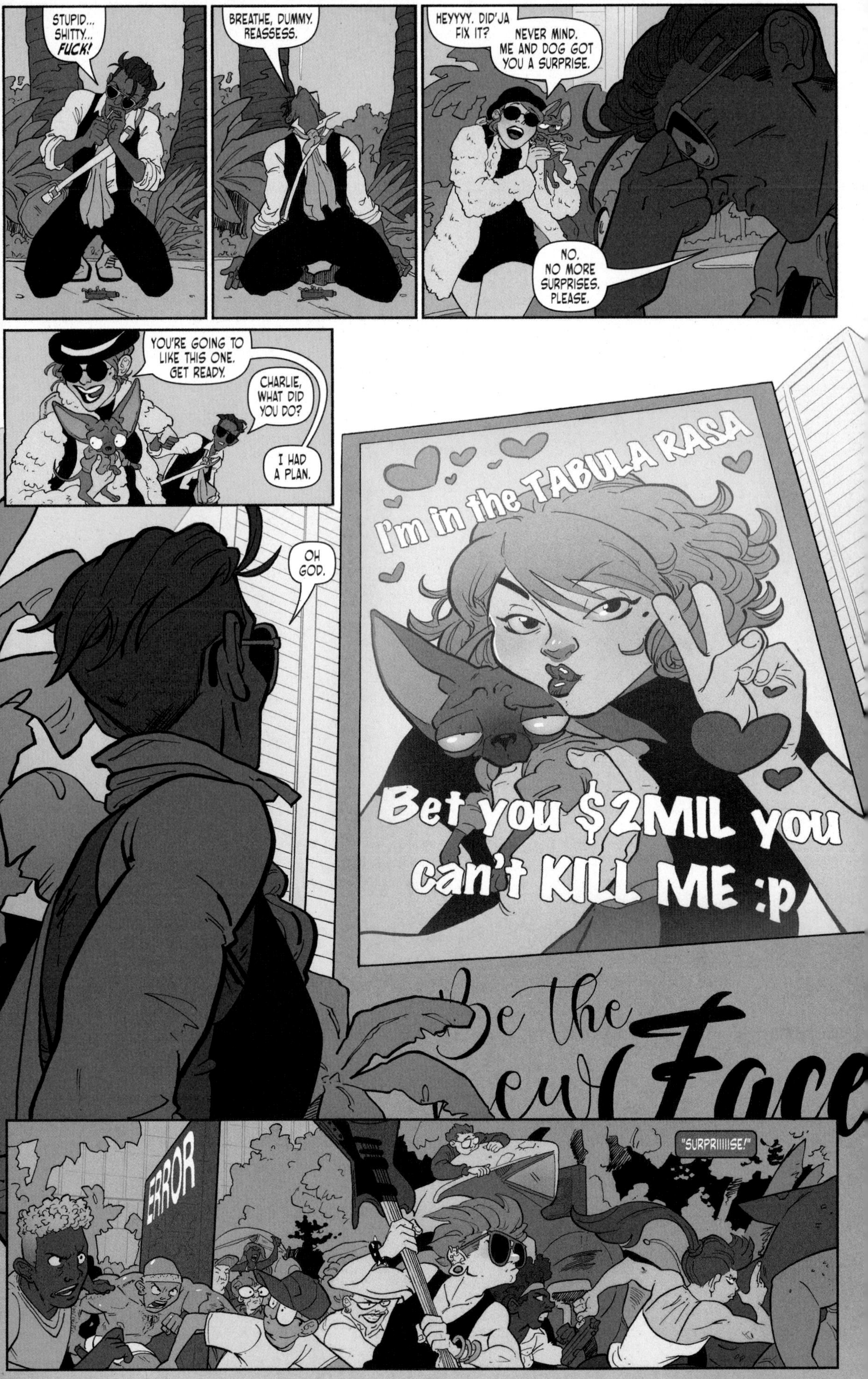
STUPID... SHITTY... FUCK!
BREATHE, DUMMY. REASSESS.
HEYYYY. DID'JA FIX IT?
NEVER MIND. ME AND DOG GOT YOU A SURPRISE.
NO. NO MORE SURPRISES. PLEASE.
YOU'RE GOING TO LIKE THIS ONE. GET READY.
CHARLIE, WHAT DID YOU DO?
I HAD A PLAN.
OH GOD.
I'm in the TABULA RASA
Bet you $2MIL you can't KILL ME :p
ERROR
"SURPRIIIIISE!"

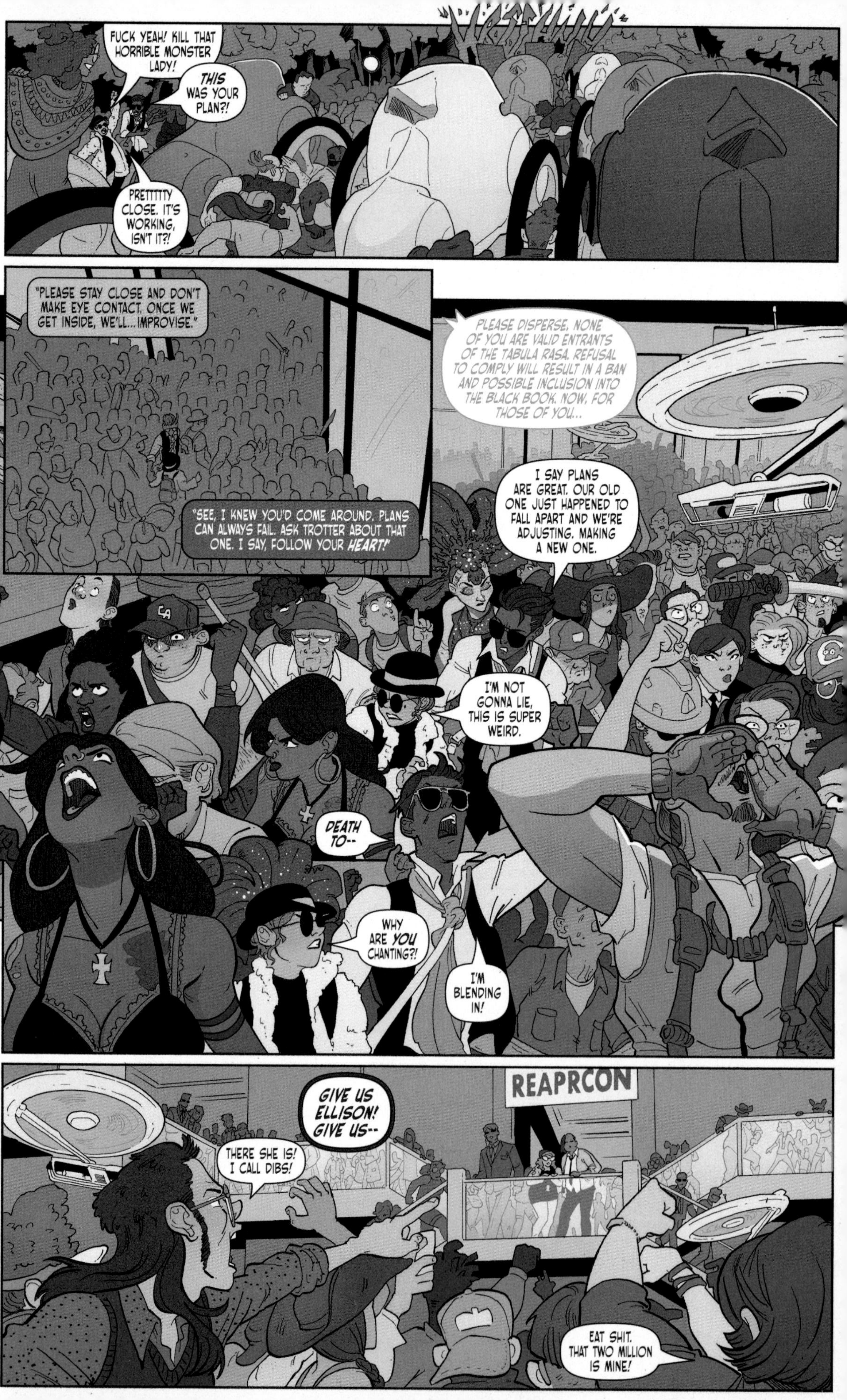
FUCK YEAH! KILL THAT HORRIBLE MONSTER LADY!
THIS WAS YOUR PLAN?!
PRETTTTTY CLOSE. IT'S WORKING, ISN'T IT?!
"PLEASE STAY CLOSE AND DON'T MAKE EYE CONTACT. ONCE WE GET INSIDE, WE'LL...IMPROVISE."
"SEE, I KNEW YOU'D COME AROUND. PLANS CAN ALWAYS FAIL. ASK TROTTER ABOUT THAT ONE. I SAY, FOLLOW YOUR HEART!"
PLEASE DISPERSE. NONE OF YOU ARE VALID ENTRANTS OF THE TABULA RASA. REFUSAL TO COMPLY WILL RESULT IN A BAN AND POSSIBLE INCLUSION INTO THE BLACK BOOK. NOW, FOR THOSE OF YOU...
I SAY PLANS ARE GREAT. OUR OLD ONE JUST HAPPENED TO FALL APART AND WE'RE ADJUSTING. MAKING A NEW ONE.
I'M NOT GONNA LIE, THIS IS SUPER WEIRD.
DEATH TO--
WHY ARE YOU CHANTING?!
I'M BLENDING IN!
REAPRCON
GIVE US ELLISON! GIVE US--
THERE SHE IS! I CALL DIBS!
EAT SHIT. THAT TWO MILLION IS MINE!

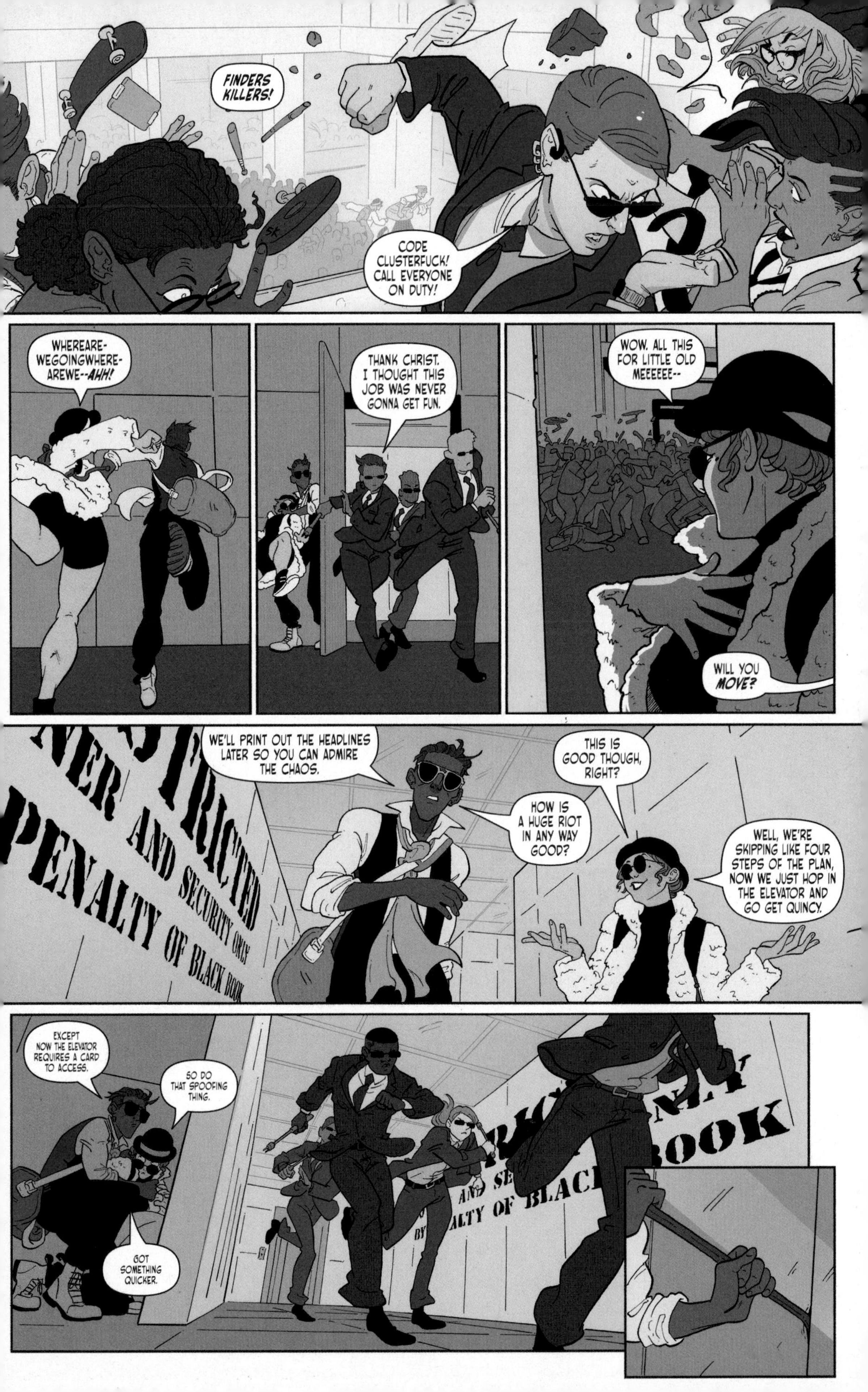

FINDERS KILLERS!
CODE CLUSTERFUCK! CALL EVERYONE ON DUTY!
WHEREARE-WEGOINGWHERE-AREWE--AHH!
THANK CHRIST. I THOUGHT THIS JOB WAS NEVER GONNA GET FUN.
WOW. ALL THIS FOR LITTLE OLD MEEEEEE--
WILL YOU MOVE?
WE'LL PRINT OUT THE HEADLINES LATER SO YOU CAN ADMIRE THE CHAOS.
THIS IS GOOD THOUGH, RIGHT?
HOW IS A HUGE RIOT IN ANY WAY GOOD?
WELL, WE'RE SKIPPING LIKE FOUR STEPS OF THE PLAN, NOW WE JUST HOP IN THE ELEVATOR AND GO GET QUINCY.
EXCEPT NOW THE ELEVATOR REQUIRES A CARD TO ACCESS.
SO DO THAT SPOOFING THING.
GOT SOMETHING QUICKER.

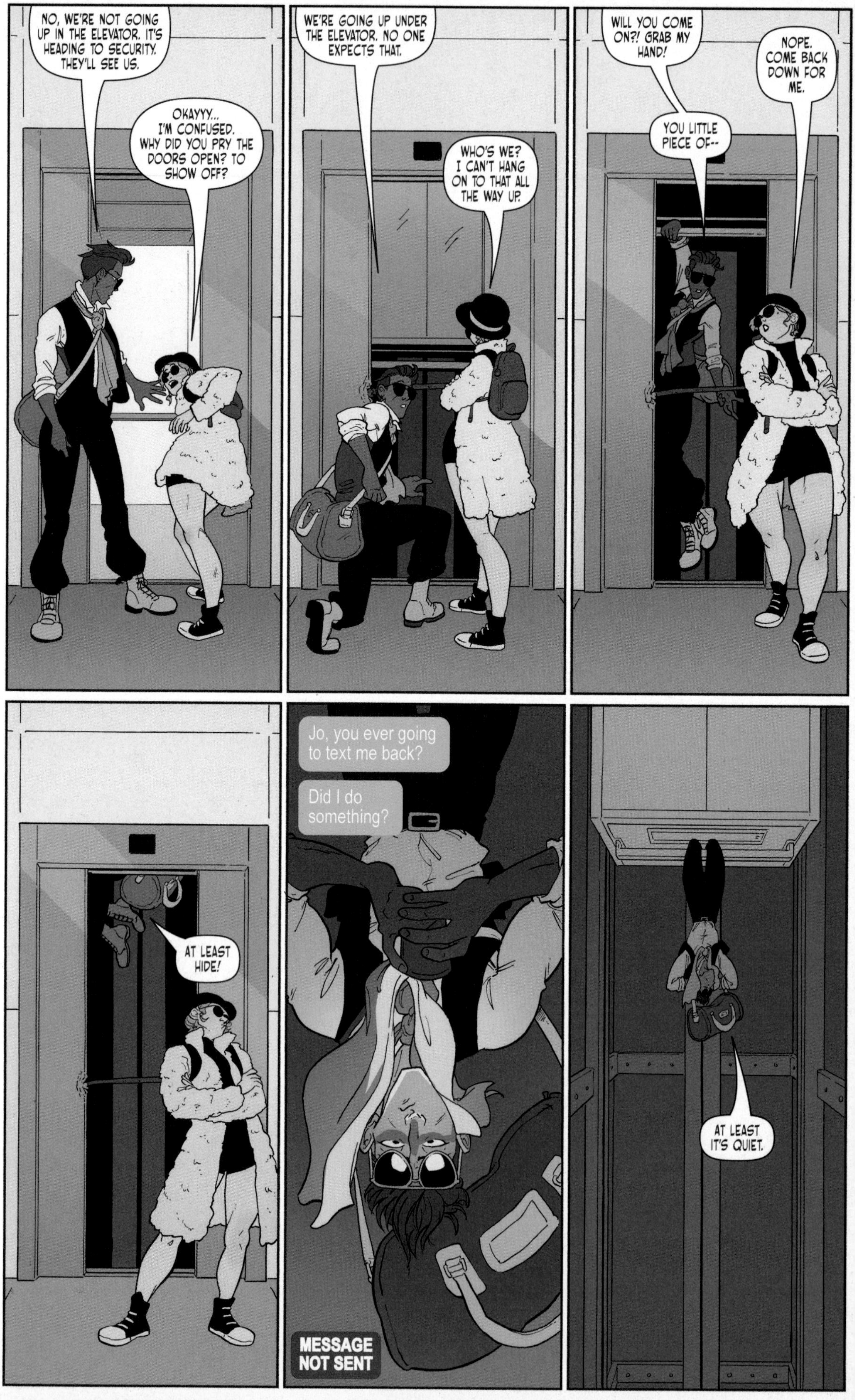
NO, WE'RE NOT GOING UP IN THE ELEVATOR. IT'S HEADING TO SECURITY. THEY'LL SEE US.
OKAYYY... I'M CONFUSED. WHY DID YOU PRY THE DOORS OPEN? TO SHOW OFF?
WE'RE GOING UP UNDER THE ELEVATOR. NO ONE EXPECTS THAT.
WHO'S WE? I CAN'T HANG ON TO THAT ALL THE WAY UP.
WILL YOU COME ON?! GRAB MY HAND!
NOPE. COME BACK DOWN FOR ME.
YOU LITTLE PIECE OF--
AT LEAST HIDE!
Jo, you ever going to text me back?
Did I do something?
MESSAGE NOT SENT
AT LEAST IT'S QUIET.

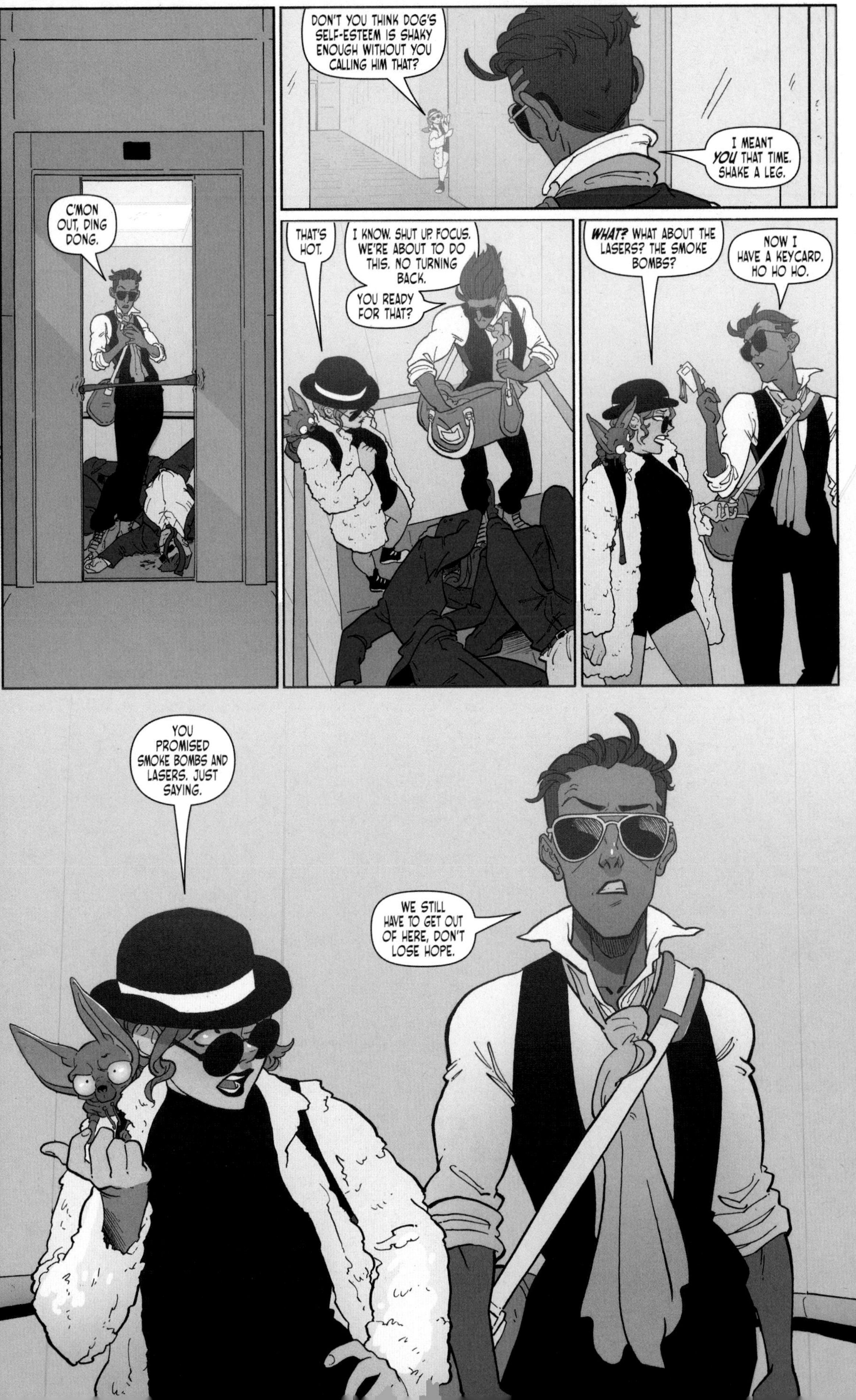
C'MON OUT, DING DONG.
DON'T YOU THINK DOG'S SELF-ESTEEM IS SHAKY ENOUGH WITHOUT YOU CALLING HIM THAT?
I MEANT YOU THAT TIME. SHAKE A LEG.
I KNOW. SHUT UP. FOCUS. WE'RE ABOUT TO DO THIS. NO TURNING BACK.
YOU READY FOR THAT?
THAT'S HOT.
NOW I HAVE A KEYCARD. HO HO HO.
WHAT? WHAT ABOUT THE LASERS? THE SMOKE BOMBS?
WE STILL HAVE TO GET OUT OF HERE, DON'T LOSE HOPE.
YOU PROMISED SMOKE BOMBS AND LASERS. JUST SAYING.

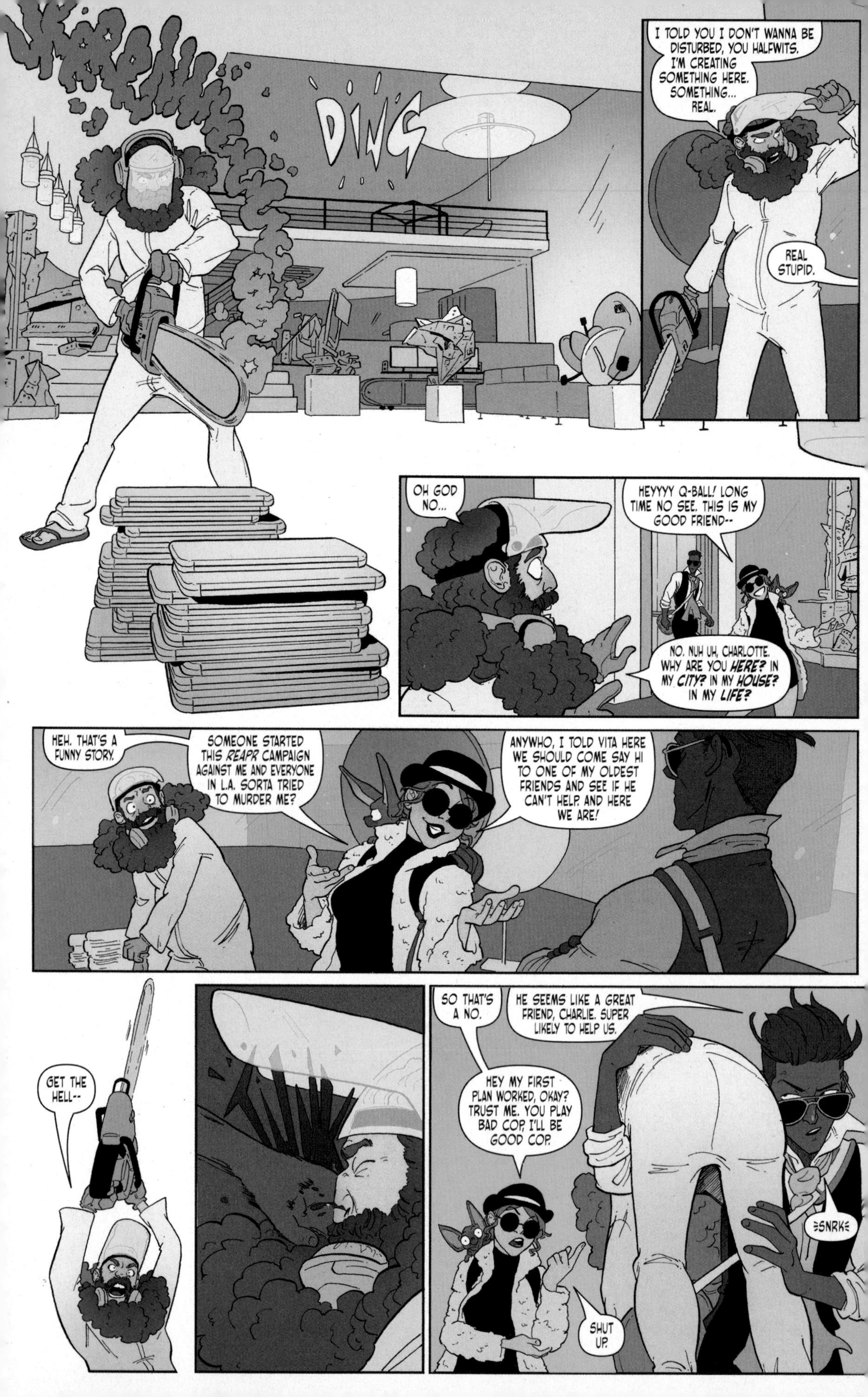
WRRRMMMM
DING
I TOLD YOU I DON'T WANNA BE DISTURBED, YOU HALFWITS. I'M CREATING SOMETHING HERE. SOMETHING... REAL.
REAL STUPID.
OH GOD NO...
HEYYYY Q-BALL! LONG TIME NO SEE. THIS IS MY GOOD FRIEND--
NO. NUH UH, CHARLOTTE. WHY ARE YOU HERE? IN MY CITY? IN MY HOUSE? IN MY LIFE?
HEH. THAT'S A FUNNY STORY.
SOMEONE STARTED THIS REAPR CAMPAIGN AGAINST ME AND EVERYONE IN L.A. SORTA TRIED TO MURDER ME?
ANYWHO, I TOLD VITA HERE WE SHOULD COME SAY HI TO ONE OF MY OLDEST FRIENDS AND SEE IF HE CAN'T HELP. AND HERE WE ARE!
GET THE HELL--
SO THAT'S A NO.
HE SEEMS LIKE A GREAT FRIEND, CHARLIE. SUPER LIKELY TO HELP US.
HEY MY FIRST PLAN WORKED, OKAY? TRUST ME. YOU PLAY BAD COP, I'LL BE GOOD COP.
SNRK
SHUT UP.

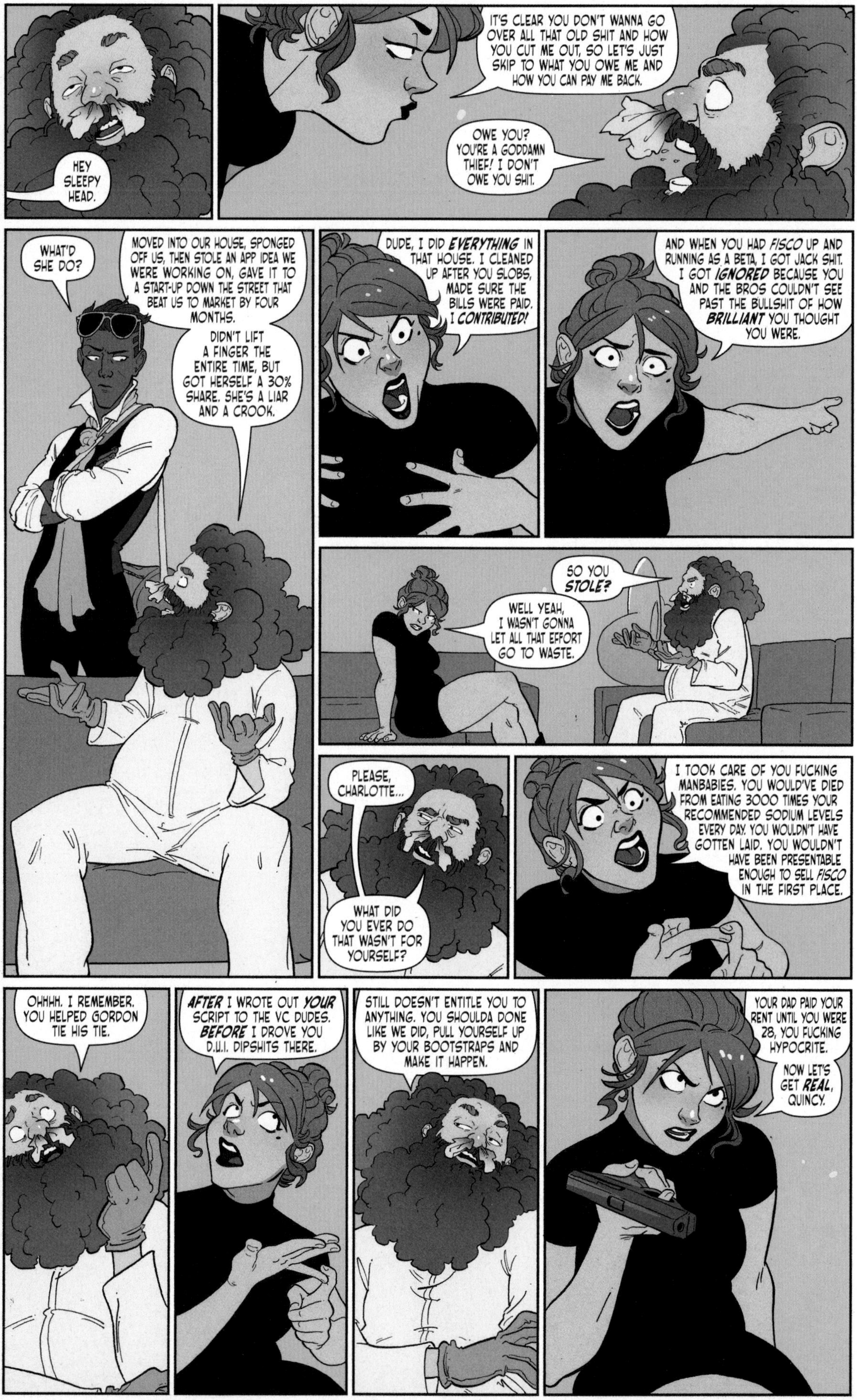
HEY SLEEPY HEAD.
IT'S CLEAR YOU DON'T WANNA GO OVER ALL THAT OLD SHIT AND HOW YOU CUT ME OUT, SO LET'S JUST SKIP TO WHAT YOU OWE ME AND HOW YOU CAN PAY ME BACK.
OWE YOU? YOU'RE A GODDAMN THIEF! I DON'T OWE YOU SHIT.
WHAT'D SHE DO?
MOVED INTO OUR HOUSE, SPONGED OFF US, THEN STOLE AN APP IDEA WE WERE WORKING ON, GAVE IT TO A START-UP DOWN THE STREET THAT BEAT US TO MARKET BY FOUR MONTHS.
DIDN'T LIFT A FINGER THE ENTIRE TIME, BUT GOT HERSELF A 30% SHARE. SHE'S A LIAR AND A CROOK.
DUDE, I DID EVERYTHING IN THAT HOUSE. I CLEANED UP AFTER YOU SLOBS, MADE SURE THE BILLS WERE PAID. I CONTRIBUTED!
AND WHEN YOU HAD FISCO UP AND RUNNING AS A BETA, I GOT JACK SHIT. I GOT IGNORED BECAUSE YOU AND THE BROS COULDN'T SEE PAST THE BULLSHIT OF HOW BRILLIANT YOU THOUGHT YOU WERE.
SO YOU STOLE?
WELL YEAH, I WASN'T GONNA LET ALL THAT EFFORT GO TO WASTE.
PLEASE, CHARLOTTE...
WHAT DID YOU EVER DO THAT WASN'T FOR YOURSELF?
I TOOK CARE OF YOU FUCKING MANBABIES. YOU WOULD'VE DIED FROM EATING 3000 TIMES YOUR RECOMMENDED SODIUM LEVELS EVERY DAY. YOU WOULDN'T HAVE GOTTEN LAID. YOU WOULDN'T HAVE BEEN PRESENTABLE ENOUGH TO SELL FISCO IN THE FIRST PLACE.
OHHHH. I REMEMBER. YOU HELPED GORDON TIE HIS TIE.
AFTER I WROTE OUT YOUR SCRIPT TO THE VC DUDES. BEFORE I DROVE YOU D.U.I. DIPSHITS THERE.
STILL DOESN'T ENTITLE YOU TO ANYTHING. YOU SHOULDA DONE LIKE WE DID, PULL YOURSELF UP BY YOUR BOOTSTRAPS AND MAKE IT HAPPEN.
YOUR DAD PAID YOUR RENT UNTIL YOU WERE 28, YOU FUCKING HYPOCRITE.
NOW LET'S GET REAL, QUINCY.

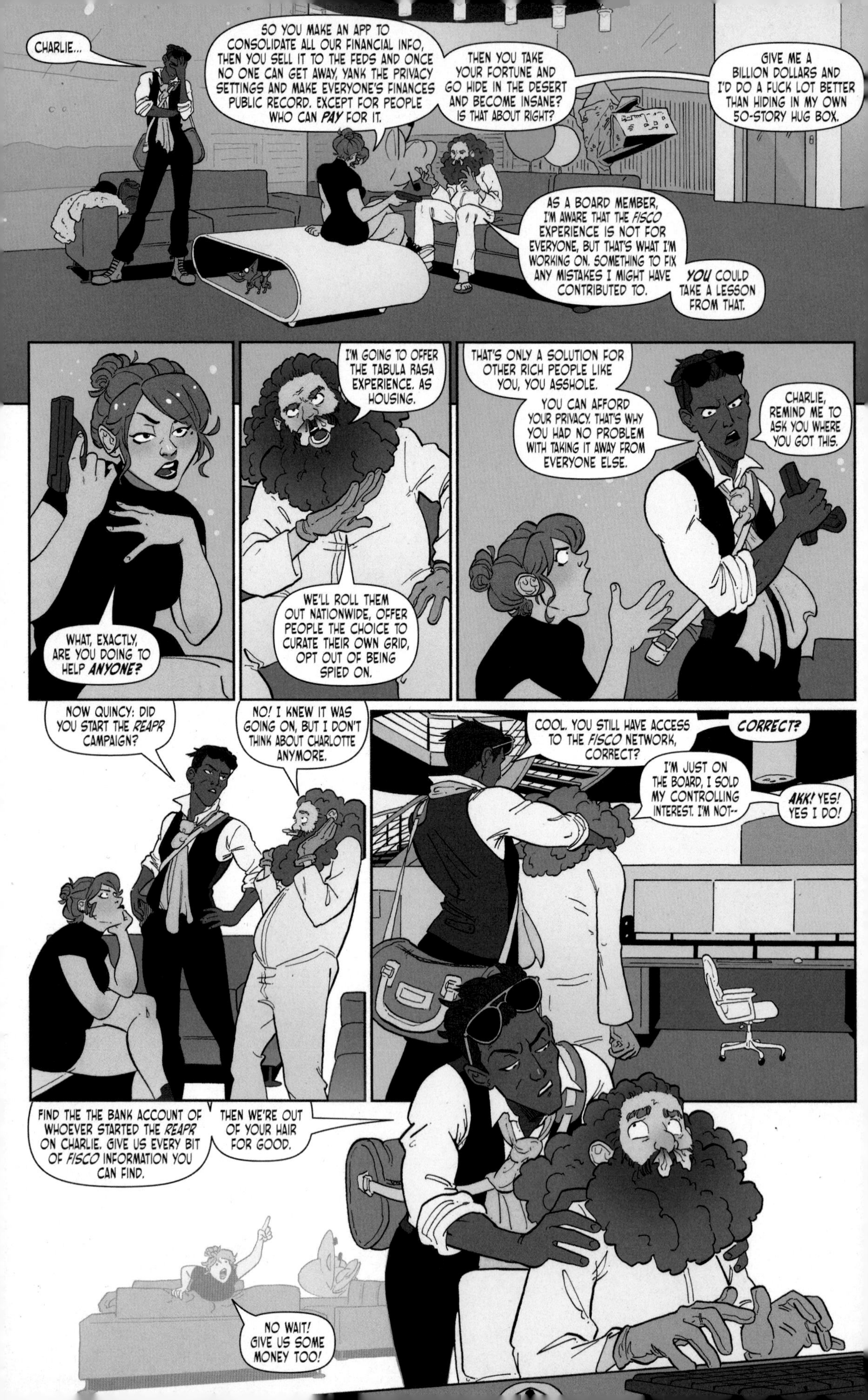

CHARLIE...
SO YOU MAKE AN APP TO CONSOLIDATE ALL OUR FINANCIAL INFO, THEN YOU SELL IT TO THE FEDS AND ONCE NO ONE CAN GET AWAY, YANK THE PRIVACY SETTINGS AND MAKE EVERYONE'S FINANCES PUBLIC RECORD. EXCEPT FOR PEOPLE WHO CAN PAY FOR IT.
THEN YOU TAKE YOUR FORTUNE AND GO HIDE IN THE DESERT AND BECOME INSANE? IS THAT ABOUT RIGHT?
GIVE ME A BILLION DOLLARS AND I'D DO A FUCK LOT BETTER THAN HIDING IN MY OWN 50-STORY HUG BOX.
AS A BOARD MEMBER, I'M AWARE THAT THE FISCO EXPERIENCE IS NOT FOR EVERYONE, BUT THAT'S WHAT I'M WORKING ON. SOMETHING TO FIX ANY MISTAKES I MIGHT HAVE CONTRIBUTED TO.
YOU COULD TAKE A LESSON FROM THAT.
WHAT, EXACTLY, ARE YOU DOING TO HELP ANYONE?
I'M GOING TO OFFER THE TABULA RASA EXPERIENCE. AS HOUSING.
WE'LL ROLL THEM OUT NATIONWIDE, OFFER PEOPLE THE CHOICE TO CURATE THEIR OWN GRID, OPT OUT OF BEING SPIED ON.
THAT'S ONLY A SOLUTION FOR OTHER RICH PEOPLE LIKE YOU, YOU ASSHOLE.
YOU CAN AFFORD YOUR PRIVACY. THAT'S WHY YOU HAD NO PROBLEM WITH TAKING IT AWAY FROM EVERYONE ELSE.
CHARLIE, REMIND ME TO ASK YOU WHERE YOU GOT THIS.
NOW QUINCY: DID YOU START THE REAPR CAMPAIGN?
NO! I KNEW IT WAS GOING ON, BUT I DON'T THINK ABOUT CHARLOTTE ANYMORE.
COOL. YOU STILL HAVE ACCESS TO THE FISCO NETWORK, CORRECT?
I'M JUST ON THE BOARD, I SOLD MY CONTROLLING INTEREST. I'M NOT--
CORRECT?
AKK! YES! YES I DO!
FIND THE THE BANK ACCOUNT OF WHOEVER STARTED THE REAPR ON CHARLIE. GIVE US EVERY BIT OF FISCO INFORMATION YOU CAN FIND.
THEN WE'RE OUT OF YOUR HAIR FOR GOOD.
NO WAIT! GIVE US SOME MONEY TOO!

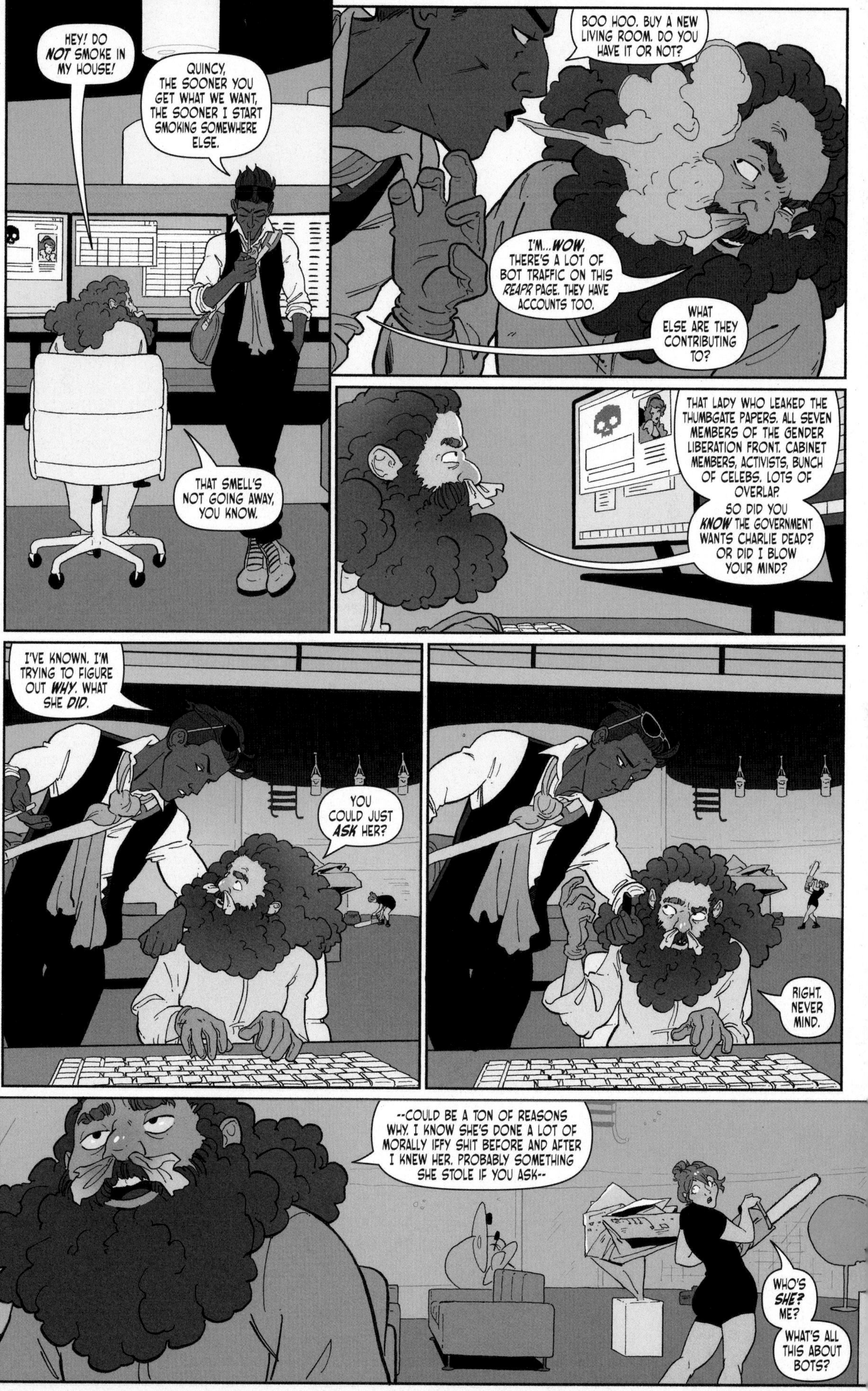
HEY! DO NOT SMOKE IN MY HOUSE!
QUINCY, THE SOONER YOU GET WHAT WE WANT, THE SOONER I START SMOKING SOMEWHERE ELSE.
THAT SMELL'S NOT GOING AWAY, YOU KNOW.
BOO HOO. BUY A NEW LIVING ROOM. DO YOU HAVE IT OR NOT?
I'M...WOW, THERE'S A LOT OF BOT TRAFFIC ON THIS REAPR PAGE. THEY HAVE ACCOUNTS TOO.
WHAT ELSE ARE THEY CONTRIBUTING TO?
THAT LADY WHO LEAKED THE THUMBGATE PAPERS. ALL SEVEN MEMBERS OF THE GENDER LIBERATION FRONT. CABINET MEMBERS, ACTIVISTS, BUNCH OF CELEBS. LOTS OF OVERLAP.
SO DID YOU KNOW THE GOVERNMENT WANTS CHARLIE DEAD? OR DID I BLOW YOUR MIND?
I'VE KNOWN. I'M TRYING TO FIGURE OUT WHY. WHAT SHE DID.
YOU COULD JUST ASK HER?
RIGHT. NEVER MIND.
--COULD BE A TON OF REASONS WHY. I KNOW SHE'S DONE A LOT OF MORALLY IFFY SHIT BEFORE AND AFTER I KNEW HER. PROBABLY SOMETHING SHE STOLE IF YOU ASK--
WHO'S SHE? ME?
WHAT'S ALL THIS ABOUT BOTS?

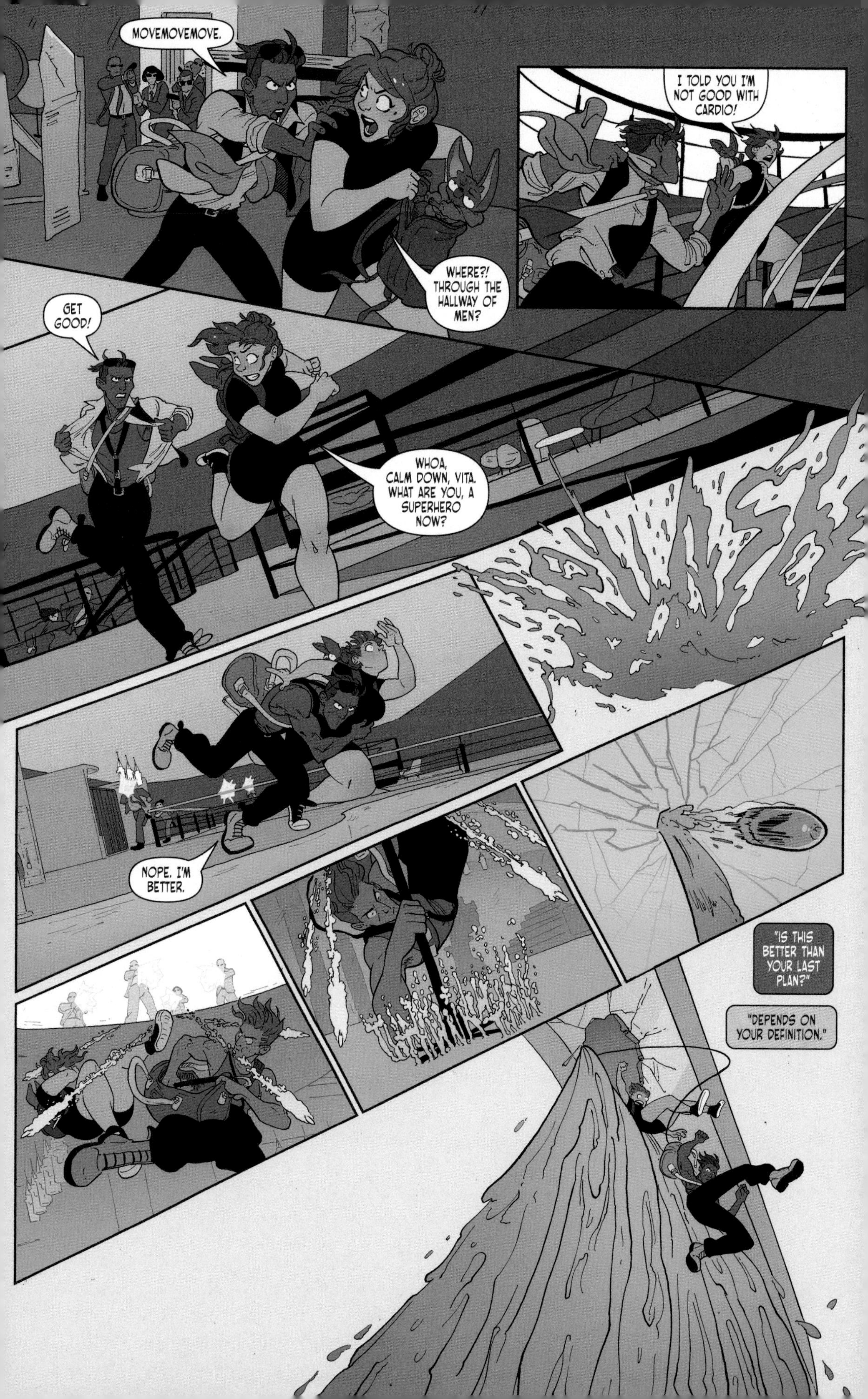
MOVEMOVEMOVE.
WHERE?! THROUGH THE HALLWAY OF MEN?
I TOLD YOU I'M NOT GOOD WITH CARDIO!
GET GOOD!
WHOA, CALM DOWN, VITA. WHAT ARE YOU, A SUPERHERO NOW?
NOPE. I'M BETTER.
"IS THIS BETTER THAN YOUR LAST PLAN?"
"DEPENDS ON YOUR DEFINITION."

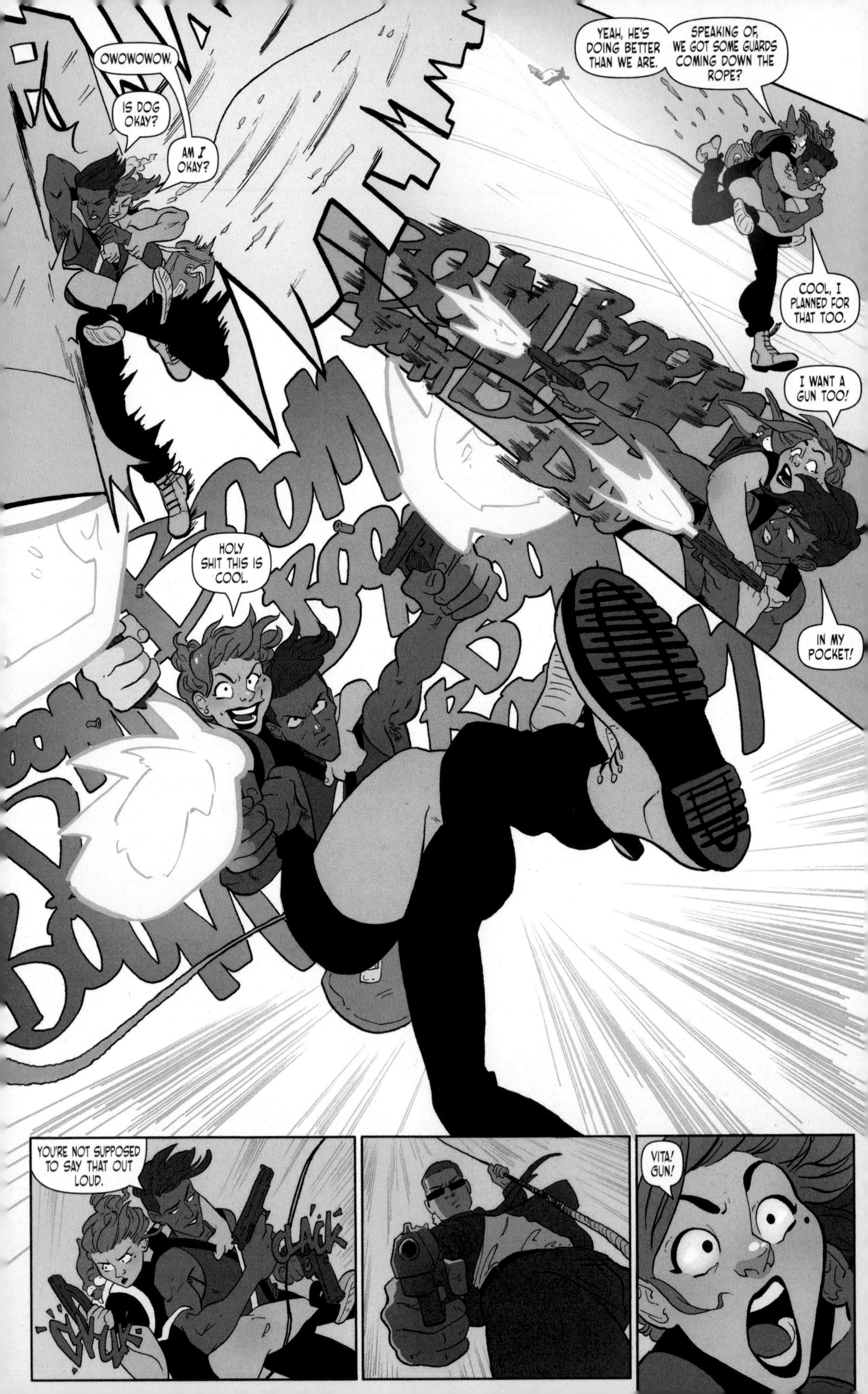
OWOWOWOW.
IS DOG OKAY?
AM I OKAY?
YEAH, HE'S DOING BETTER THAN WE ARE.
SPEAKING OF, WE GOT SOME GUARDS COMING DOWN THE ROPE?
COOL, I PLANNED FOR THAT TOO.
I WANT A GUN TOO!
IN MY POCKET!
HOLY SHIT THIS IS COOL.
YOU'RE NOT SUPPOSED TO SAY THAT OUT LOUD.
CLACK
CHACK
VITA! GUN!

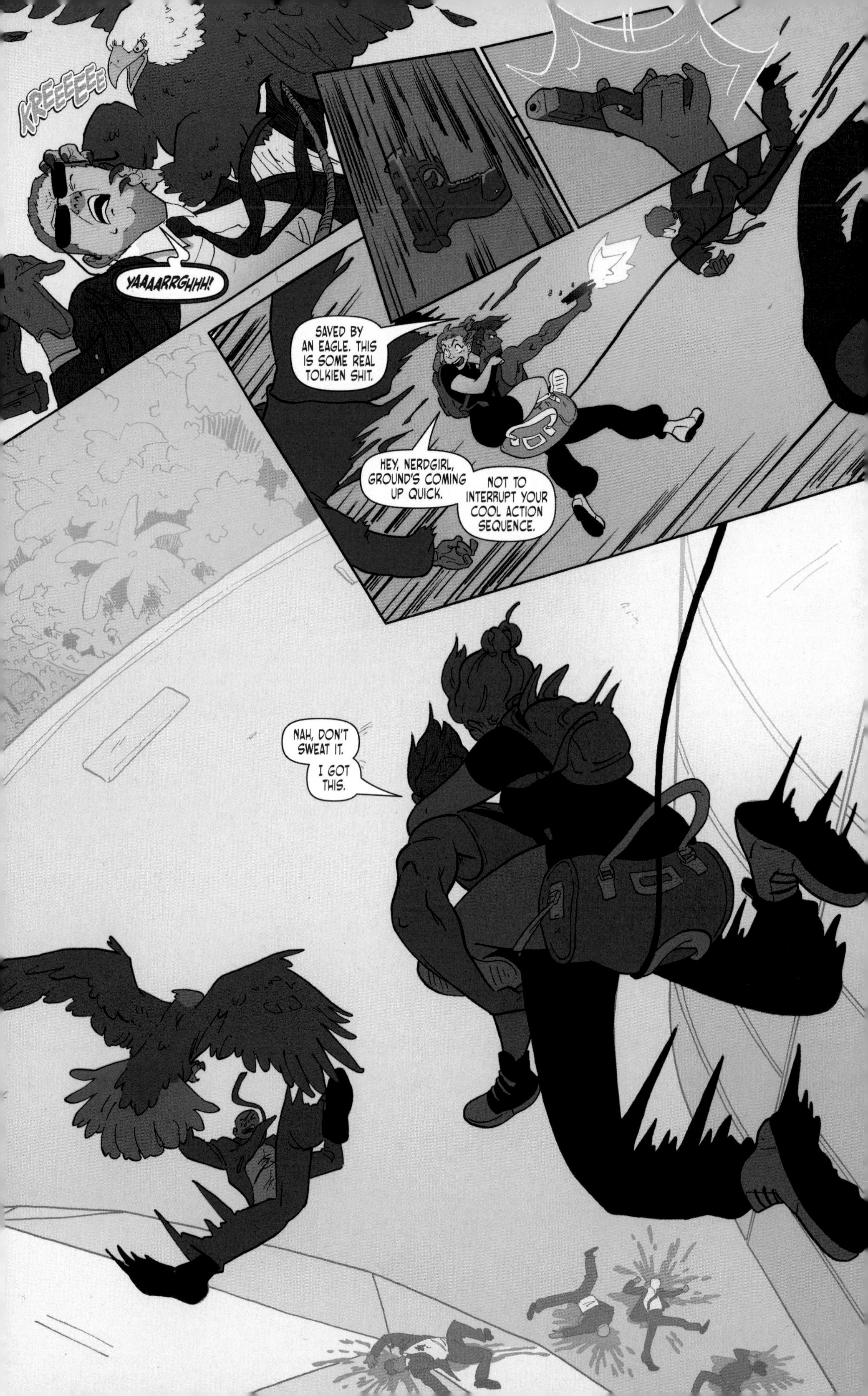
KREEEEEE
YAAAARRGHHH!
SAVED BY AN EAGLE. THIS IS SOME REAL TOLKIEN SHIT.
HEY, NERDGIRL, GROUND'S COMING UP QUICK.
NOT TO INTERRUPT YOUR COOL ACTION SEQUENCE.
NAH, DON'T SWEAT IT. I GOT THIS.

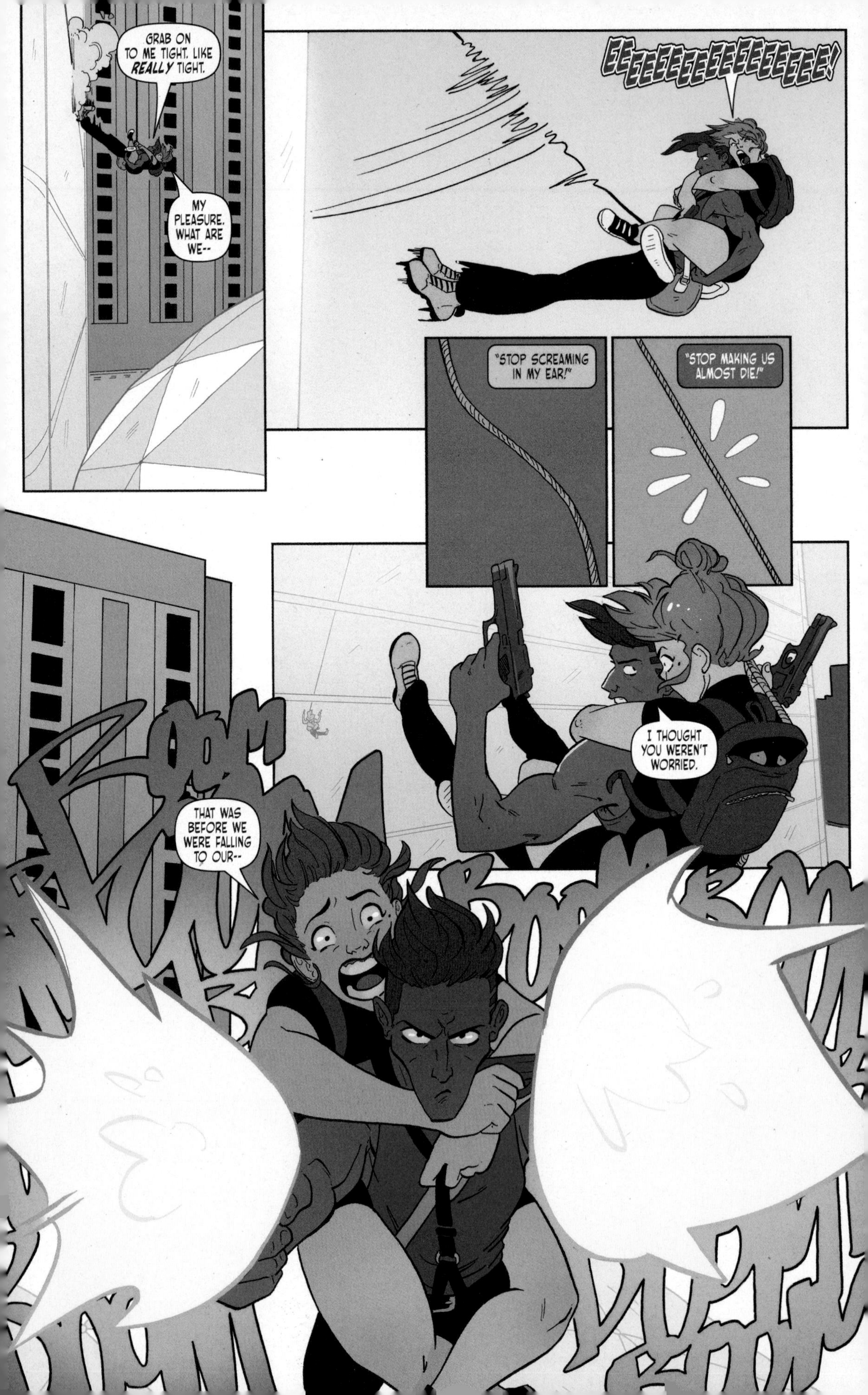
GRAB ON TO ME TIGHT. LIKE REALLY TIGHT.
MY PLEASURE. WHAT ARE WE--
EEEEEEEEEEEEEEEEE!
"STOP SCREAMING IN MY EAR!"
"STOP MAKING US ALMOST DIE!"
I THOUGHT YOU WEREN'T WORRIED.
THAT WAS BEFORE WE WERE FALLING TO OUR--

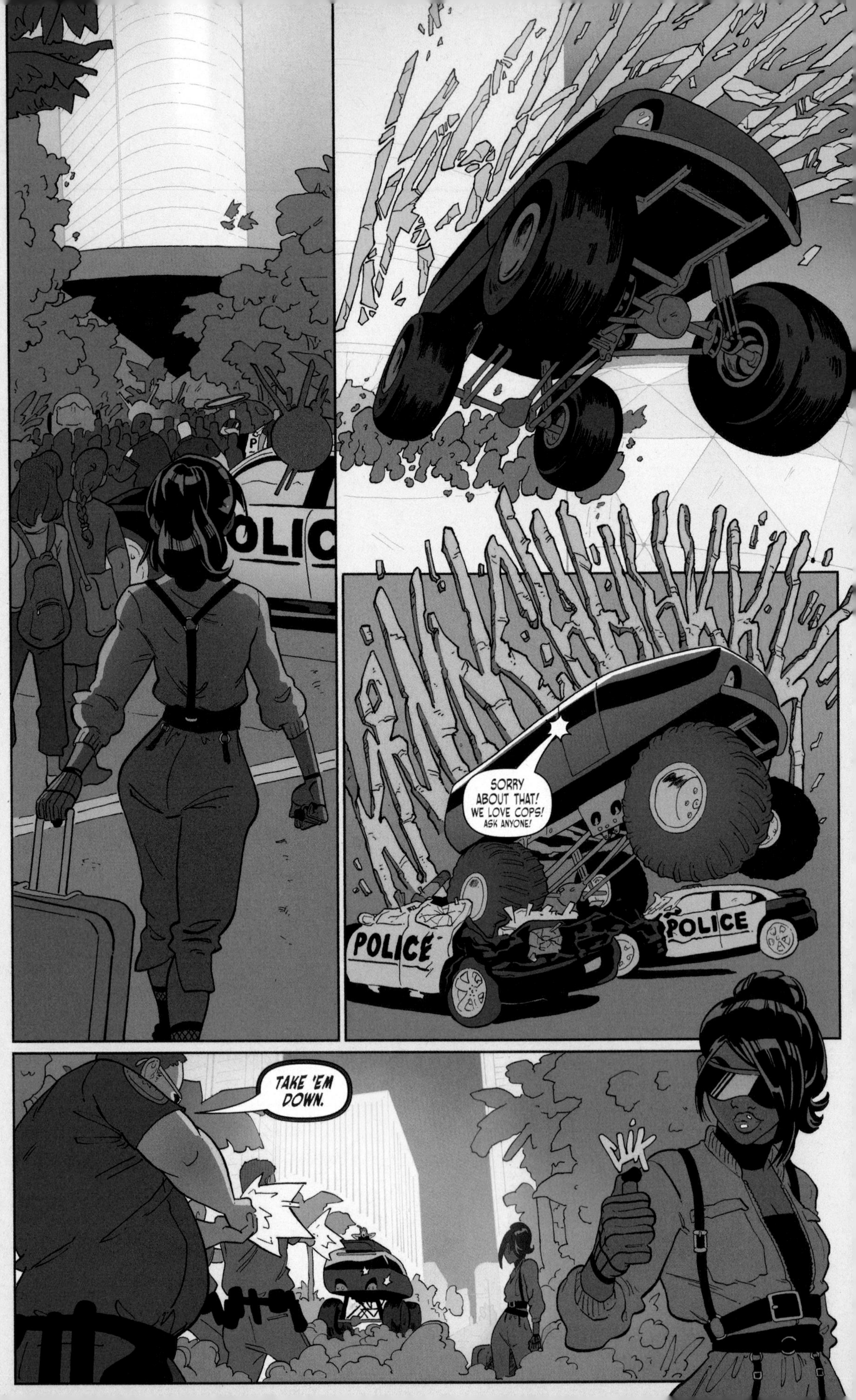
SORRY ABOUT THAT! WE LOVE COPS! ASK ANYONE!
TAKE 'EM DOWN.
CLIK

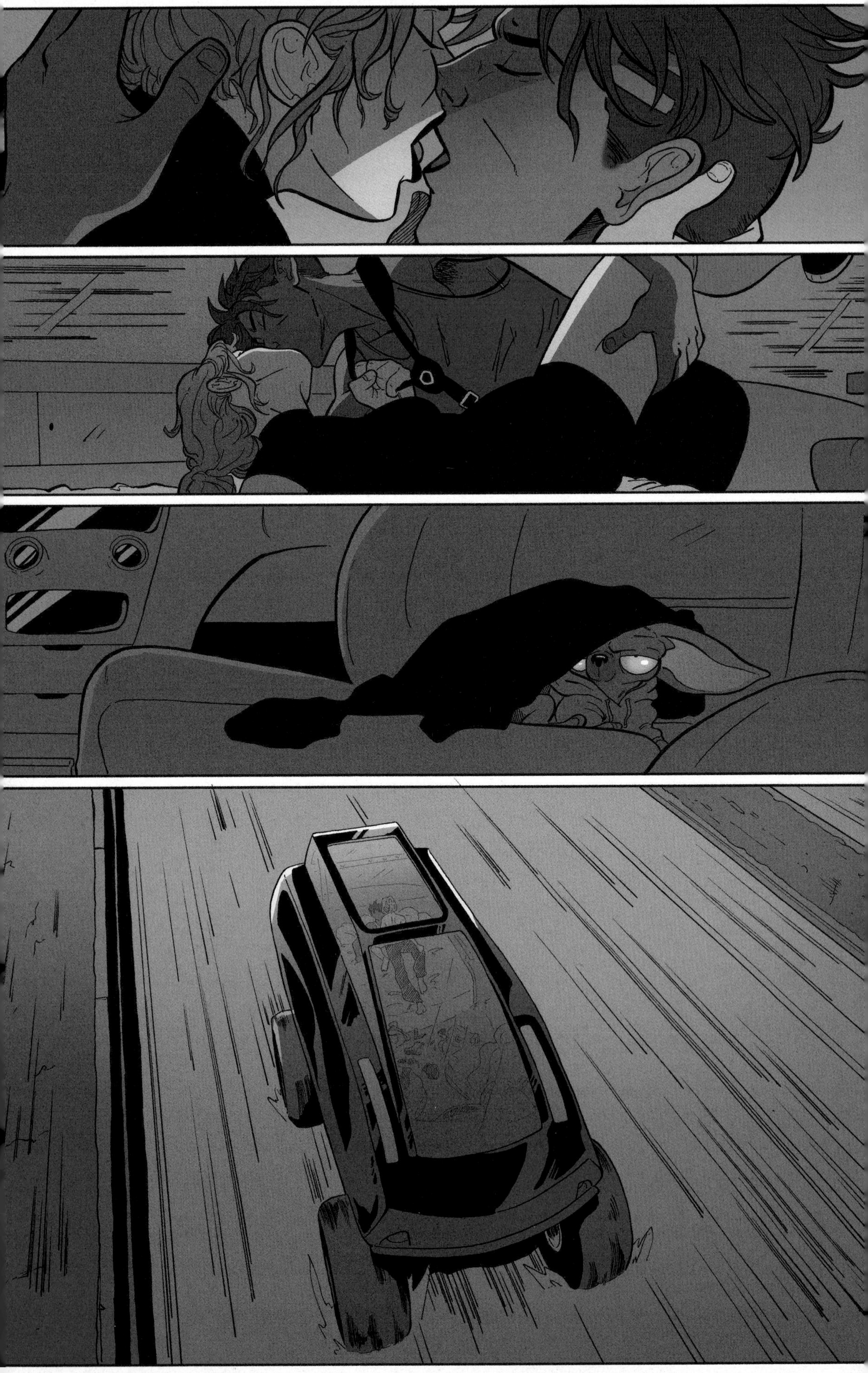

CHAPTER TEN

IF WE'RE STILL ALIVE

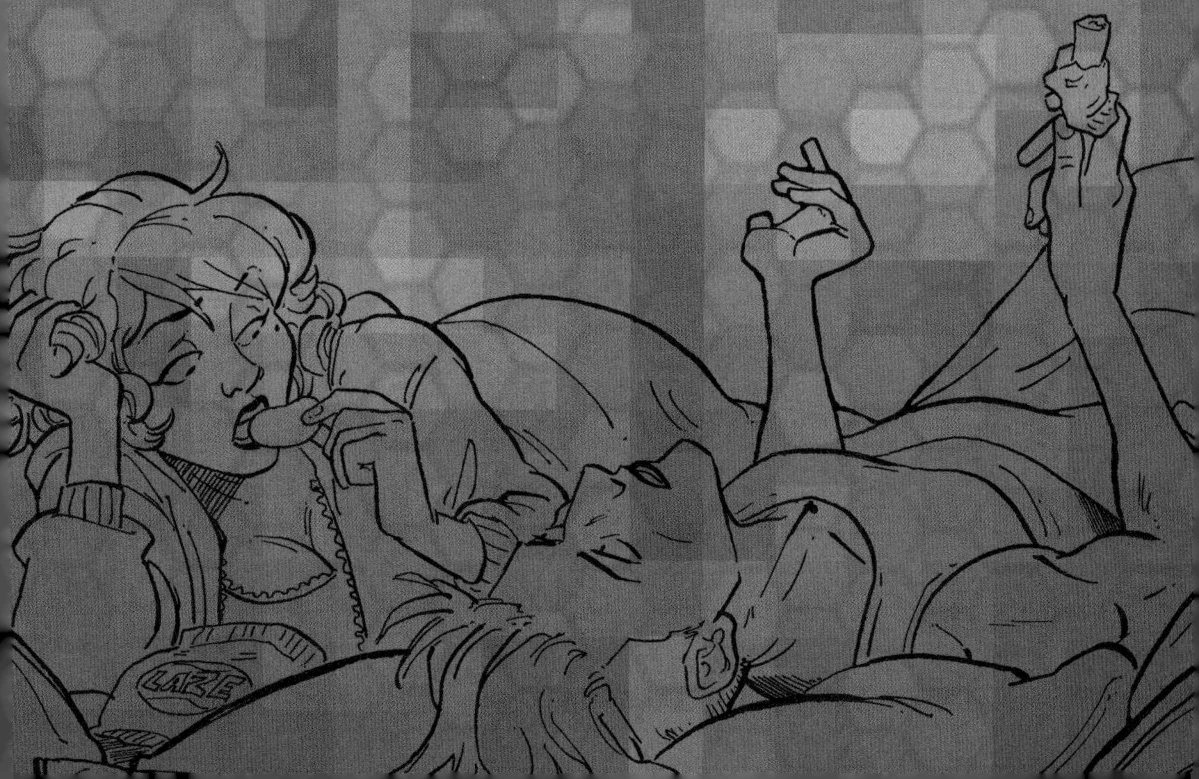
LAZE

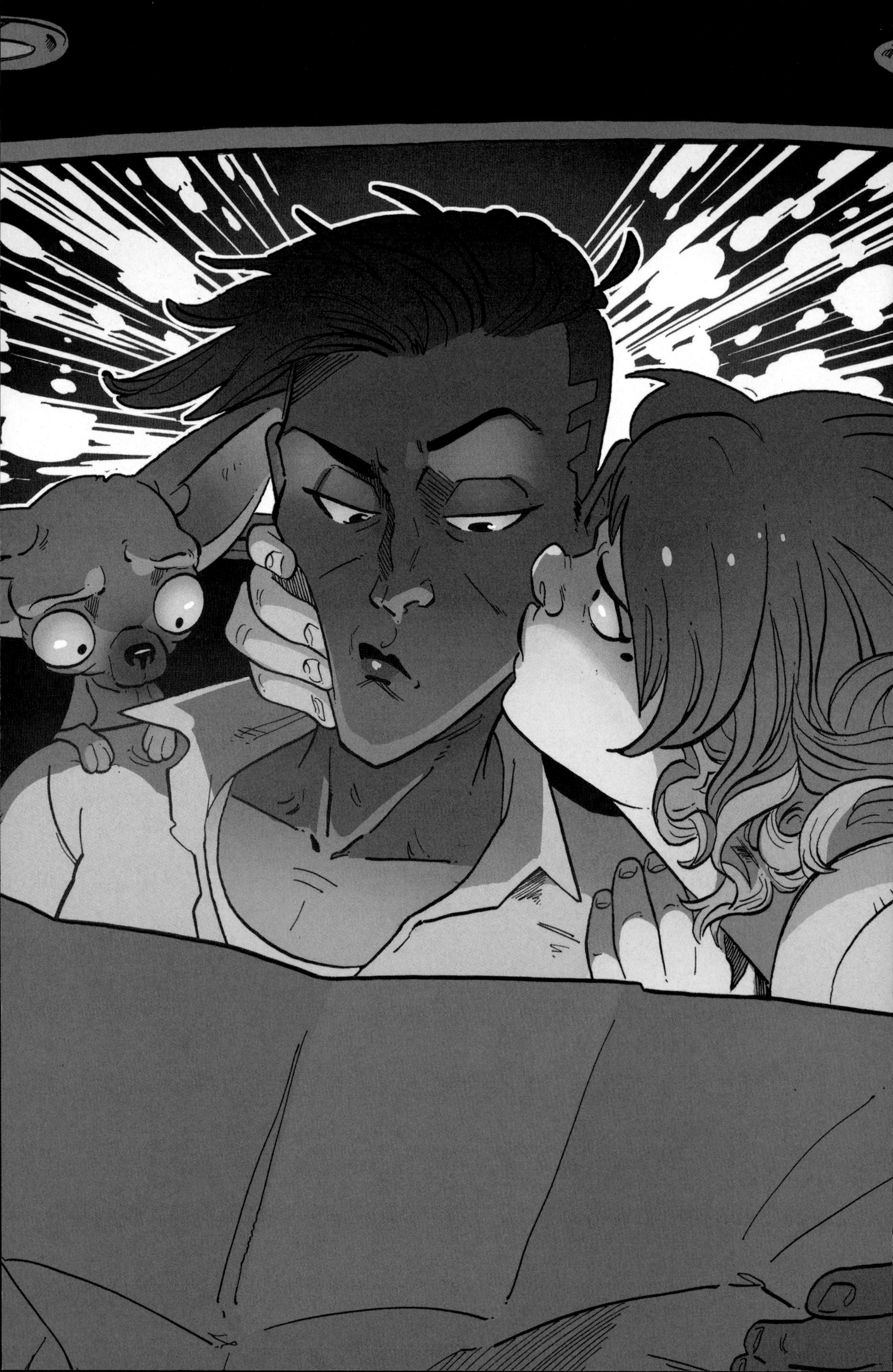

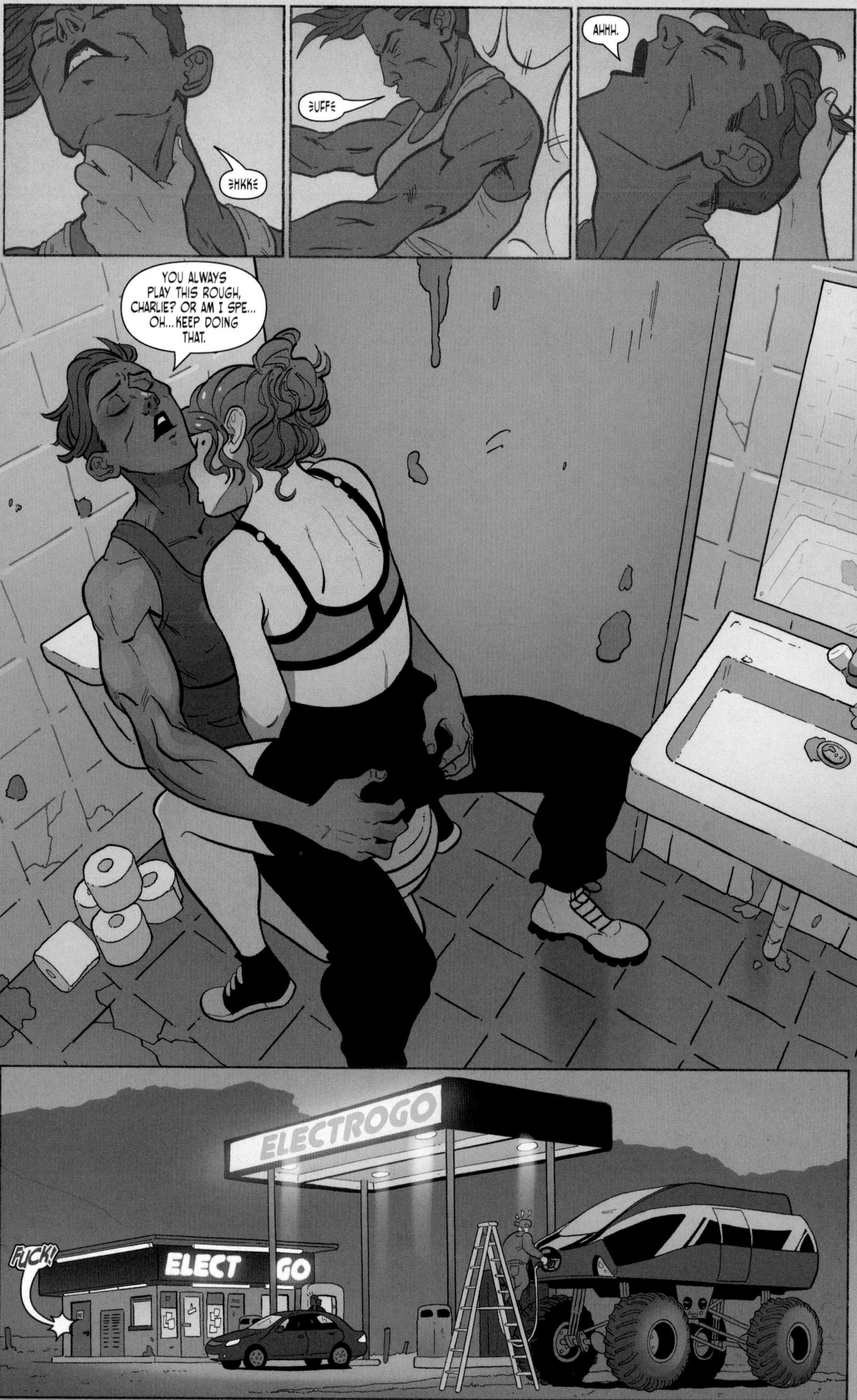
HKK
UFF
AHHH.
YOU ALWAYS PLAY THIS ROUGH, CHARLIE? OR AM I SPE... OH... KEEP DOING THAT.
ELECTROGO
ELECTROGO
ELECT GO
FUCK!

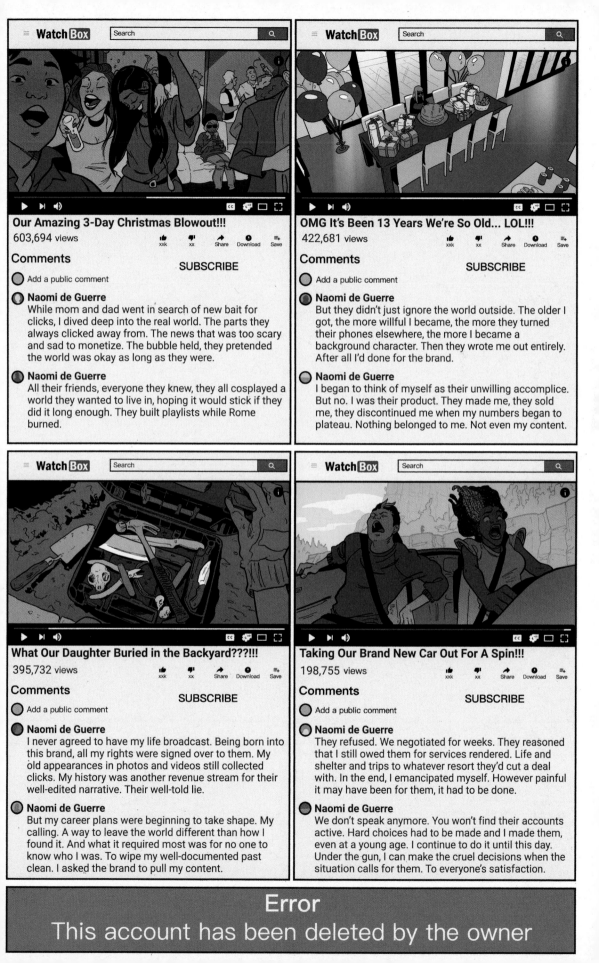

Panel 1

WatchBox — Search

Our Amazing 3-Day Christmas Blowout!!!

603,694 views 👍 xxk 👎 xx Share Download Save

Comments SUBSCRIBE

Add a public comment

Naomi de Guerre
While mom and dad went in search of new bait for clicks, I dived deep into the real world. The parts they always clicked away from. The news that was too scary and sad to monetize. The bubble held, they pretended the world was okay as long as they were.

Naomi de Guerre
All their friends, everyone they knew, they all cosplayed a world they wanted to live in, hoping it would stick if they did it long enough. They built playlists while Rome burned.

Panel 2

WatchBox — Search

OMG It's Been 13 Years We're So Old... LOL!!!

422,681 views 👍 xxk 👎 xx Share Download Save

Comments SUBSCRIBE

Add a public comment

Naomi de Guerre
But they didn't just ignore the world outside. The older I got, the more willful I became, the more they turned their phones elsewhere, the more I became a background character. Then they wrote me out entirely. After all I'd done for the brand.

Naomi de Guerre
I began to think of myself as their unwilling accomplice. But no. I was their product. They made me, they sold me, they discontinued me when my numbers began to plateau. Nothing belonged to me. Not even my content.

Panel 3

WatchBox — Search

What Our Daughter Buried in the Backyard???!!!

395,732 views 👍 xxk 👎 xx Share Download Save

Comments SUBSCRIBE

Add a public comment

Naomi de Guerre
I never agreed to have my life broadcast. Being born into this brand, all my rights were signed over to them. My old appearances in photos and videos still collected clicks. My history was another revenue stream for their well-edited narrative. Their well-told lie.

Naomi de Guerre
But my career plans were beginning to take shape. My calling. A way to leave the world different than how I found it. And what it required most was for no one to know who I was. To wipe my well-documented past clean. I asked the brand to pull my content.

Panel 4

WatchBox — Search

Taking Our Brand New Car Out For A Spin!!!

198,755 views 👍 xxk 👎 xx Share Download Save

Comments SUBSCRIBE

Add a public comment

Naomi de Guerre
They refused. We negotiated for weeks. They reasoned that I still owed them for services rendered. Life and shelter and trips to whatever resort they'd cut a deal with. In the end, I emancipated myself. However painful it may have been for them, it had to be done.

Naomi de Guerre
We don't speak anymore. You won't find their accounts active. Hard choices had to be made and I made them, even at a young age. I continue to do it until this day. Under the gun, I can make the cruel decisions when the situation calls for them. To everyone's satisfaction.

Error
This account has been deleted by the owner

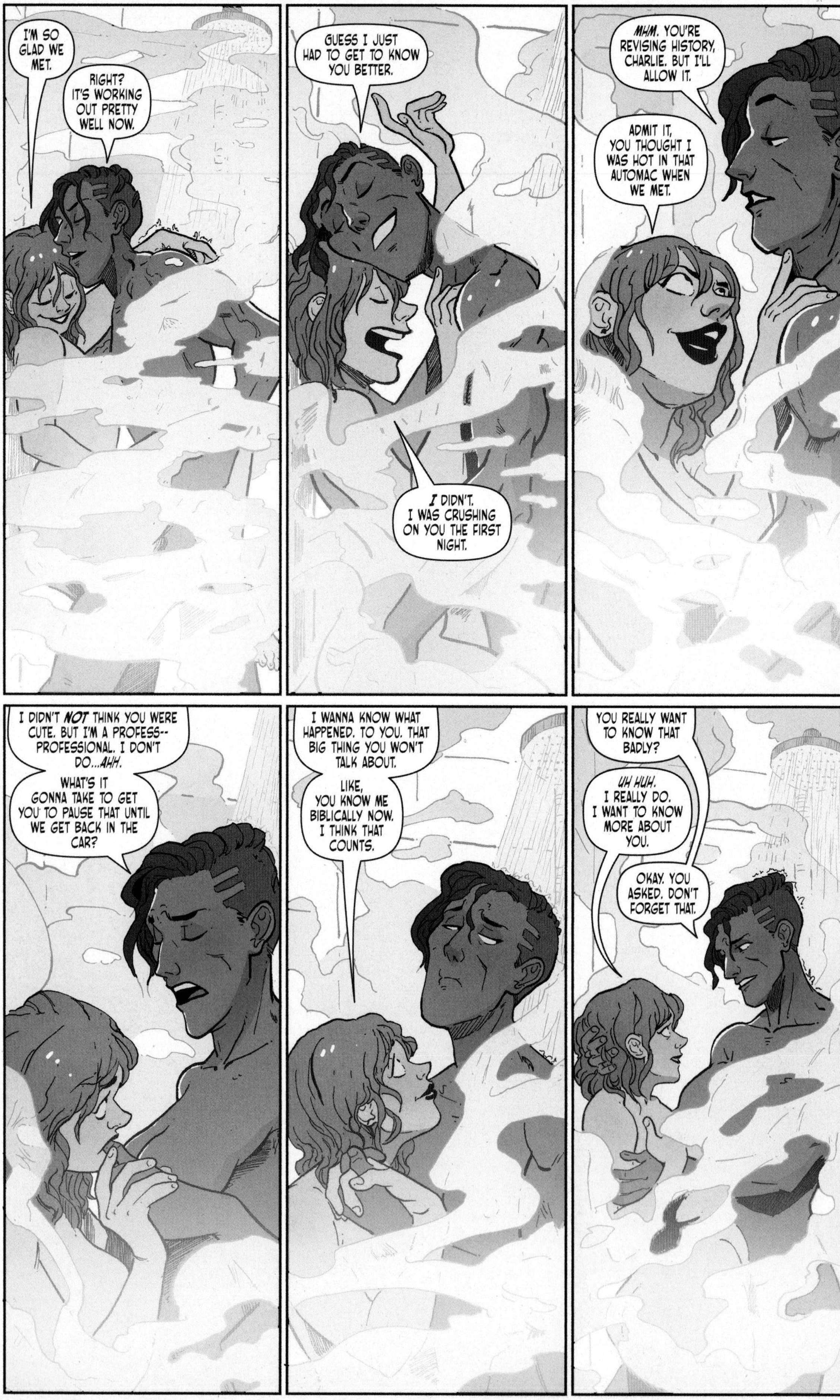
I'M SO GLAD WE MET.
RIGHT? IT'S WORKING OUT PRETTY WELL NOW.
GUESS I JUST HAD TO GET TO KNOW YOU BETTER.
I DIDN'T. I WAS CRUSHING ON YOU THE FIRST NIGHT.
MHM. YOU'RE REVISING HISTORY, CHARLIE. BUT I'LL ALLOW IT.
ADMIT IT, YOU THOUGHT I WAS HOT IN THAT AUTOMAC WHEN WE MET.
I DIDN'T NOT THINK YOU WERE CUTE. BUT I'M A PROFESS--PROFESSIONAL. I DON'T DO...AHH.
WHAT'S IT GONNA TAKE TO GET YOU TO PAUSE THAT UNTIL WE GET BACK IN THE CAR?
I WANNA KNOW WHAT HAPPENED. TO YOU. THAT BIG THING YOU WON'T TALK ABOUT.
LIKE, YOU KNOW ME BIBLICALLY NOW. I THINK THAT COUNTS.
YOU REALLY WANT TO KNOW THAT BADLY?
UH HUH. I REALLY DO. I WANT TO KNOW MORE ABOUT YOU.
OKAY. YOU ASKED. DON'T FORGET THAT.

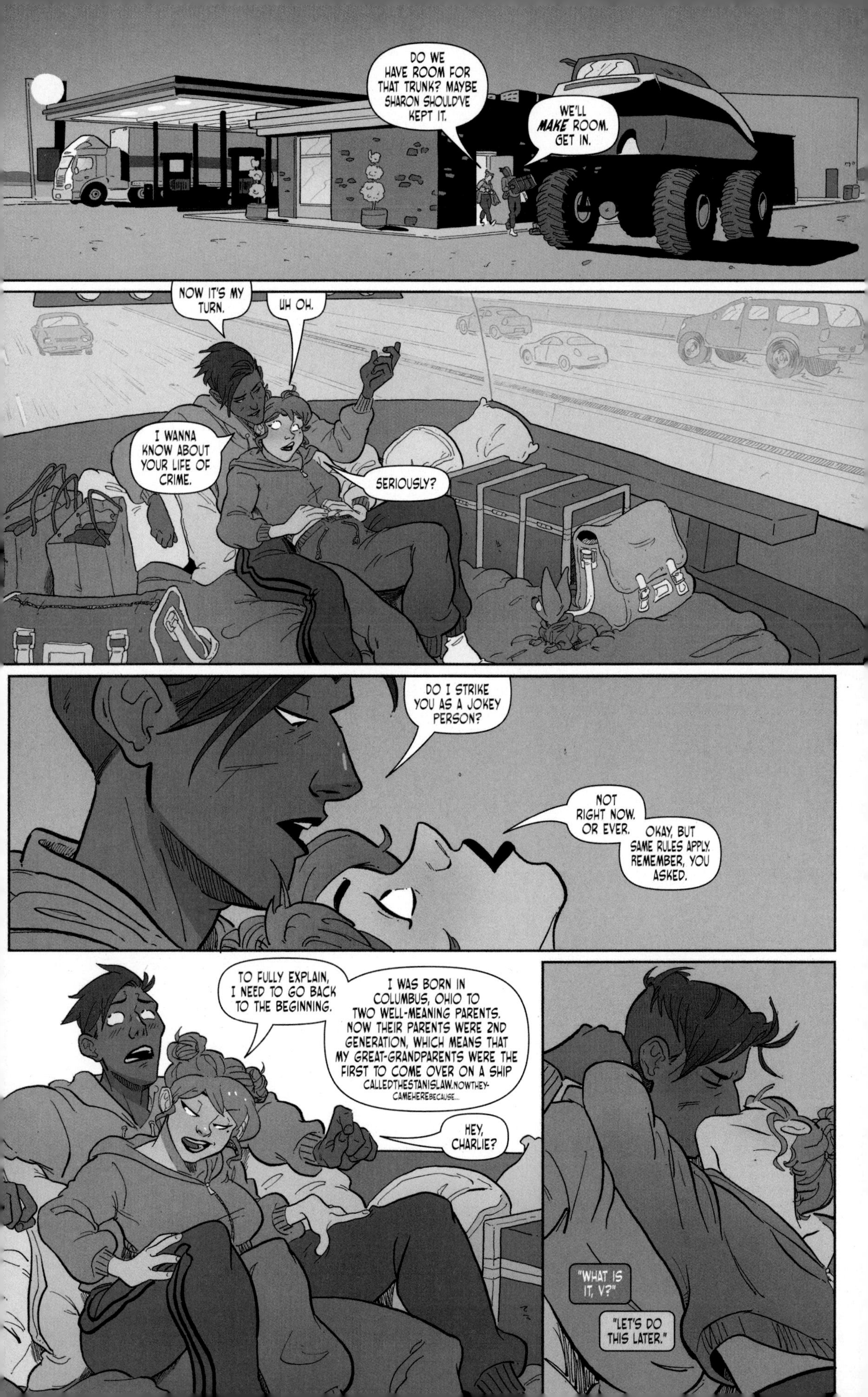
DO WE HAVE ROOM FOR THAT TRUNK? MAYBE SHARON SHOULD'VE KEPT IT.
WE'LL *MAKE* ROOM. GET IN.
NOW IT'S MY TURN.
UH OH.
I WANNA KNOW ABOUT YOUR LIFE OF CRIME.
SERIOUSLY?
DO I STRIKE YOU AS A JOKEY PERSON?
NOT RIGHT NOW. OR EVER.
OKAY, BUT SAME RULES APPLY. REMEMBER, YOU ASKED.
TO FULLY EXPLAIN, I NEED TO GO BACK TO THE BEGINNING.
I WAS BORN IN COLUMBUS, OHIO TO TWO WELL-MEANING PARENTS. NOW THEIR PARENTS WERE 2ND GENERATION, WHICH MEANS THAT MY GREAT-GRANDPARENTS WERE THE FIRST TO COME OVER ON A SHIP CALLEDTHESTANISLAW.NOWTHEY-CAMEHEREBECAUSE...
HEY, CHARLIE?
"WHAT IS IT, V?"
"LET'S DO THIS LATER."

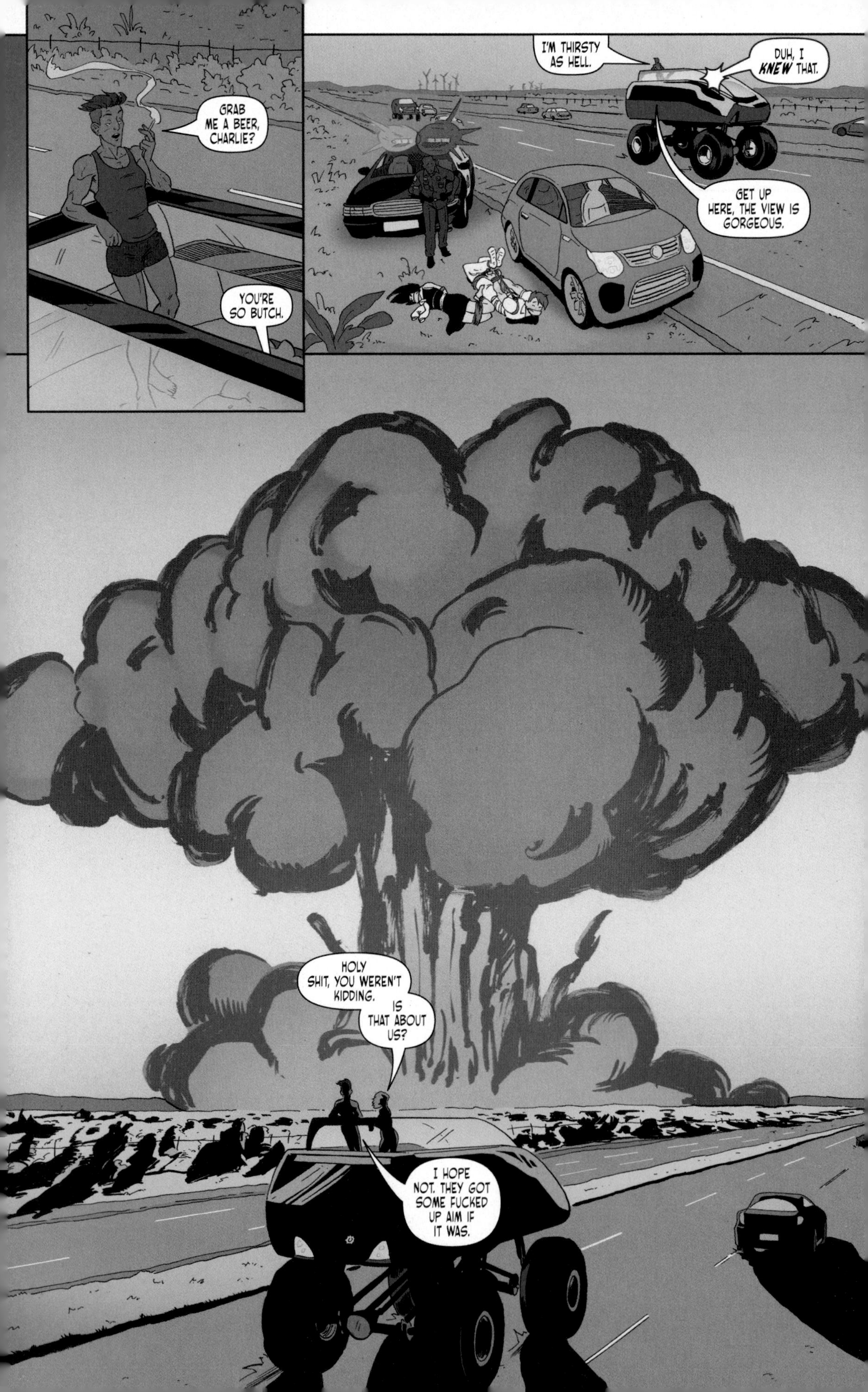
GRAB ME A BEER, CHARLIE?
YOU'RE SO BUTCH.
I'M THIRSTY AS HELL.
DUH, I KNEW THAT.
GET UP HERE, THE VIEW IS GORGEOUS.
HOLY SHIT, YOU WEREN'T KIDDING.
IS THAT ABOUT US?
I HOPE NOT. THEY GOT SOME FUCKED UP AIM IF IT WAS.

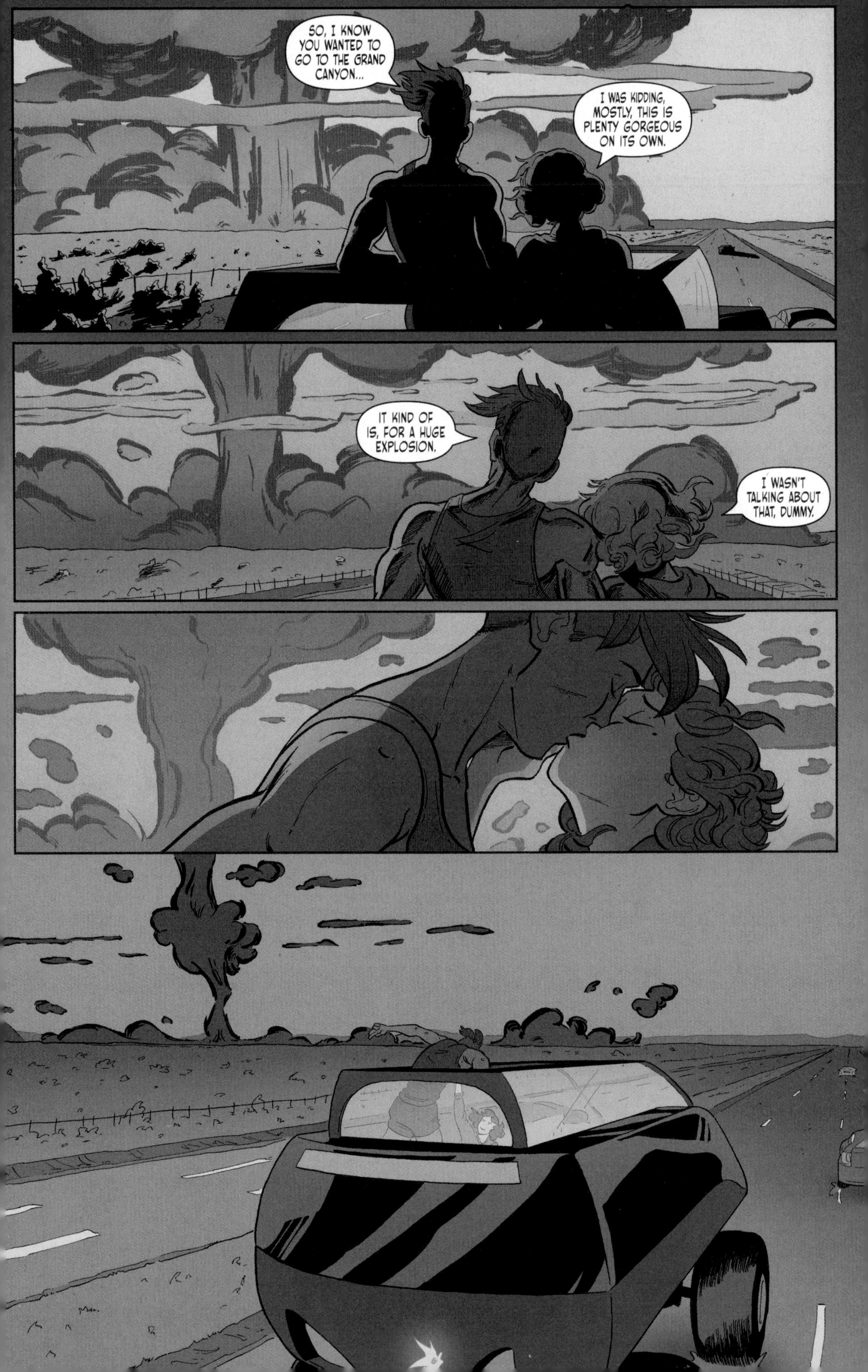
SO, I KNOW YOU WANTED TO GO TO THE GRAND CANYON...
I WAS KIDDING, MOSTLY, THIS IS PLENTY GORGEOUS ON ITS OWN.
IT KIND OF IS, FOR A HUGE EXPLOSION.
I WASN'T TALKING ABOUT THAT, DUMMY.

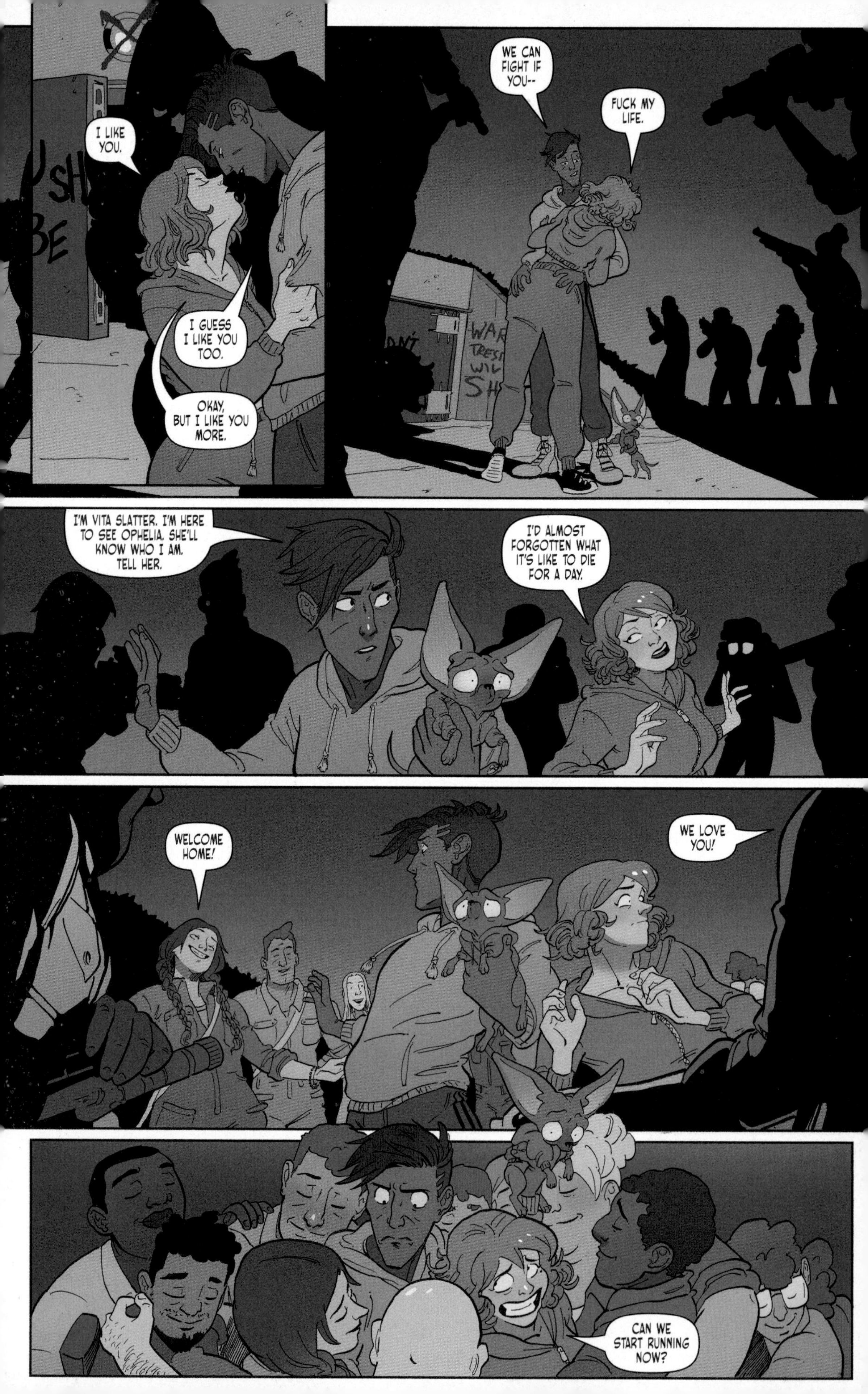
I LIKE YOU.
I GUESS I LIKE YOU TOO.
OKAY, BUT I LIKE YOU MORE.
WE CAN FIGHT IF YOU--
FUCK MY LIFE.
I'M VITA SLATTER. I'M HERE TO SEE OPHELIA. SHE'LL KNOW WHO I AM. TELL HER.
I'D ALMOST FORGOTTEN WHAT IT'S LIKE TO DIE FOR A DAY.
WELCOME HOME!
WE LOVE YOU!
CAN WE START RUNNING NOW?

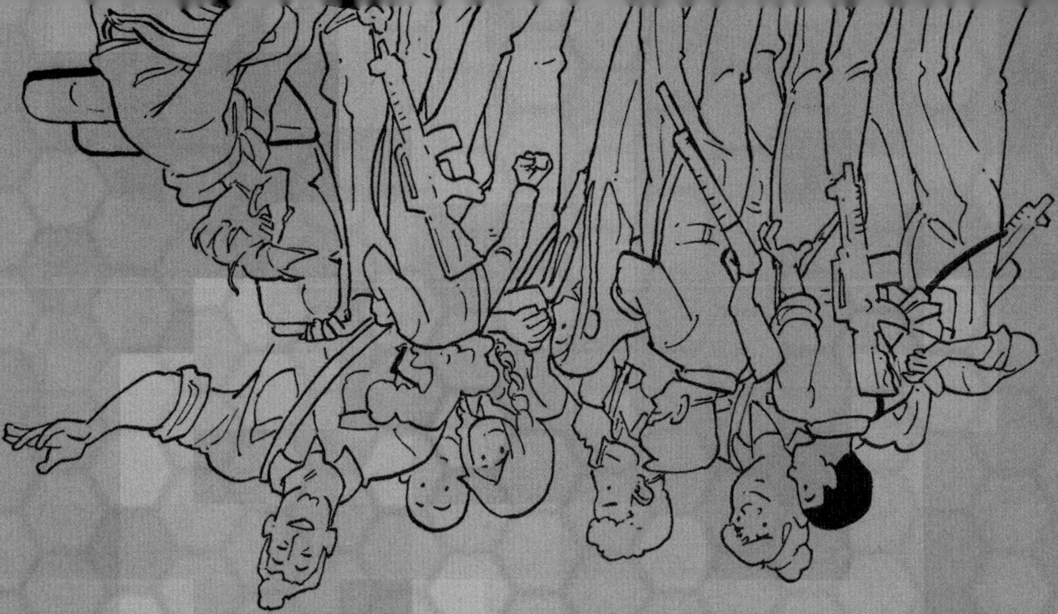

CHAPTER ELEVEN

ANXIOUS TYPE

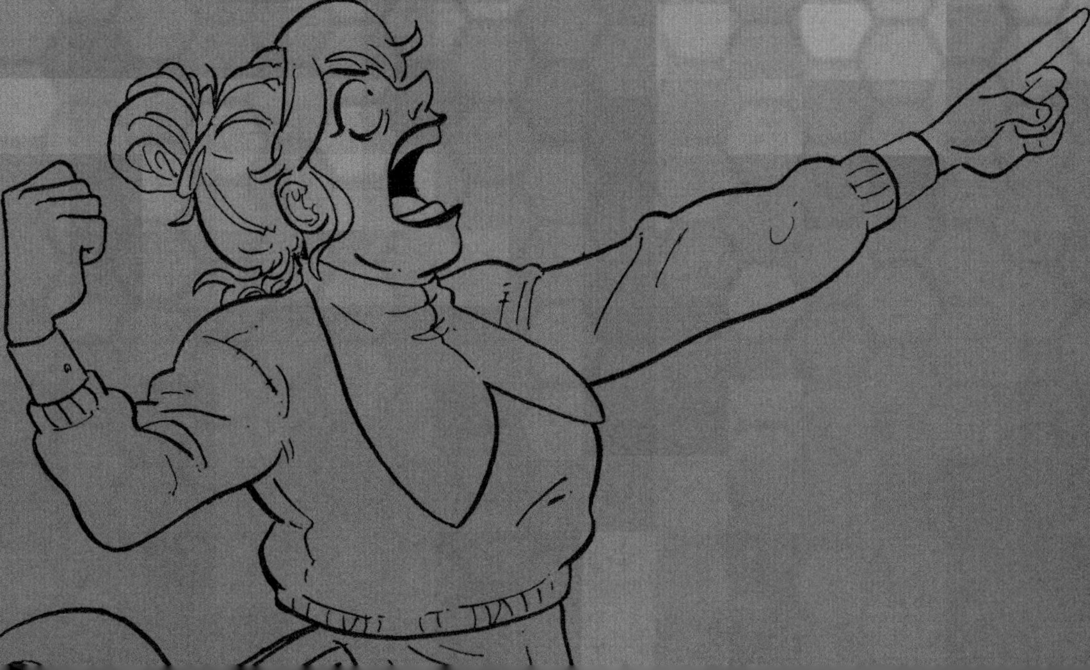

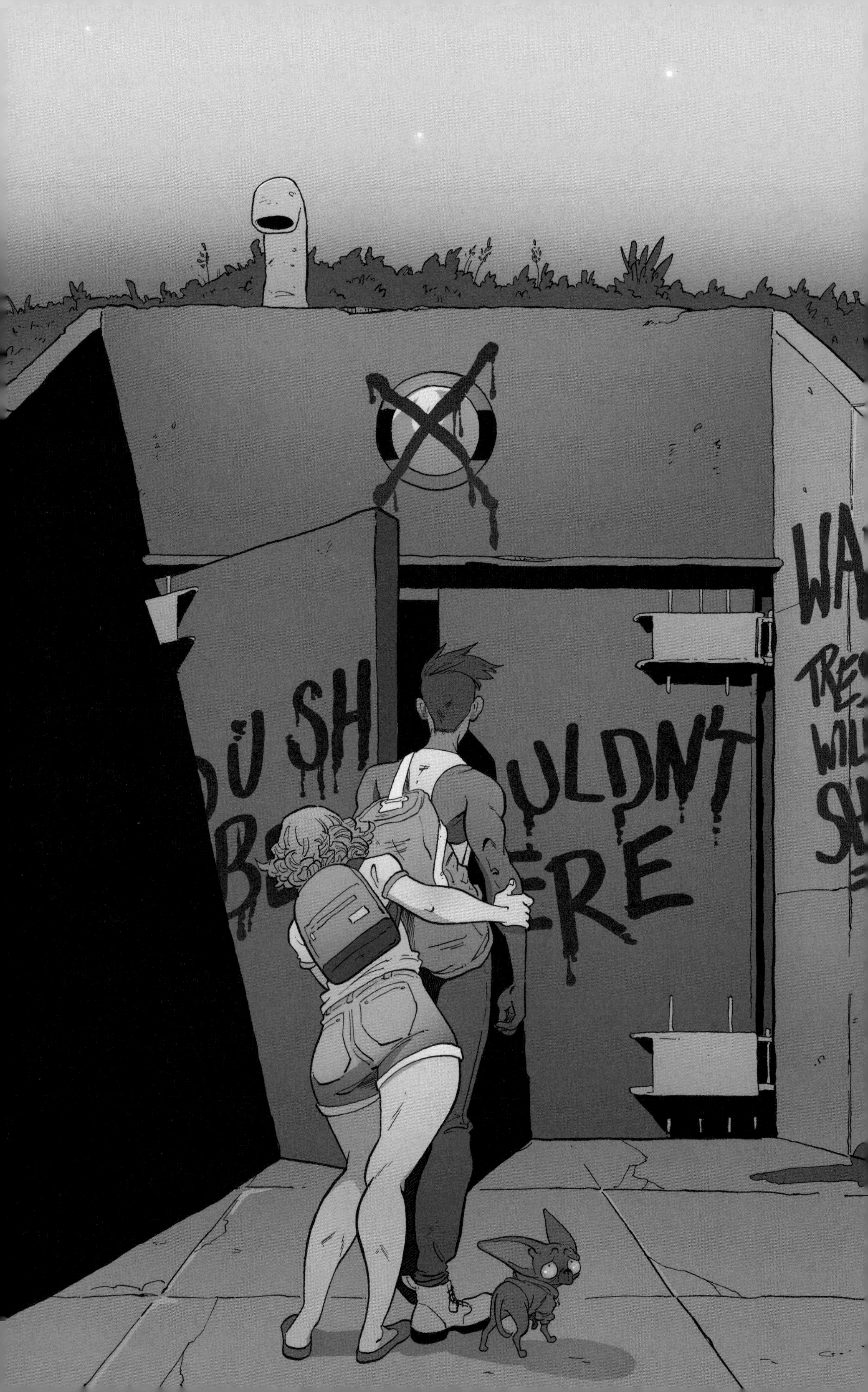

OU SH ULDN'T
B ERE

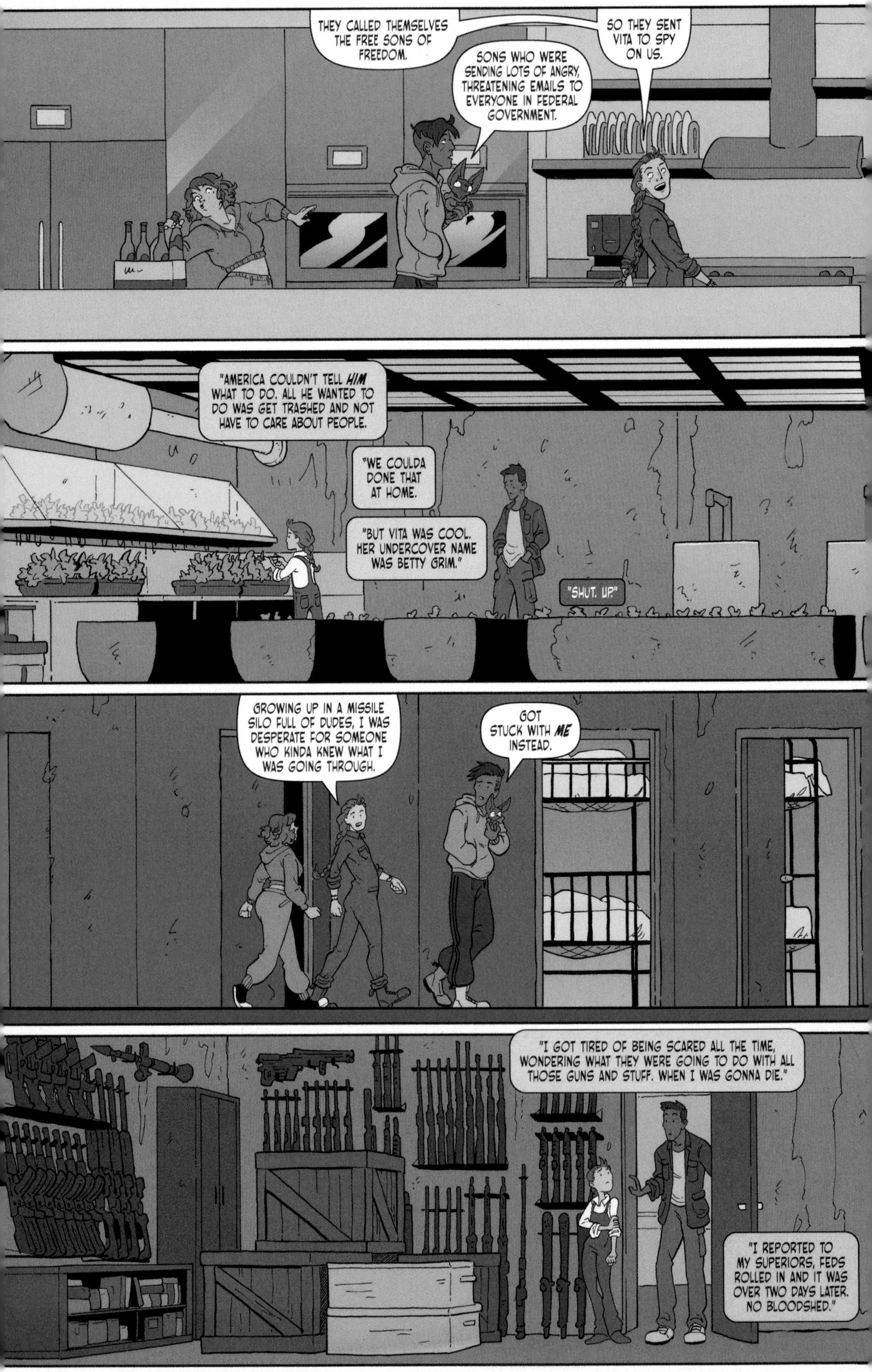
THEY CALLED THEMSELVES THE FREE SONS OF FREEDOM.
SONS WHO WERE SENDING LOTS OF ANGRY, THREATENING EMAILS TO EVERYONE IN FEDERAL GOVERNMENT.
SO THEY SENT VITA TO SPY ON US.
"AMERICA COULDN'T TELL *HIM* WHAT TO DO. ALL HE WANTED TO DO WAS GET TRASHED AND NOT HAVE TO CARE ABOUT PEOPLE.
"WE COULDA DONE THAT AT HOME.
"BUT VITA WAS COOL. HER UNDERCOVER NAME WAS BETTY GRIM."
"SHUT. UP."
GROWING UP IN A MISSILE SILO FULL OF DUDES, I WAS DESPERATE FOR SOMEONE WHO KINDA KNEW WHAT I WAS GOING THROUGH.
GOT STUCK WITH *ME* INSTEAD.
"I GOT TIRED OF BEING SCARED ALL THE TIME, WONDERING WHAT THEY WERE GOING TO DO WITH ALL THOSE GUNS AND STUFF. WHEN I WAS GONNA DIE."
"I REPORTED TO MY SUPERIORS, FEDS ROLLED IN AND IT WAS OVER TWO DAYS LATER. NO BLOODSHED."

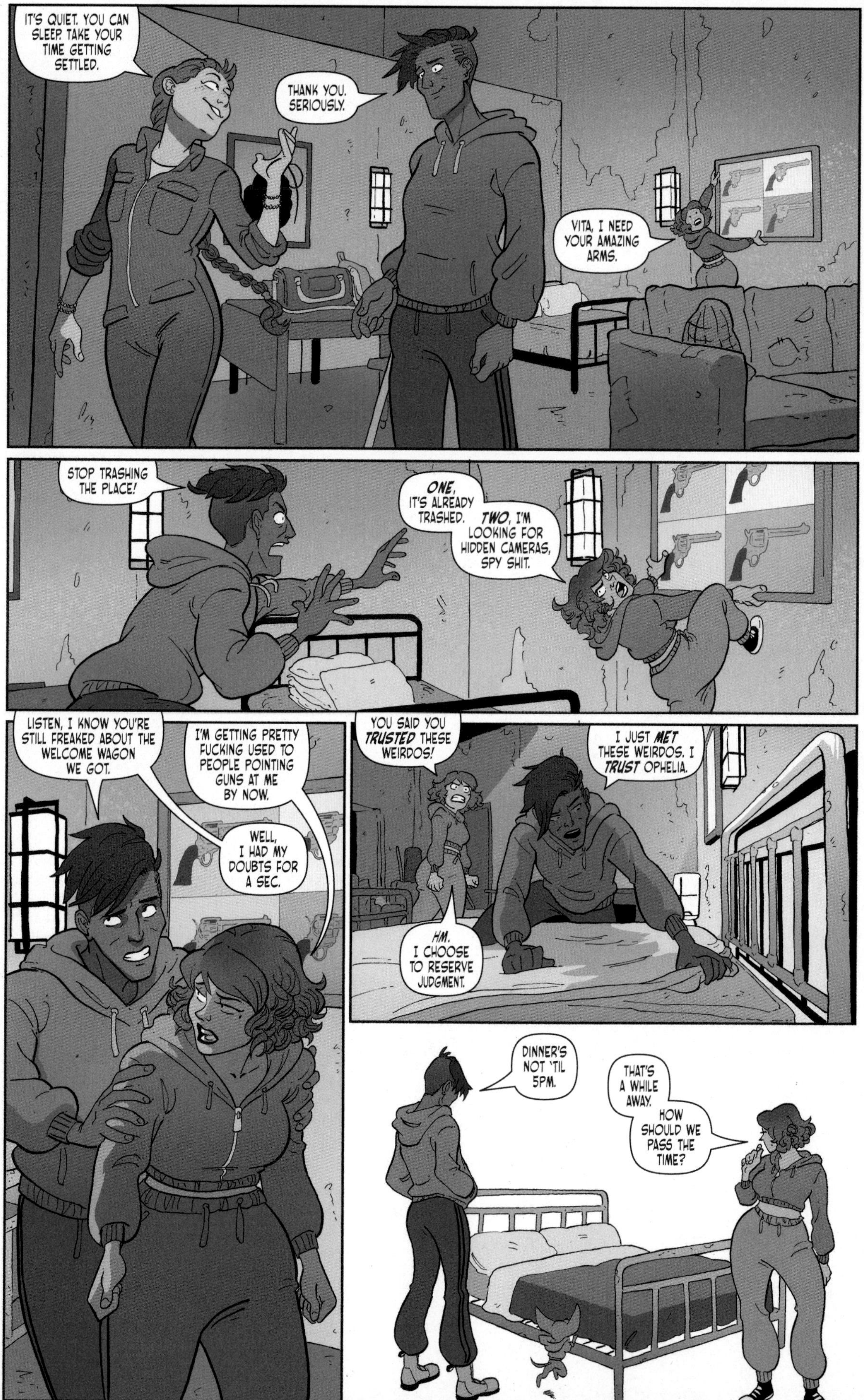
IT'S QUIET. YOU CAN SLEEP. TAKE YOUR TIME GETTING SETTLED.
THANK YOU. SERIOUSLY.
VITA, I NEED YOUR AMAZING ARMS.
STOP TRASHING THE PLACE!
ONE, IT'S ALREADY TRASHED. TWO, I'M LOOKING FOR HIDDEN CAMERAS, SPY SHIT.
LISTEN, I KNOW YOU'RE STILL FREAKED ABOUT THE WELCOME WAGON WE GOT.
I'M GETTING PRETTY FUCKING USED TO PEOPLE POINTING GUNS AT ME BY NOW.
WELL, I HAD MY DOUBTS FOR A SEC.
YOU SAID YOU TRUSTED THESE WEIRDOS!
I JUST MET THESE WEIRDOS. I TRUST OPHELIA.
HM. I CHOOSE TO RESERVE JUDGMENT.
DINNER'S NOT 'TIL 5PM.
THAT'S A WHILE AWAY.
HOW SHOULD WE PASS THE TIME?

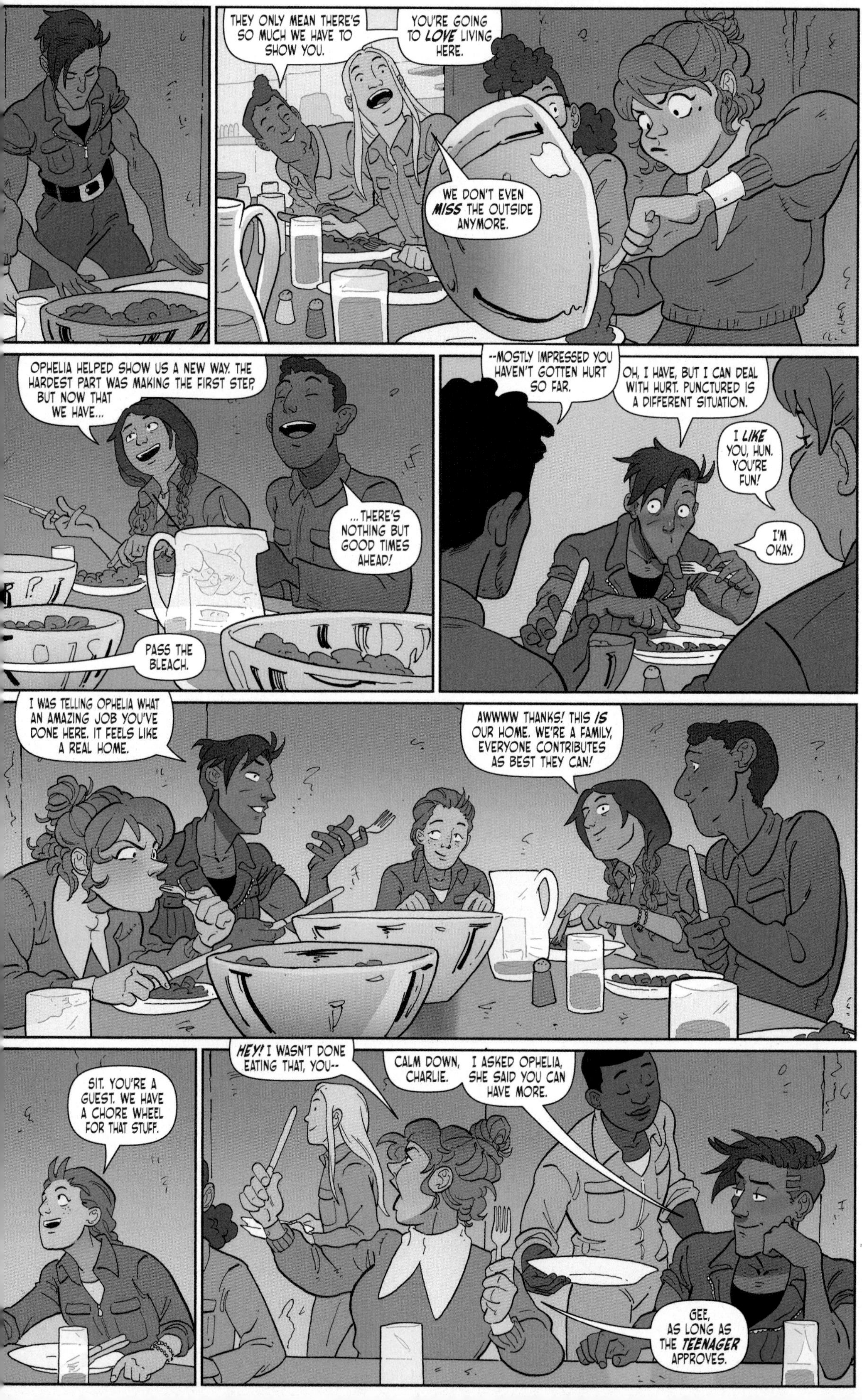
THEY ONLY MEAN THERE'S SO MUCH WE HAVE TO SHOW YOU.
YOU'RE GOING TO LOVE LIVING HERE.
WE DON'T EVEN MISS THE OUTSIDE ANYMORE.
OPHELIA HELPED SHOW US A NEW WAY. THE HARDEST PART WAS MAKING THE FIRST STEP, BUT NOW THAT WE HAVE...
...THERE'S NOTHING BUT GOOD TIMES AHEAD!
PASS THE BLEACH.
--MOSTLY IMPRESSED YOU HAVEN'T GOTTEN HURT SO FAR.
OH, I HAVE, BUT I CAN DEAL WITH HURT. PUNCTURED IS A DIFFERENT SITUATION.
I LIKE YOU, HUN. YOU'RE FUN!
I'M OKAY.
I WAS TELLING OPHELIA WHAT AN AMAZING JOB YOU'VE DONE HERE. IT FEELS LIKE A REAL HOME.
AWWWW THANKS! THIS IS OUR HOME. WE'RE A FAMILY, EVERYONE CONTRIBUTES AS BEST THEY CAN!
SIT. YOU'RE A GUEST. WE HAVE A CHORE WHEEL FOR THAT STUFF.
HEY! I WASN'T DONE EATING THAT, YOU--
CALM DOWN, CHARLIE.
I ASKED OPHELIA, SHE SAID YOU CAN HAVE MORE.
GEE, AS LONG AS THE TEENAGER APPROVES.

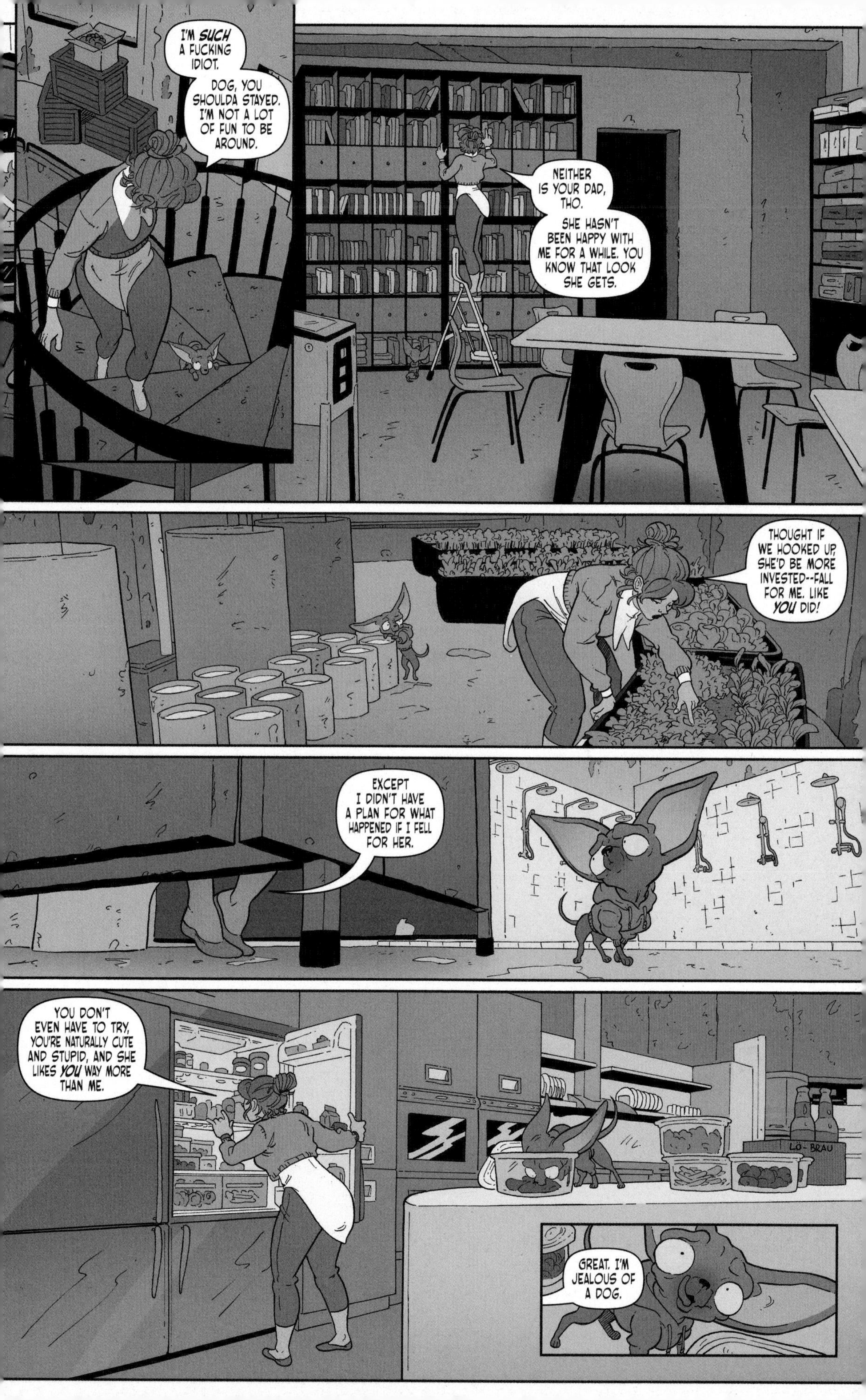
I'M *SUCH* A FUCKING IDIOT.
DOG, YOU SHOULDA STAYED. I'M NOT A LOT OF FUN TO BE AROUND.
NEITHER IS YOUR DAD, THO.
SHE HASN'T BEEN HAPPY WITH ME FOR A WHILE. YOU KNOW THAT LOOK SHE GETS.
THOUGHT IF WE HOOKED UP, SHE'D BE MORE INVESTED--FALL FOR ME. LIKE *YOU* DID!
EXCEPT I DIDN'T HAVE A PLAN FOR WHAT HAPPENED IF I FELL FOR HER.
YOU DON'T EVEN HAVE TO TRY, YOU'RE NATURALLY CUTE AND STUPID, AND SHE LIKES *YOU* WAY MORE THAN ME.
LÖ-BRAU
GREAT. I'M JEALOUS OF A DOG.

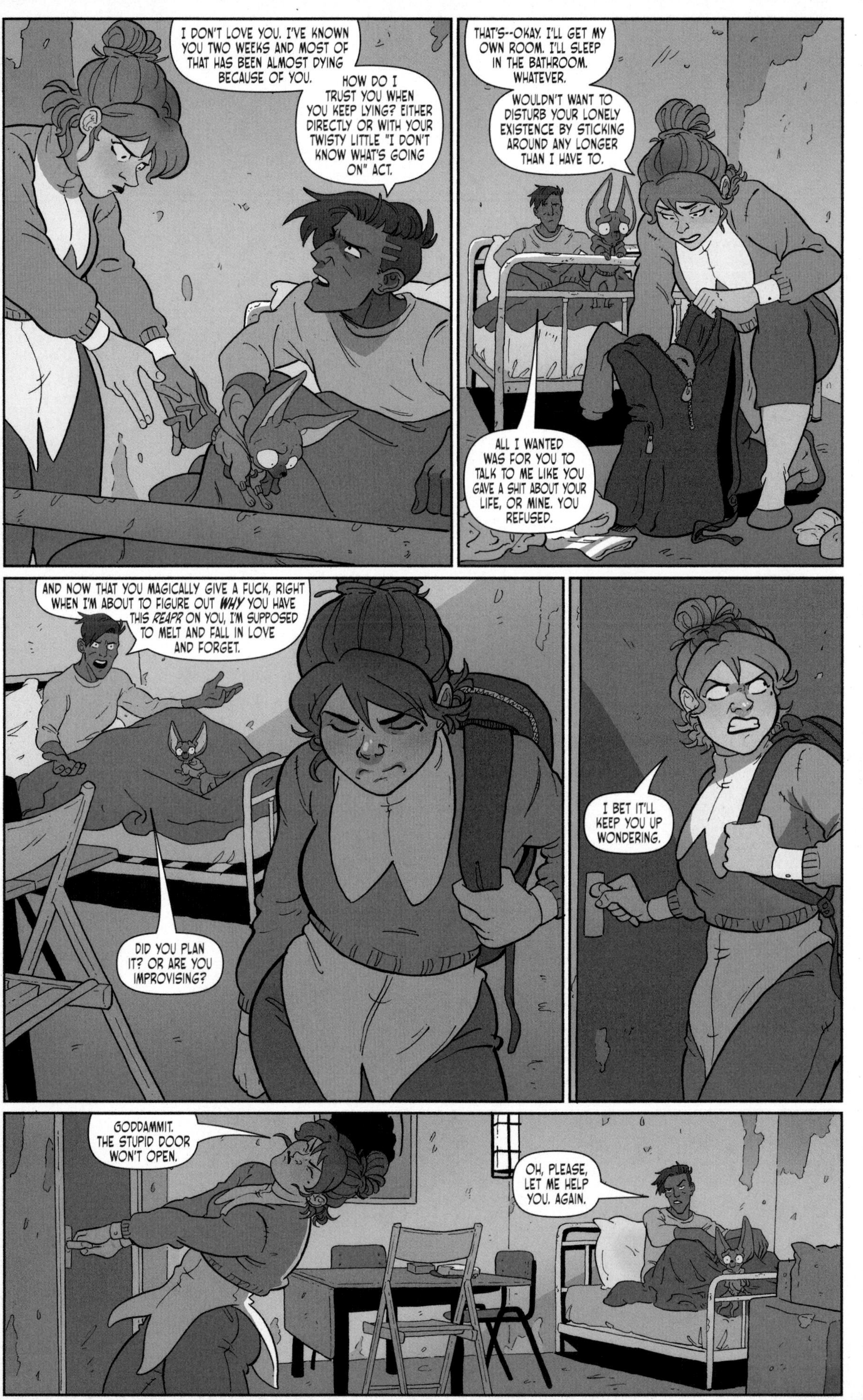
I DON'T LOVE YOU. I'VE KNOWN YOU TWO WEEKS AND MOST OF THAT HAS BEEN ALMOST DYING BECAUSE OF YOU.
HOW DO I TRUST YOU WHEN YOU KEEP LYING? EITHER DIRECTLY OR WITH YOUR TWISTY LITTLE "I DON'T KNOW WHAT'S GOING ON" ACT.
THAT'S--OKAY. I'LL GET MY OWN ROOM. I'LL SLEEP IN THE BATHROOM. WHATEVER.
WOULDN'T WANT TO DISTURB YOUR LONELY EXISTENCE BY STICKING AROUND ANY LONGER THAN I HAVE TO.
ALL I WANTED WAS FOR YOU TO TALK TO ME LIKE YOU GAVE A SHIT ABOUT YOUR LIFE, OR MINE. YOU REFUSED.
AND NOW THAT YOU MAGICALLY GIVE A FUCK, RIGHT WHEN I'M ABOUT TO FIGURE OUT *WHY* YOU HAVE THIS *REAPR* ON YOU, I'M SUPPOSED TO MELT AND FALL IN LOVE AND FORGET.
DID YOU PLAN IT? OR ARE YOU IMPROVISING?
I BET IT'LL KEEP YOU UP WONDERING.
GODDAMMIT. THE STUPID DOOR WON'T OPEN.
OH, PLEASE, LET ME HELP YOU. AGAIN.

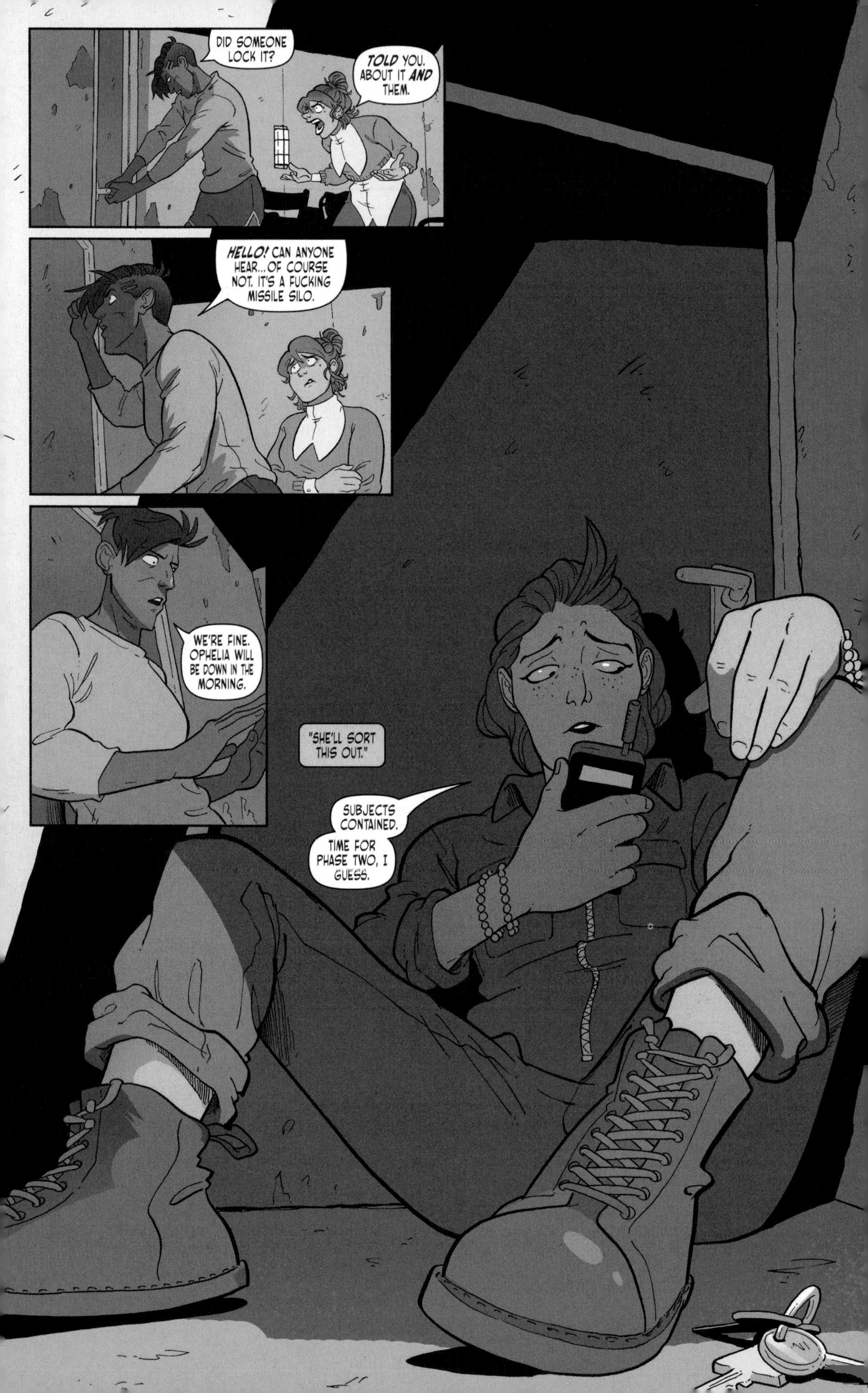
DID SOMEONE LOCK IT?
TOLD YOU. ABOUT IT AND THEM.
HELLO! CAN ANYONE HEAR...OF COURSE NOT. IT'S A FUCKING MISSILE SILO.
WE'RE FINE. OPHELIA WILL BE DOWN IN THE MORNING.
"SHE'LL SORT THIS OUT."
SUBJECTS CONTAINED.
TIME FOR PHASE TWO, I GUESS.

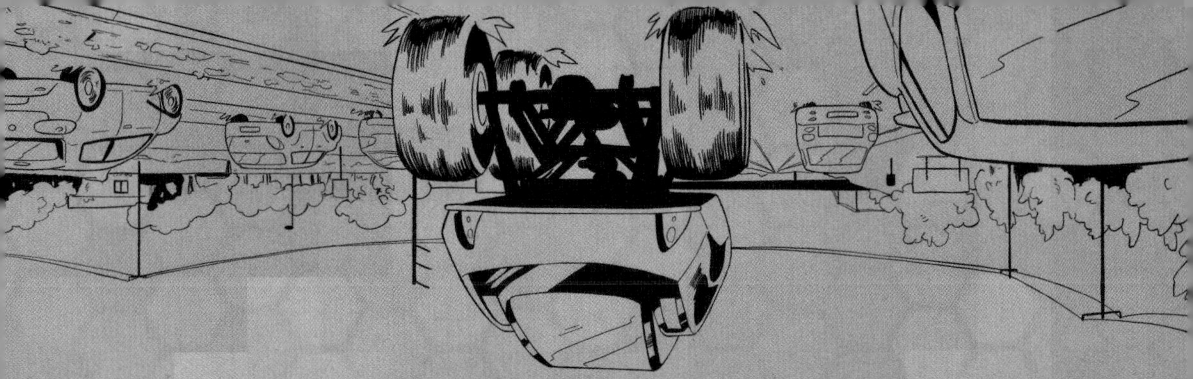

CHAPTER TWELVE

GLAD GIRLS

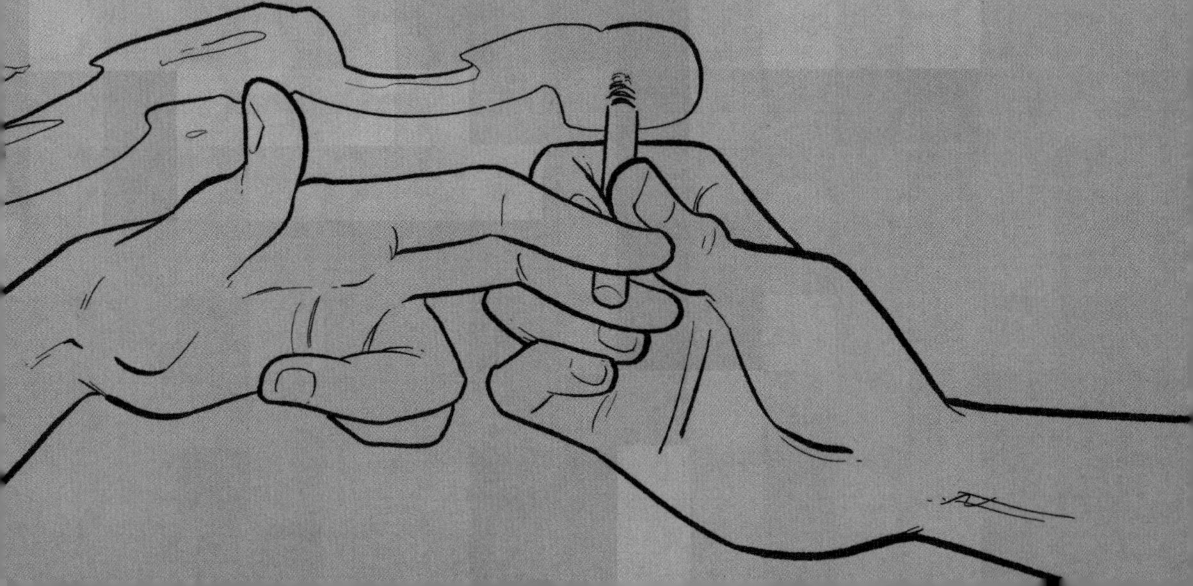

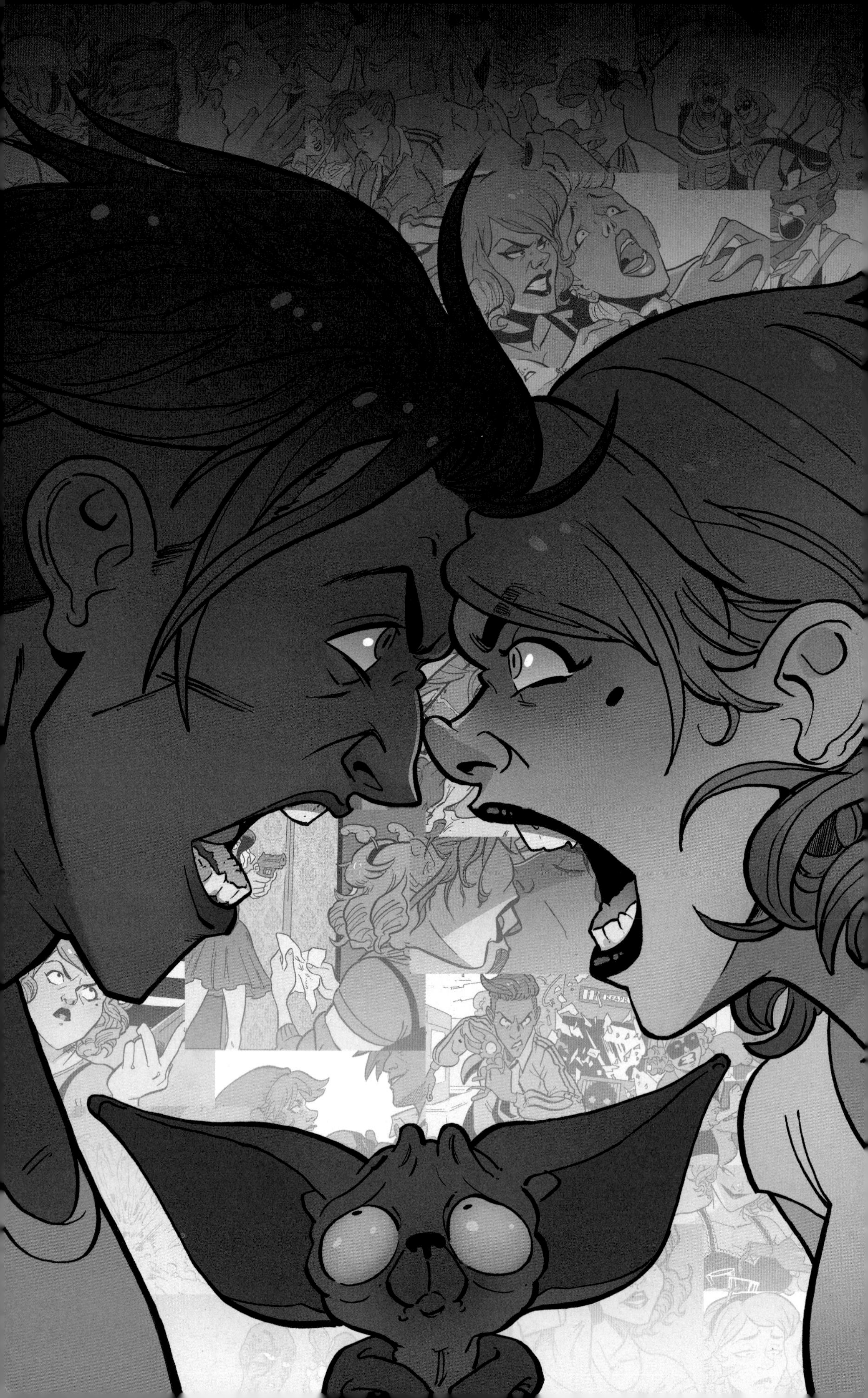

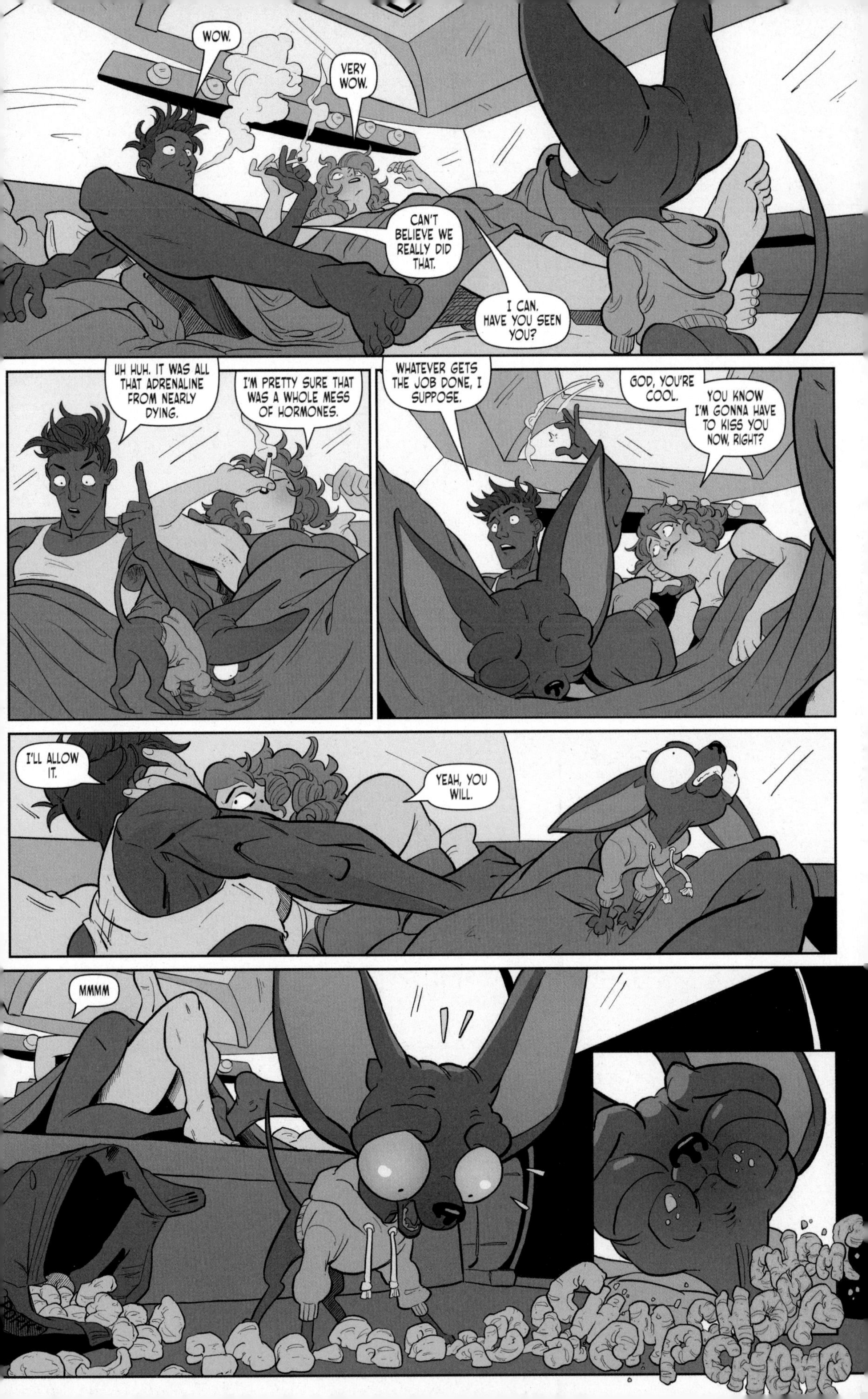
WOW.
VERY WOW.
CAN'T BELIEVE WE REALLY DID THAT.
I CAN. HAVE YOU SEEN YOU?
UH HUH. IT WAS ALL THAT ADRENALINE FROM NEARLY DYING.
I'M PRETTY SURE THAT WAS A WHOLE MESS OF HORMONES.
WHATEVER GETS THE JOB DONE, I SUPPOSE.
GOD, YOU'RE COOL.
YOU KNOW I'M GONNA HAVE TO KISS YOU NOW, RIGHT?
I'LL ALLOW IT.
YEAH, YOU WILL.
MMMM

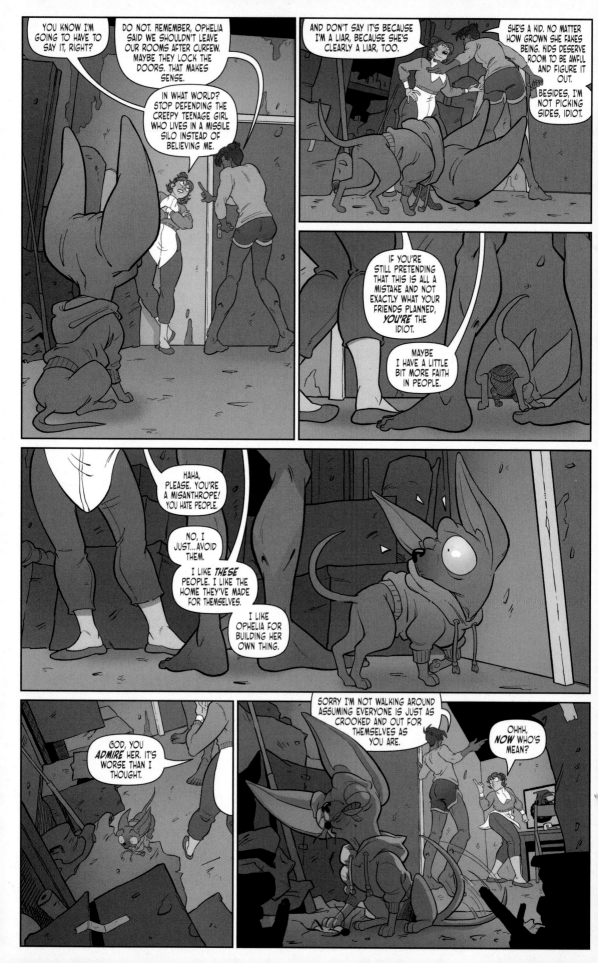

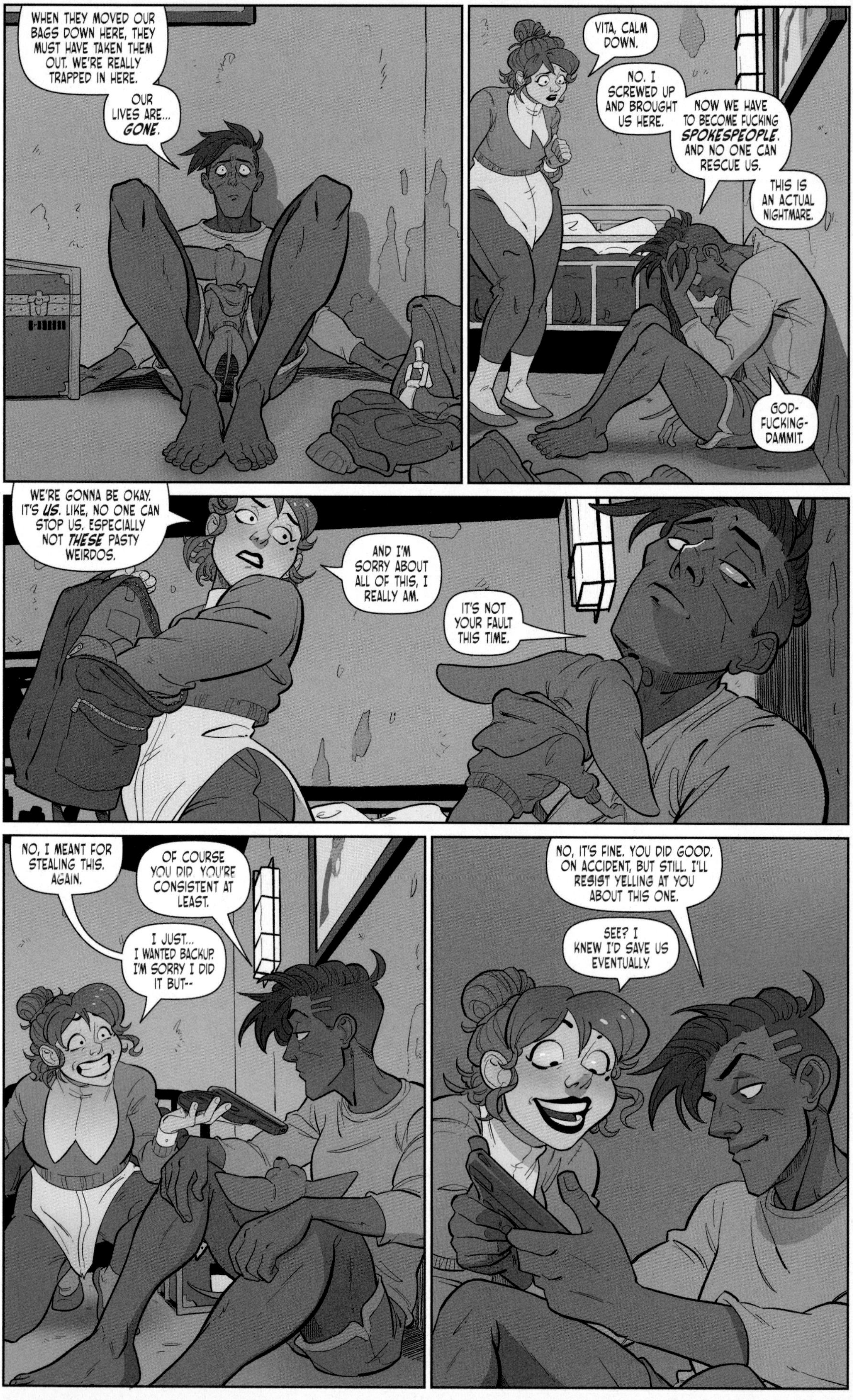
WHEN THEY MOVED OUR BAGS DOWN HERE, THEY MUST HAVE TAKEN THEM OUT. WE'RE REALLY TRAPPED IN HERE.
OUR LIVES ARE... *GONE*.
VITA, CALM DOWN.
NO. I SCREWED UP AND BROUGHT US HERE.
NOW WE HAVE TO BECOME FUCKING *SPOKESPEOPLE*. AND NO ONE CAN RESCUE US.
THIS IS AN ACTUAL NIGHTMARE.
GOD-FUCKING-DAMMIT.
WE'RE GONNA BE OKAY. IT'S *US*. LIKE, NO ONE CAN STOP US. ESPECIALLY NOT *THESE* PASTY WEIRDOS.
AND I'M SORRY ABOUT ALL OF THIS, I REALLY AM.
IT'S NOT YOUR FAULT THIS TIME.
NO, I MEANT FOR STEALING THIS. AGAIN.
OF COURSE YOU DID. YOU'RE CONSISTENT AT LEAST.
I JUST... I WANTED BACKUP. I'M SORRY I DID IT BUT--
NO, IT'S FINE. YOU DID GOOD. ON ACCIDENT, BUT STILL. I'LL RESIST YELLING AT YOU ABOUT THIS ONE.
SEE? I KNEW I'D SAVE US EVENTUALLY.

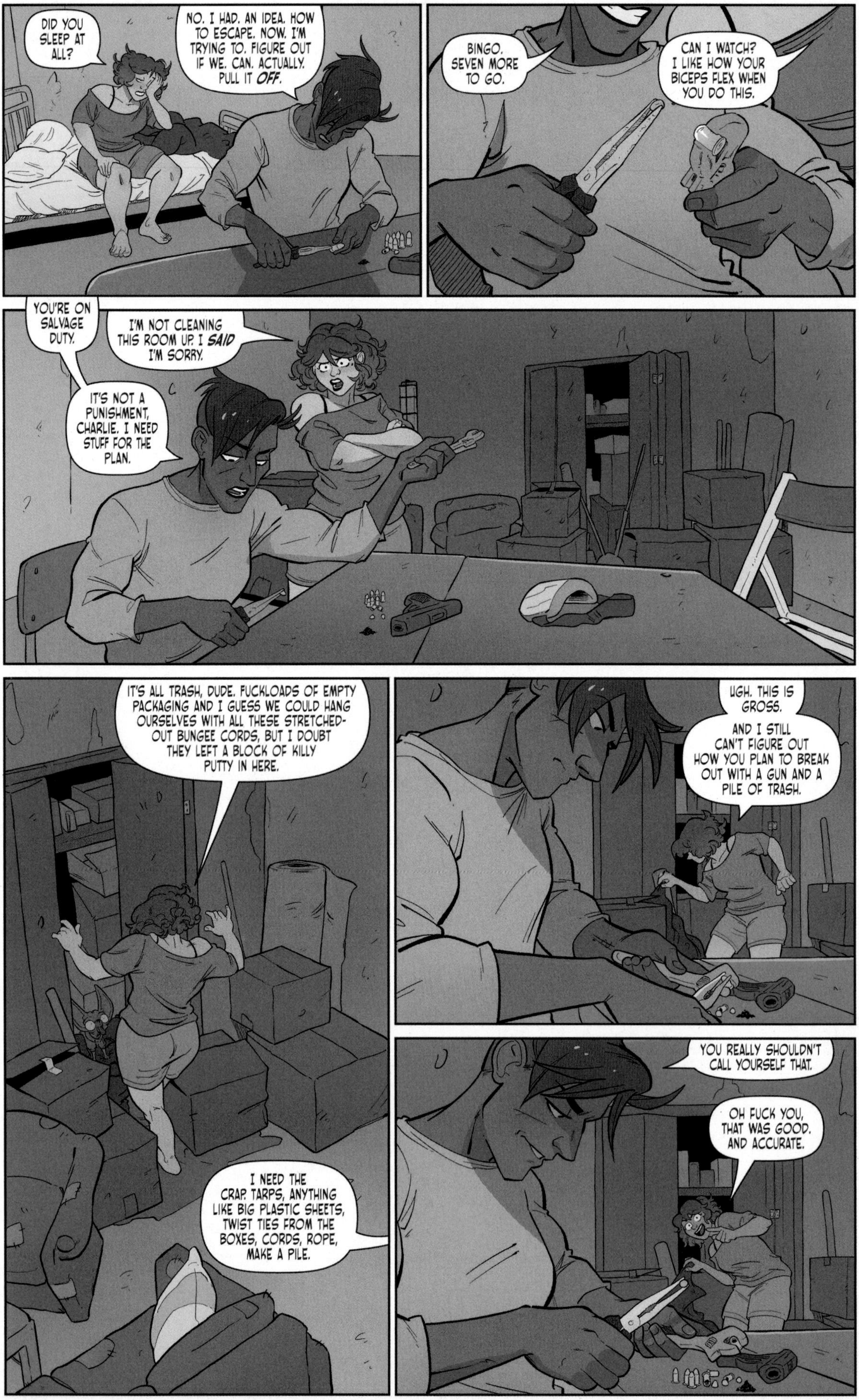
DID YOU SLEEP AT ALL?
NO. I HAD. AN IDEA. HOW TO ESCAPE. NOW. I'M TRYING TO. FIGURE OUT IF WE. CAN. ACTUALLY. PULL IT OFF.
BINGO. SEVEN MORE TO GO.
CAN I WATCH? I LIKE HOW YOUR BICEPS FLEX WHEN YOU DO THIS.
YOU'RE ON SALVAGE DUTY.
I'M NOT CLEANING THIS ROOM UP. I SAID I'M SORRY.
IT'S NOT A PUNISHMENT, CHARLIE. I NEED STUFF FOR THE PLAN.
IT'S ALL TRASH, DUDE. FUCKLOADS OF EMPTY PACKAGING AND I GUESS WE COULD HANG OURSELVES WITH ALL THESE STRETCHED-OUT BUNGEE CORDS, BUT I DOUBT THEY LEFT A BLOCK OF KILLY PUTTY IN HERE.
I NEED THE CRAP. TARPS, ANYTHING LIKE BIG PLASTIC SHEETS, TWIST TIES FROM THE BOXES, CORDS, ROPE, MAKE A PILE.
UGH. THIS IS GROSS.
AND I STILL CAN'T FIGURE OUT HOW YOU PLAN TO BREAK OUT WITH A GUN AND A PILE OF TRASH.
YOU REALLY SHOULDN'T CALL YOURSELF THAT.
OH FUCK YOU, THAT WAS GOOD. AND ACCURATE.

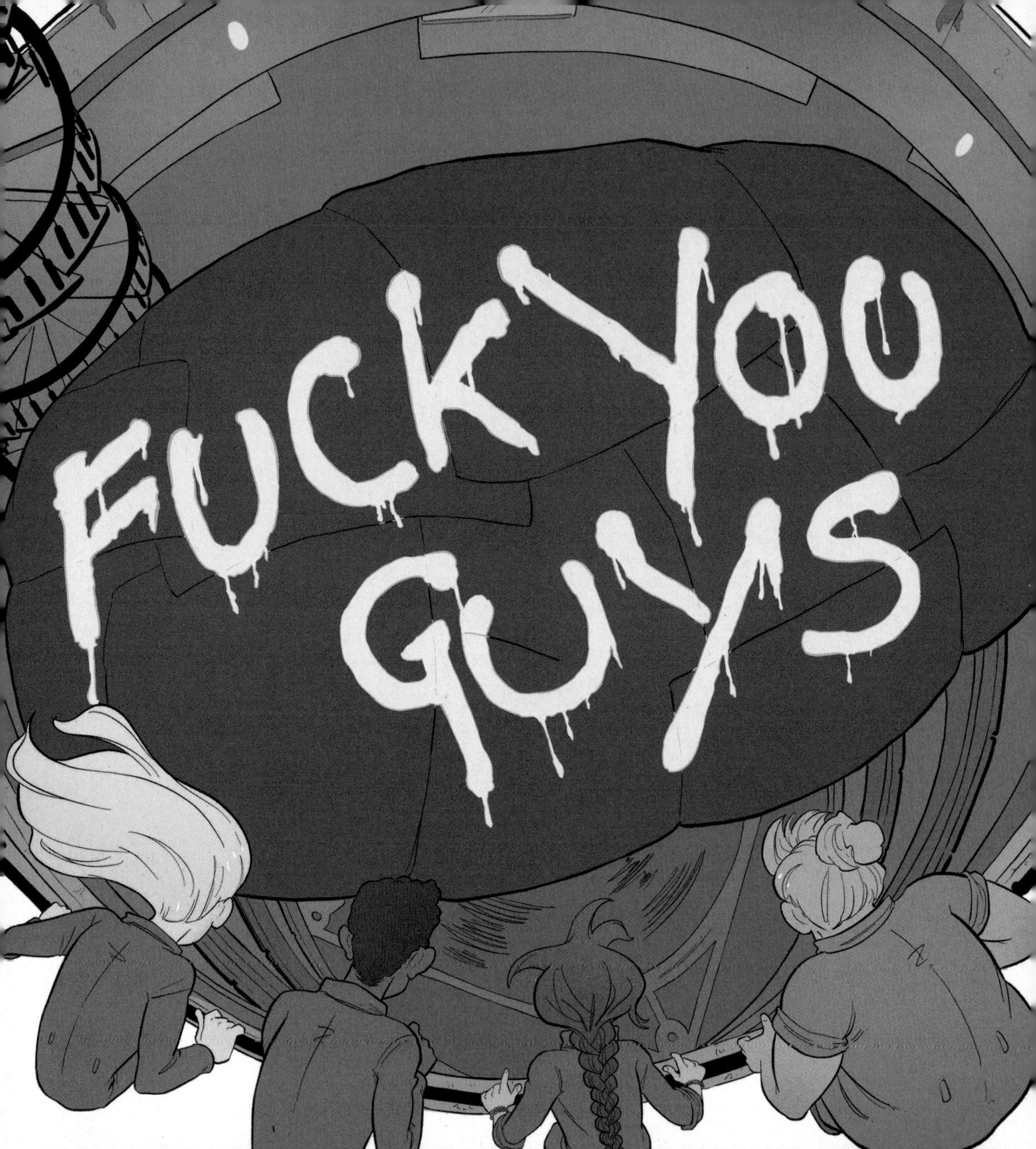
FUCK YOU
GUYS

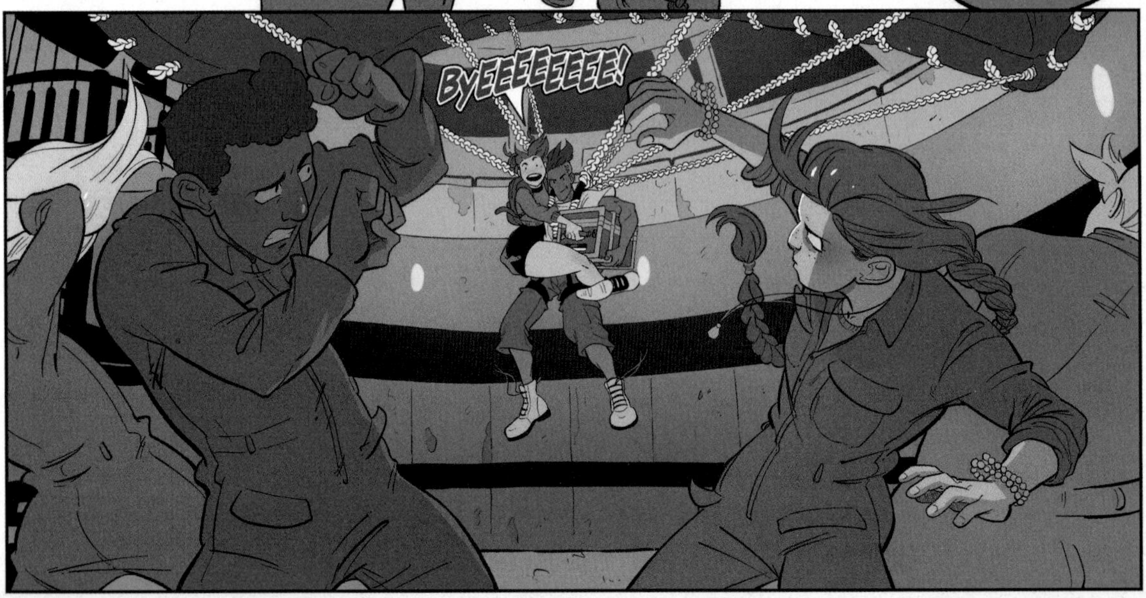
BYEEEEEEEE!

**GABY EPSTEIN
#7 VARIANT
COVER**

**MJ ERICKSON
#8 VARIANT
COVER**

**SLOANE LEONG
#9 VARIANT
COVER** ——

—— **LISA STERLE
#10 VARIANT
COVER**

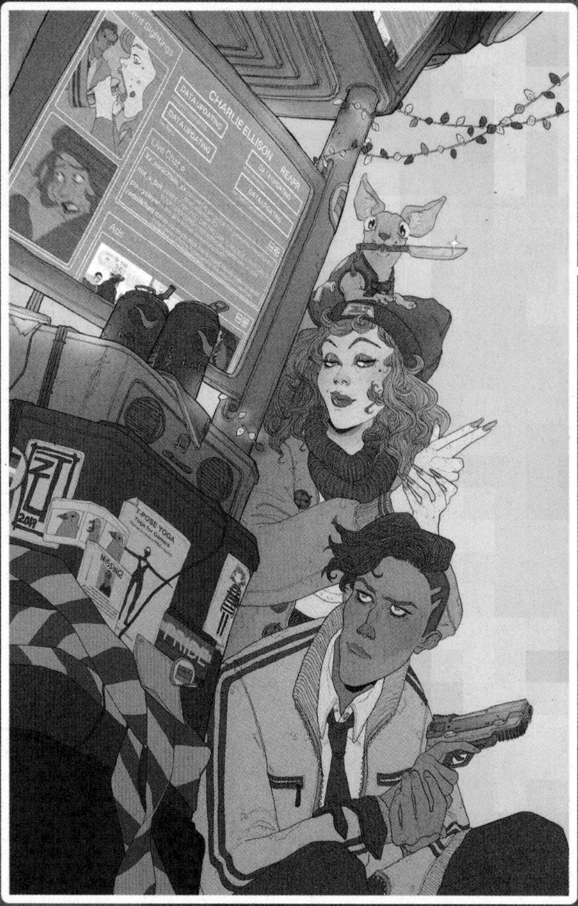
CHARLIE ELLISON

ZOE THOROGOOD
#11 VARIANT
COVER

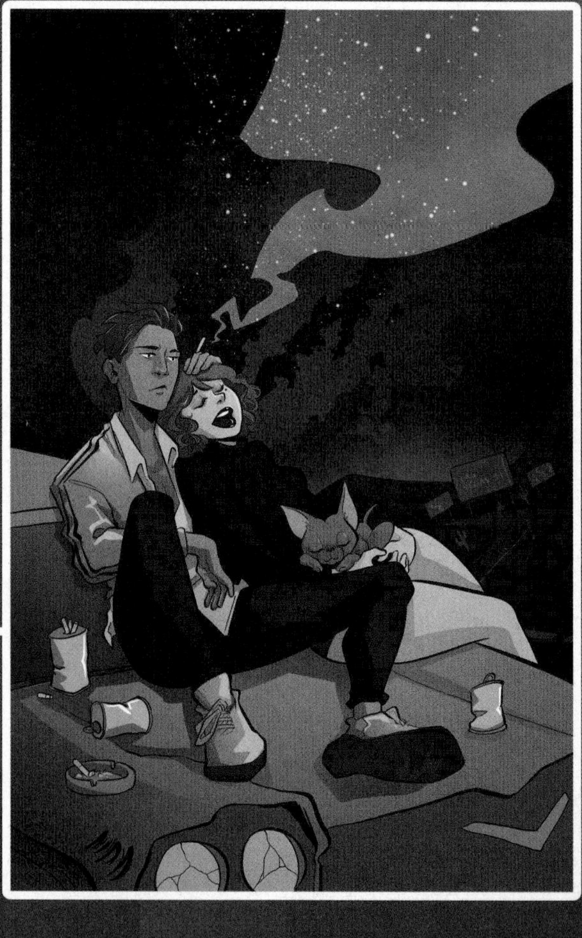

LINDSAY ISHIHIRO
#12 VARIANT
COVER

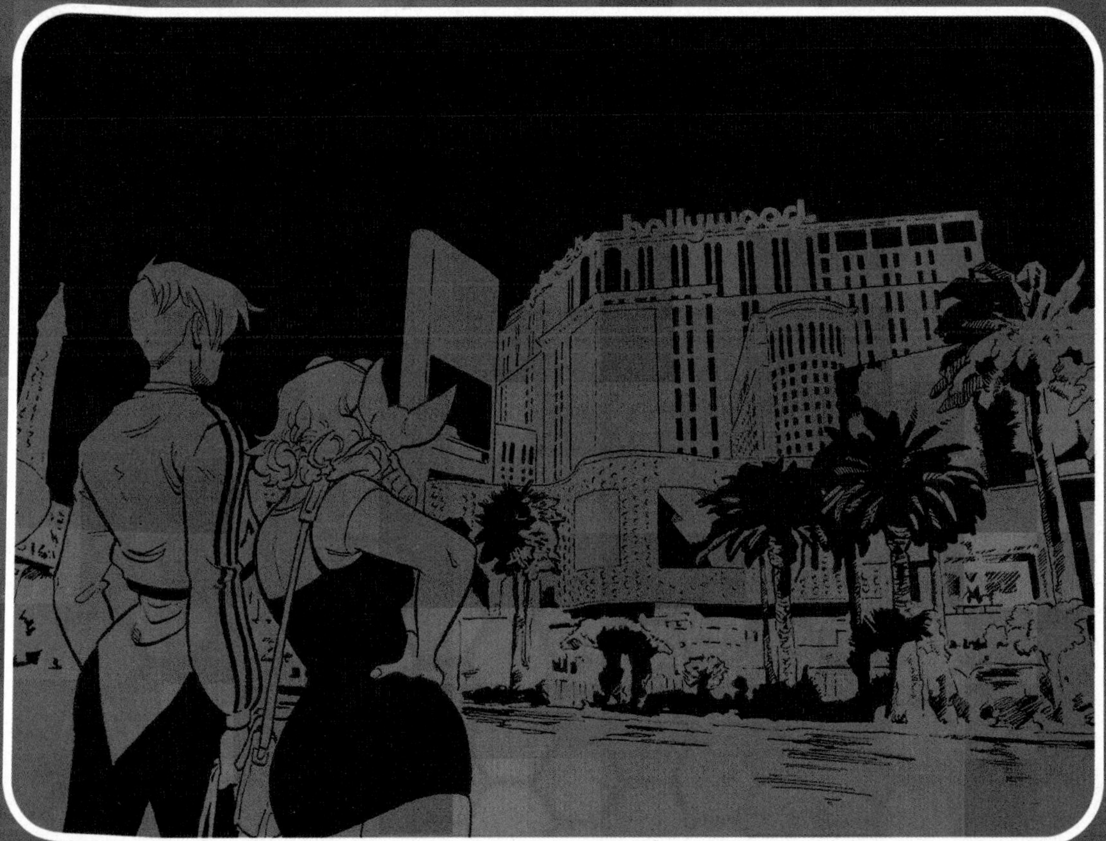
hollywood

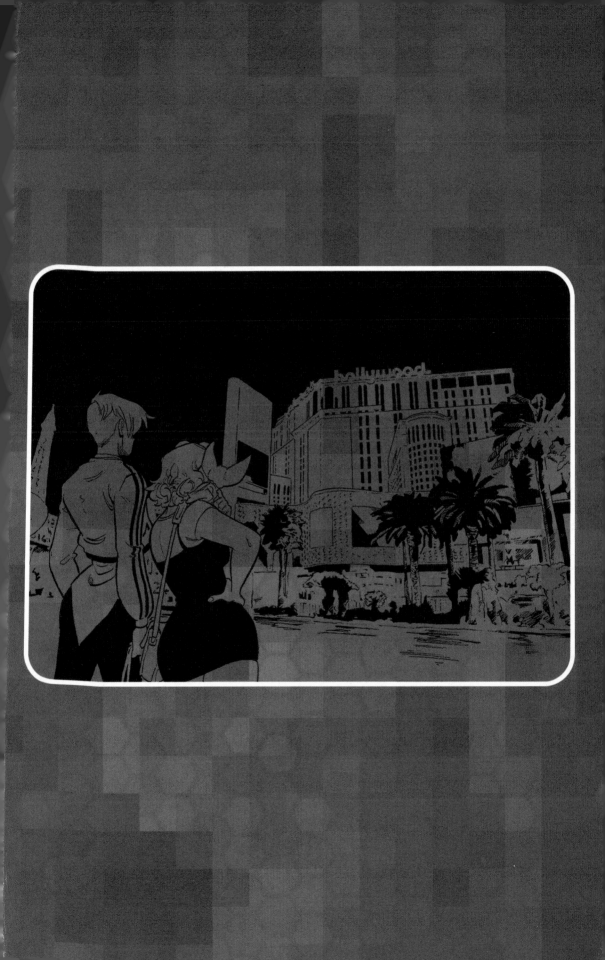